INTERNAL FAMILY SYSTEMS THERAPY

Internal family systems therapy, or IFS, is widely recognized as one of the most compassionate and comprehensive psychotherapies available. Its nonpathologizing approach to behavior, consciousness and personality have been adopted by clinicians around the world, but with the exception of Richard Schwartz's foundational introductory text, few texts give clinicians the information they need on adapting the IFS framework to patients' complex and diverse needs and circumstances. *Internal Family Systems Therapy: New Dimensions* changes that. The chapters focus on topics common in therapists' practice, and each provides both a refreshing approach to sometimes thorny issues, and clear, practical guidance for how best to explore them in treatment. For any practitioner interested in learning about this vital, vibrant form of therapy, *Internal Family Systems Therapy: New Dimensions* is the perfect introduction. For clinicians already a part of the IFS community, this book is bound to become one of the most essential tools in their toolbox.

Martha Sweezy, PhD, is the associate director and director of training for the dialectical behavioral therapy (DBT) program at the Cambridge Health Alliance, a lecturer on psychiatry at Cambridge Health Alliance, Harvard Medical School, and assists at IFS trainings. She is the author of two articles on IFS, "Treating Trauma After Dialectical Behavioral Therapy" in the *Journal of Psychotherapy Integration* (2011, Vol. 21, No. 1, pp. 90–102) and "The Teenager's Confession: Regulating Shame in Internal Family Systems Therapy" in the *American Journal of Psychotherapy* (2011, Vol. 65, No. 2, pp. 179–188). She also has a therapy and consultation practice in Northampton, Massachusetts.

Ellen L. Ziskind, LICSW, has been affiliated with Harvard Medical School at Cambridge Hospital, Beth Israel Deaconess Medical Center, Boston Institute for Psychotherapy and Two Brattle Center, leading staff groups and doing group consultation. Currently she is on the faculty at Northeastern Society for Group Psychotherapy. IFS is an integral part of her work with individuals, couples and groups. She has a private practice in Brookline, Massachusetts.

CE credit is available to purchasers of this book at www.mensanapublications.com.

INTERNAL FAMILY SYSTEMS THERAPY

New Dimensions

Edited by Martha Sweezy
Ellen L. Ziskind

Foreword by
Richard C. Schwartz

Routledge
Taylor & Francis Group

NEW YORK AND LONDON

First published 2013
by Routledge
711 Third Avenue, New York, NY 10017

Simultaneously published in the UK
by Routledge
27 Church Road, Hove, East Sussex BN3 2FA

Library of Congress Cataloging-in-Publication Data

Internal family systems therapy : new dimensions / edited by Martha Sweezy and Ellen L. Ziskind.
      pages cm
   Includes bibliographical references and index.
   1. Psychotherapy patients—Family relationships.   2. Family psychotherapy.
I. Sweezy, Martha.   II. Ziskind, Ellen L.
RC489.F33I58   2013
616.89'156—dc23   2012037413

ISBN: 978-0-415-50683-0 (hbk)
ISBN: 978-0-415-50684-7 (pbk)
ISBN: 978-0-203-12669-1 (ebk)

Typeset in ACaslon
by Apex CoVantage, LLC

To my sine qua non, Rob and Theo.

—Martha Sweezy

To Maggie, friend and sister—the best of each.

—Ellen L. Ziskind

CONTENTS

About the Contributors   ix

Foreword   xiii
Richard C. Schwartz

Acknowledgments   xv

An Introduction to IFS   xvii
Jack Engler

1   The Therapist–Client Relationship and the Transformative
Power of Self   1
Richard C. Schwartz

2   Emotional Cannibalism: Shame in Action   24
Martha Sweezy

3   IFS with Children and Adolescents   35
Pamela K. Krause

4   Self in Relationship: An Introduction to IFS Couple Therapy   55
Toni Herbine-Blank

5   Integrating IFS with Phase-Oriented Treatment of
Clients with Dissociative Disorder   72
Joanne H. Twombly

6 Embodying the Internal Family   90
   Susan McConnell

7 "Who's Taking What?" Connecting Neuroscience,
   Psychopharmacology and Internal Family Systems for Trauma   107
   Frank Guastella Anderson

8 The Internal Family System and Adult Health: Changing the
   Course of Chronic Illness   127
   Nancy Sowell

9 IFS and Health Coaching: A New Model of Behavior
   Change and Medical Decision Making   143
   John B. Livingstone and Joanne Gaffney

10 Treating Pornography Addiction with IFS   159
   Nancy Wonder

11 Welcoming All Erotic Parts: Our Reactions to the Sexual
   and Using Polarities to Enhance Erotic Excitement   166
   Lawrence G. Rosenberg

Glossary   187
Index   191

ABOUT THE CONTRIBUTORS

Frank Guastella Anderson, MD, has spoken extensively on the psychopharmacology of posttraumatic stress disorder and dissociation, and has integrated IFS with neuroscience in relation to trauma. There are two video productions of his work, "Psychiatric Medications Through a Trauma Lens" (2008) and "Psychopharmacologic Approaches to Complex Trauma" (2012), available at www.traumacenter.org. In addition to IFS, Frank is trained in EMDR and sensorimotor psychotherapy. He is affiliated with the Center for Self Leadership as well as the Trauma Center in Boston and maintains a private practice in Concord, Massachusetts.

Jack Engler, PhD, is an instructor in psychology at Harvard Medical School where he teaches and supervises psychotherapy in the department of psychiatry at the Cambridge Health Alliance. He helped found the Insight Meditation Society and the Barre Center for Buddhist Studies, where he taught for many years. He has written and spoken extensively on the integration of meditation and psychotherapy, and eastern and western approaches to health and healing. He coauthored *Transformations of Consciousness* with Ken Wilbur, PhD, and Daniel Brown, PhD, and *A Consumer's Guide to Psychotherapy* with Daniel Goleman, PhD. He has a full-time private practice in Cambridge, Massachusetts.

Joanne Gaffney, RN, LICSW, is trained in a broad range of psychotherapeutic methods and is certified in IFS, EMDR and Rubenfeld Synergy (mind/body). She has studied health behavior change and medical decision-making processes and designed new training programs in health coaching for midcareer nurse health coaches at Health Dialog, Inc. She has a private,

IFS-informed psychotherapy and consulting practice for individuals and couples in Provincetown, Massachusetts. Contact: www.gaffney-livingstone.com

Toni Herbine-Blank, MS, RN, Cs-P, is a psychiatric clinical nurse specialist. As a senior lead trainer for the Center for Self Leadership, she developed curricula for both basic and advanced trainings. She also developed the concepts and created the curriculum for her own training program in IFS couple therapy, *Intimacy from the Inside Out©*. Toni has a private practice in Durango, Colorado, where she lives with her husband, Jordan, and a menagerie of animals.

Pamela K. Krause, LCSW, has worked inpatient and outpatient with children and adolescents and, as a board member of two nonprofit organizations, has helped develop programs for at-risk youth. Pamela is a senior lead trainer for the Center for Self Leadership, where she teaches Levels 1 and 2 of the IFS trainings. In addition, she developed and teaches workshops on using IFS with children and adolescents. Pamela maintains a private practice near Harrisburg, Pennsylvania, with children, adolescents and adults.

John B. Livingstone, MD, is a chaired assistant clinical professor in psychiatry, Harvard Medical School at McLean Hospital, where he founded Children's Outpatient Services and Team Clinic. He has a long-standing commitment to improving medical care and preventing illness. His most recent project involves adapting the IFS model to the processes of health behavior change and decision making. He spent three years designing and researching an updated training program for midcareer nurse health coaches at Health Dialog, Inc. His clinical practice in Provincetown, Massachusetts, with children, parents and couples is heavily informed by his training in IFS. Contact: www.gaffney-livingstone.com

Susan McConnell, MA, senior lead trainer for the Center for Self Leadership (CSL), teaches IFS therapy in the United States and Europe. Her involvement with CSL includes developing training curricula, training the IFS training staff and designing and leading retreats and seminars. Susan's master's degree emphasized somatic psychotherapy. She developed, uses and teaches a somatic application of IFS, and has a private clinical practice in Chicago, Illinois.

Lawrence G. Rosenberg, PhD, is a specialist in human sexuality and brings an integrative perspective to psychotherapy. He has taught and published on themes pertaining to gay/lesbian/bisexual/transgender development, power dynamics in sexual relationships, erotic fantasy and compulsive sexual behavior. He presents IFS workshops and assists at IFS trainings. Larry is an instructor in psychology at Cambridge Health Alliance, Harvard Medical School, and has a clinical and consultation practice for individuals and couples in Cambridge, Massachusetts.

Richard C. Schwartz, PhD, began his career as a systemic family therapist and an academic at the University of Illinois and at Northwestern University. Grounded in systems thinking, Dr. Schwartz developed the Internal Family Systems model (IFS) in response to clients' descriptions of various parts within themselves. In 2000, he founded the Center for Self Leadership (www.selfleadership.org), which offers three levels of trainings and workshops in IFS for professionals and the general public, both in this country and abroad. A featured speaker for national professional organizations, Dr. Schwartz has published five books and over fifty articles about IFS.

Nancy Sowell, LICSW, is a trainer for the Center for Self Leadership. She consults and teaches IFS in the United States and Europe and runs workshops to train clinicians in the use of IFS with medical problems. Specializing in the use of IFS to promote health, she developed a treatment program for medical patients in a research study at Brigham and Women's Hospital in Boston and coauthored its IFS research treatment protocol. Nancy is a teaching associate at Harvard Medical School and maintains a private practice on Cape Cod as well as in Newton, Massachusetts.

Joanne H. Twombly, LICSW, specializes in treating complex posttraumatic stress disorder and dissociative disorders. She provides training and consultation in IFS, EMDR and hypnosis, and has written articles and chapters on diagnosis and treatment of dissociative disorders, the use of EMDR in treating dissociative disorders, EMDR and IFS. She is a past board member for the International Society for the Study of Trauma and Dissociation, where she received a Distinguished Achievement Award, and the past president of the New England Society for the Treatment of Trauma and Dissociation. She is in private practice in Waltham, Massachusetts.

Nancy Wonder, PhD, is an assistant trainer with the Center for Self Leadership. She has focused on sexual addiction, sexual offending and sexual abuse in her individual, group and consulting work and has used IFS to enhance therapy for sexual concerns. She has presented nationally on pornography addiction, couples and victim empathy with juveniles who commit sexual offenses. She has a private practice is in Tallahassee, Florida.

FOREWORD

Whenever I think about this book, the part who drove me to birth IFS relaxes a little. Here is concrete evidence that I'm no longer alone on this journey. These chapters contain the accumulated wisdom of 12 highly respected therapists who have been using IFS for many years in their respective specialties. In doing so, they have taken the model places I never could while broadening and deepening it.

They are making my inner life easier in other ways as well. As I've presented IFS over the last three decades, someone has invariably asked, "How do you use it with children?" "What do you think about medication?" "What about transference and countertransference?" "How does it work with DID, couples, medical symptoms, sex addiction?" and so forth. I would give a couple of sentences in answer to those questions based on my limited experience but a part of me would feel ashamed, thinking, "If this model were substantial, experts would be writing about these topics." Now that I can proudly say, "Read chapter X in *Internal Family Systems Therapy: New Dimensions*," that part, too, has begun to relax.

In addition to helping ease some of my burdens, this book is a major contribution to the literature on IFS, and, in turn, to the movement in psychotherapy and medicine toward a more collaborative, nonpathologizing, empowering approach. Each of the contributors is not only well versed in IFS but is also an authority on the topic about which they write. Martha and Ellen, the editors, took their jobs seriously. They selected key topics that fill holes in the IFS literature, chose authors who know the material and provided exceptional editorial support. I'm honored to be a part of this volume as it represents a large step forward in the history of IFS.

—*Richard C. Schwartz*

ACKNOWLEDGMENTS

MARTHA'S ACKNOWLEDGMENT OF ELLEN

On the certainty that multiplicity in human realms is a good thing, I wanted two editors for this project. So, with intuition as my guide, I invited Ellen to join me. Along the way I learned that I could not have done it without her. In addition to being smart, kind, insightful and an excellent editor, Ellen has been my anchor in hard moments and the partner who made this project fun and exciting week after week, day by day, e-mail after e-mail. I am deeply grateful.

ELLEN'S ACKNOWLEDGMENT OF MARTHA

When Martha asked me to join her as coeditor, I was surprised because we did not know each other well, and excited by the prospect of collaborating with someone I held in high regard on a project of such interest to me. I knew her to be a person with integrity and perspective. And I sensed in her a steadfast spirit full of playfulness and ingenuity. How right I was. Martha has been, without exaggeration, a dream of a partner: gracious, openhearted, generous and supremely capable. My only regret is that our work has come to an end.

OTHER ACKNOWLEDGMENTS

We thank Patricia Papernow for introducing us to Anna Moore, our editor at Routledge, who has been a gentle guide, genuine collaborator and supportive presence from start to finish. We also thank Sam Rosenthal, Anna's editorial assistant, who answered all our questions with reassurance and alacrity. And we thank Susan Callaghan, Director of Marketing and Communications at Boston College Graduate School of Social Work, for her beautiful cover design.

We particularly thank our authors, from whom we have learned so much, for their deep commitment to expanding the boundaries of the IFS model. Our editorial parts have been the happy recipients of their patience and gracious good humor. We thank Dick Schwartz for his masterful clinical work, his leadership in developing the model and his generosity in contributing both the Foreword for this book and a seminal chapter on the evolution of his thinking about the relational aspects of IFS.

We also thank the following people: Maggie Brenner, who offered invaluable perspective and insight on both content and process throughout book; and Lisa Ferentz, Matt Leeds and Janna Smith, who gave their time and expertise by reading and supporting our book proposal.

AN INTRODUCTION TO IFS

Jack Engler

BEGINNINGS

Ironically, I was introduced to one of the newest and fastest growing therapies in the United States in the First Parish Church of Cambridge, one of the oldest public buildings in the Boston area, on a cold, wet winter afternoon in 2005. I have come to view this as fitting because IFS has affinities with some of the world's great spiritual traditions. Although Boston has become the epicenter of growth for IFS, at the time it was an eastern outpost hosting a workshop given by the founder, Richard Schwartz.

I had been practicing psychodynamic psychotherapy in Cambridge for 25 years, so initially I wasn't all that enthusiastic about learning a new system. But this first exposure to IFS turned out to be compelling. I was impressed by Dr. Schwartz' presentation, by the basic concepts and structure of the IFS model, and by his description of how IFS emerged from a paradox he encountered while doing structural family therapy: "A family would make the structural changes the theory said should help them function better," I recall him saying, "but when I began to ask individual family members about their actual subjective experience of the changes the family had made, they would often say they didn't feel any better than before."

PARTS AND THE MULTIPLICITY OF MIND

Exploring this paradox eventually led him to discover an *internal* family system similarly composed of separate components in complex relationships with each other, very much like members of the external family.

That is, the mind is not a singular entity or self, but is multiple, composed of *parts*. This principle of multiplicity is at the core of the IFS model. Each of our parts, Dr. Schwartz found, has its own history, outlook and approach, its own idiosyncratic beliefs, characteristic moods and feelings, and its own relationships with other parts. More important, each part has its own distinct role or function within the internal system. A part, in other words, is not just a temporary emotional state or habitual thought pattern; it is a discrete and autonomous mental system with its own unique range of emotion, style of expression, set of abilities, desires and view of the world (Schwartz, 1995: 34). IFS views this multiplicity of mind as normal. In fact, we talk this way about ourselves all the time. We say, for instance, "A part of me wanted to do it. A part of me didn't." Assagioli's (1976) notion of "subpersonality," Jung's idea of "complexes" (1969) and Perls's (1969) gestalt therapy all capture something of this idea of multiplicity. As psychoanalytic thinking has become more re-lational, it too has wrestled with the question of whether the self is singular or multiple (Mitchell, 1993; Engler, 2003). Although the idea that the mind is multiple is very old, the concept runs against our preferred way of repre-senting ourselves to ourselves as a separate, autonomous self, an "I" or "me" whom we view as an independent center of consciousness and initiative. This idea of a separate, singular self is actually quite modern and western, only three or four hundred years old, a product of the European enlightenment (Taylor, 1989). So though Schwartz described arriving at his conceptualiza-tion independently, largely from asking clients a set of questions that were new to family therapists, IFS has distinguished antecedents.

Parts, as understood by IFS, cluster into three groups, each with a differ-ent function. The first is a protective group of parts called *managers*. These strategic, task-oriented parts strive to keep us organized and safe. They may push perfectionism, worry obsessively, exhaust with care taking, or more pas-sively avoid, deny, discourage and devalue. Ironically, as they become extreme in the pursuit of safety and exile our injured parts to protect the system, they inflict more harm. The injured parts who get exiled are invariably burdened with emotional pain and dysfunctional beliefs about their worth and lovability that threaten the equilibrium protectors crave. When exiles override manag-ers with emotional pain, they take us over, literally become us. IFS says they are now *blended* with us. Before we realize it, we identify with our exiles and take them to be who we are. We see ourselves and the world through their eyes and believe it is "the" world. In this state it won't occur to us that we have been hijacked.

When exiles blend with us, another set of protective parts called *firefight-ers* are activated. Their role is to put out the emotional fire at any cost, often by starting backfires. This is the heavy artillery: alcohol, drugs, eating disorders, promiscuous sex, pornography, self-mutilation and suicidality, exacting a steep cost in collateral damage. Exiles, managers and firefighters are the trio we encounter in symptomatic behavior. Although exiles have been forced into a position not of their own choosing, protectors are volunteers who have often been playing their part since early in life, sometimes since infancy, to keep the system functioning.

From the point of view of IFS, therefore, many behaviors typically viewed as symptoms of underlying psychiatric disorders are actually strategies of protection. Common examples include anxiety-related symptoms such as obsessions, compulsions, phobias and panic attacks; or depression-related symptoms like passivity, withdrawal or insomnia and somatic complaints; or more self-destructive behaviors like eating disorders, self-harm and suicide. The IFS conceptualization of parts appealed to me because it is experience-near and nonpathologizing. Behaviors seem less entrenched and intimidating, more workable and open to change.

How are these parts actually experienced? Some experience them as internal people, though this may be the least common. More frequently they are experienced as internal "voices," images or sensations. Contact with a part can be made through any mode of perception, including imagery, memory or physical sensation. They may manifest differently at different times, and be experienced as more or less distinct. But this doesn't prevent connection with them, or make the work less effective. The key is approaching every part with genuine interest and respect.

Sooner or later most practitioners wonder what type of reality parts have. This question remains unresolved because IFS has developed, as with most psychotherapies, phenomenologically. Dr. Schwartz deliberately deferred the process of grounding IFS in theory and research until later to make IFS immediately available to clinicians. Research is now beginning, as are attempts to approach philosophical issues like the nature of parts.

SELF

Dr. Schwartz introduced another finding in the introductory workshop that I have come to feel is the most important and innovative aspect of the entire IFS model: the notion of Self. This term *Self* (capital S) can be controversial because it carries certain connotations and invites associations with other therapeutic and spiritual systems that use the same term. Beginning with Freud, psychoanalysis has felt compelled to find a place for the concept of self. In fact it has become the most debated notion in contemporary analytic thinking (Mitchell, 1993). Long before IFS, I was familiar with a similar discussion in the great spiritual traditions, for which the term is central. "Self" in the Upanishads or Vedanta, for instance, points to Ultimate Reality, Absolute Being, our innermost being behind all transient appearances and outside space and time. But there is no agreed upon meaning. The term is used inconsistently within the therapeutic and spiritual traditions themselves. Buddhism, for instance, uses the diametrically opposite term "No-Self" for what is arguably the same reality (Engler & Fulton, 2012). But although certainly aware of its usage in the spiritual traditions (Schwartz, 2001, 29ff), Dr. Schwartz said he discovered what he came to call Self by listening closely to his clients.

He attempted to anchor this term, too, in direct experience. When a part steps back and releases its grip on us so that we no longer take it to be part of our core identity, what do we discover? First of all, a state of pure, open receptive awareness and acceptance without judgment or agendas. Self is what remains when parts are willing to unblend from us. When we relax into being that which is not any of our parts, IFS says we find our core, our essence, our true nature. Our natural state is a state of wholeness and completeness.

And from that core, uncontrived state, we discover that basic wholesome qualities emanate spontaneously. For instance, we don't become compassionate and kind. Kindness and compassion are already there, as are many other positive attributes. We cannot acquire or generate them, and we don't need to because they are innate. They are not transient states of consciousness that come and go, but timeless qualities of being. Self is like a beam of light that refracts into all the colors of the rainbow as it passes through a prism and illuminates our parts and external objects in the world. Interestingly, these "colors" overlap with many of the same qualities that all the Great Traditions identify. Dr. Schwartz used a mnemonic of Cs to identify eight of them, though this list is not exhaustive: calmness, clarity (or wisdom), curiosity, compassion, confidence, courage, creativity and connectedness. This is the same group of qualities that Buddhist teaching has long called *paramis*, or "perfections," qualities of mind considered essential to awakening. IFS uses the term "Self" for this unblended state. The term Self-energy is also useful to designate the flow of feeling from Self to parts, and to recognize the different degrees to which a part is blended.

Two things about the notion of Self as described by Dr. Schwartz struck me as original. First, unlike most of the Great Traditions, which typically assume that years of disciplined practice are necessary to access Self-energy, practitioners of IFS find that any time a part becomes willing to unblend, we will experience some degree of inherent wisdom and compassion, some sense of freedom, lucidity and connection. At the same time, IFS recognizes the reality that our parts are seldom completely unblended from us. The part we are working with may need to stay partially blended to feel safe enough for interaction with us. Moreover, as one part unblends we may still be blended or partially blended with others. This means we are seldom completely "in Self." Instead we move into Self by degrees. This idea may be original with IFS and is crucial in working with parts.

Second, the description Dr. Schwartz gave of Self playing an interactive role with parts was new and stimulating to me. In his conceptualization, Self doesn't only witness or passively observe as in some meditation traditions; it has an active leadership role. One of his metaphors likens Self to the conductor of an orchestra, helping parts find new roles and function more harmoniously resulting in a symphony rather than a cacophony. From Self, curiosity, compassion and wisdom arise spontaneously, helping us to get to know and care for our parts. More surprising still was the idea that if we are even somewhat unblended, we are capable of providing the leadership our parts need.[1] The assumption—repeatedly borne out in my experience since—is that only Self-led leadership is trustworthy and effective. That which is whole and complete, aware and awake in us, is very unlike parts. It is unbiased, impartial and does not need things to be "this" way or "that" but instead expresses interest, concern, care and compassion. Parts have agendas. Self does not.

This was the overall view of IFS that Dr. Schwartz presented on that cold, wet winter weekend in Cambridge. I liked the experience-near conceptualizations and language. I also had been trying for some time to formulate a notion of self as both singular and multiple from the perspectives of psychoanalytic and Buddhist psychology (Engler, 2003). In addition, I was looking for fresh inspiration in my clinical work. I found it all that weekend.

As intrigued as I was with IFS theory at that workshop, what I remember most was a video of Dr. Schwartz working with a 21-year-old woman diagnosed with borderline personality disorder, a notoriously hard-to-treat set of symptoms. In the video she sat stiff and unmoving in an overstuffed chair, staring ahead, barely able to speak. An enraged suicidal part had vowed she would not live past 21 and this was her 21st birthday. The videotape showed Dr. Schwartz working with the client to get the suicidal part to unblend, help the exile it had been protecting to feel safe and heard and then, implausibly to me at the time, help the suicidal part actually find a different and less destructive role within her internal family. As I watched, I realized this work went to a level and used a skill set with which I was not familiar. I have since learned that after this session the young woman stopped self-mutilating and ceased to be suicidal.

THE CAPE COD INSTITUTE: UNBURDENING

That summer of 2005, I attended a weeklong seminar that Dr. Schwartz offers annually at the Cape Cod Summer Institute. This seminar introduced me to *unburdening*, a process that may be unique to IFS. The notion that we accumulate burdens in the form of extreme ideas or feelings seemed self-evident to me. However, the notion that burdens are not intrinsic to parts and can be released was not. For unburdening to occur, both client and therapist must first recognize that the burden is not the part's essence, that it was imposed from the outside at some point in the individual's life, and that it need not evoke guilt or shame. Next, the part needs to have some or all of its experiences witnessed and understood by the client's Self. Only then will it let the burden go. IFS offers a stepwise protocol for the release of burdens, in which parts are invited to choose their own rituals for letting go; on the other hand, unburdening often occurs spontaneously. Dr. Schwartz acknowledged that some clients find the concept too gimmicky and easy. Or else they have trouble believing that burdens can actually be released. For others, the idea flies in the face of their all-too-long struggle with burdened parts. Still others carry a secret (or unconscious) belief that there cannot really be an end to internal conflict and suffering. Even some IFS therapists have trouble believing unburdening is possible. Among those who accept the notion, there is controversy over whether an unburdening will hold over time or will have to be repeated. In my experience, if a part carries several different burdens, or has received the same burden from several sources, the process often does need to be repeated. My first unburdening, described below, was one and done, but I know from subsequent experience this is not always the case.

I returned to my room in late afternoon after a day at the seminar introducing the unburdening process. I had a couple of hours before supper and thought I'd use the time to practice what we'd been taught. I mostly wanted to see for myself whether and how it worked. Soon after starting, it became very real. When I went inside to see which parts were asking for attention, I quickly became aware of a continuous high-pitched scream of terror, which seemed to come from the back of my mind. I gradually realized that I had been hearing this screaming for as far back as I could remember. It was in the background of almost every state of consciousness. I invited the part who was screaming to come forward. It was a 7-year-old boy. I asked if there was something he wanted me to understand about his screaming.

At once a memory surfaced of a terrifying hospital experience in which this child was strapped to a gurney while strangers slowly lowered an ether mask over his face. His parents had disappeared. All he could see was the black, foul-smelling hole coming closer and closer to engulf and suffocate him. Whether his scream was out loud or only in his mind, he didn't know, but he did suddenly know why he was screaming. I asked him if there were more he needed me to witness, or if he could finally release this burden of terror, shame, abandonment and helplessness. He said he felt ready. I asked if he wanted to come into the present to be with me and find a role in my current life. Again he said yes. I told him he could go ahead and release the burden and join me, which he did. I have not heard the screaming since.

INDIVIDUAL THERAPY

I didn't have to wait long before discovering further applications of IFS. Later that fall of 2005, I was hit broadside while driving. Fortunately the collision was low impact. Neither of us seemed hurt. Two to three weeks later, however, I began to experience pain in my neck. Over the fall and winter the pain gradually radiated down my left side until it became unbearable. A series of imaging studies revealed problems in my cervical spine. After a series of epidurals in the spring of 2006 remitted most of the pain, I approached one of Dr. Schwartz' senior assistants from the Cape Cod workshop about doing individual IFS therapy. This decision proved fortuitous, especially after a consulting neurologist told me—without sufficient data, I thought—that he "would have to think about ALS," or Lou Gehrig's disease. Hearing this threw many of my parts into panic, especially exiles who were constantly on the verge of feeling overwhelmed by fear. Initially, trying to help them un-blend was next to impossible. So I went back into therapy again, this time with a clear understanding of the task and how to approach it.

I've sought help from therapists a number of times over the past thirty years, but I experienced this two-year therapy as completely different. I have no doubt it was this therapist and the IFS approach we took that saw me through. It was the work of slowly unblending from terrified parts, befriending and reaching out to frightened protectors, and being able to work with them all from Self, that enabled me to gradually find some balance and inner peace. Even in daily mindfulness meditation, which I had been practicing for 35 years, I found myself spontaneously working with these terrified parts. Although I would not claim that IFS was the only therapeutic approach that would have worked, it proved remarkably effective in this extreme situation when living and dying seemed to hang in the balance. I can feel no deeper gratitude.

IFS IN DAILY LIFE

I include the following vignette because it shows how parts work can be done in increments, on the spot, in the middle of daily life; and because it was one of many similar experiences that engendered my trust in the method. It also shows some of the steps involved in working with a part. I had been invited to give a series of talks at four different hospitals and colleges in the spring of 2007. I had a bad feeling going into them for reasons I didn't fully understand. And indeed the first three did not go that well, each one a little less successful than the one before. I could feel my anxiety rising and my confidence sinking with each talk. I became particularly anxious as the fourth one approached, feeling a kind of dread. Why I didn't think to consult my parts earlier I don't know—probably because they were so blended with me. I finally remembered to contact the part who was making me so anxious. The part responded im-mediately. What it said made a certain sense.

"If you go down to New York feeling this anxious, you're going to make a fool of yourself in front of your professional colleagues. You know what will happen—you'll feel humiliated and ashamed. My job is to protect you from embarrassing yourself. I figure if I can make you anxious enough, you'll find some way to excuse yourself and not go. I will have spared you the shame."

I thought about this and replied, "Thank you for wanting to help. I can see you intend well. However, I committed to giving this talk. If you persist in making me more anxious and I mess up the talk, you're going to bring about the very situation you're trying to protect me from. Do you see that?"

The part immediately replied, "Oh, I didn't think about that! That's not what I intended! What can we do?"

I said, "Let me make a suggestion. Why don't you accompany me to New York? There's no point in asking you to trust me. Come see for yourself whether you need to be as protective as you think. Your over-protectiveness is partly what's creating the problem."

The part agreed. I made an additional request: "You might become anxious yourself on the way down and jump in to try to prevent me from continuing. But if that happens, we'll know what that's about and we'll deal with it so we can continue." The part agreed to this too.

The flight to JFK was uneventful. I was feeling no more than the normal anxiety I would expect. However, when I went to get a ticket for the airport shuttle to the Long Island Railroad, I suddenly became disoriented and confused. Complete brain fog. Everyone else was getting their ticket and streaming through the turnstiles, and I couldn't figure out how to operate the automated ticket machine I'd never had a problem with before. A moment of clarity: "Is that you? Did you just jump in to prevent me from getting there?"

"Yes, it's me."

"OK. You're still having problems trusting me so you're taking matters into your own hands again. No problem. Please step back so we can proceed. But keep watching and observing." Instantly the fog cleared. I knew exactly what to do. An hour later I came out of the subway, felt the cold mix of sleet and rain on City Hall Plaza, saw the inches of slush underfoot, and in a moment realized I'd left my umbrella on the train.

"Is that you again?"

"Yes, my anxiety got the better of me again. This was my last chance to stop you from trying to give the talk."

"Thank you. We anticipated this might happen. Please step back and let me cross the Plaza. But come with me and witness the talk. See if I make a fool of myself. I'll check in with you afterward to see what you think."

I turned around and discovered a kiosk selling umbrellas for $5 directly behind me. I bought one, crossed City Hall Plaza, and gave the talk—not my best, but I enjoyed giving it and enjoyed the students. I did not embarrass myself. On the way back to Grand Central Station, I checked in with the part as promised.

"What did you think?"

In reply, a deep, quiet, contented silence, which lasted all the way back to Boston. Since then I've certainly had performance anxiety before talks, but only once before this had I experienced the dread I felt that spring, and never the inner peace I felt afterward.

CLINICAL PRACTICE

I began using the frame and language of IFS in 2007. Often I use the entire therapy protocol if the client is open to working directly with parts. With some explanation and encouragement, this seems to happen easily and naturally, sometimes for the entire session. In daily living I use IFS all the time. For me, this is in some ways the most interesting and fruitful application of all. Parts don't wait—sometimes can't wait—until the therapy hour to make their presence felt and have their needs acknowledged. I've also found IFS very compatible with mindfulness and have made it part of my daily meditation practice. Having a meditation practice and using IFS helps clients to work interactively with the parts they discover when they "go inside."

INTRODUCTION TO THE CHAPTERS

In the following chapters the reader will notice the repeated appearance of the guiding axioms of IFS. Parts always intend our well-being. This is true regardless of how it may look when we first encounter a part and no matter how misdirected its actions. It is true even of aversive and afflictive mind states like the "Three Poisons" of greed, hatred and delusion in Buddhist psychology. Because all parts have some Self-energy at their core, they themselves seek balance and harmony and are ultimately open to change. Unskillful or harmful behavior derives from the extreme role a part has been forced into, not from its intentions. The goal of therapy is therefore not to eliminate parts but to help them transform. And when they do transform and change roles, they remain part of the internal family. They do not disappear.

The essential element for the transformation of parts is Self-energy; the key to accessing Self-energy lies in helping parts to unblend; and the key to unblending is curiosity and disinterested inquiry into their experience, with no intention to fix, change or eliminate. As the ground state of receptive awareness, Self provides the compassionate leadership that parts need to initiate change. It is a given in this treatment that burdens, including the burdens of feeling shamed and unlovable, can be released with the help of Self-energy. In sum, the process of IFS involves several steps, in this order: unblending, befriending, being curious about and transforming parts. The befriending of parts is fundamental. *All* parts. This is a tantric practice: adversaries become allies spontaneously. As the IFS mantra states, *All parts welcome!*

These chapters are intended both for those who are familiar with the model and for newcomers. Although serving as a rich introduction, the book also provides insight into the current thinking and practice of some of the most experienced IFS therapists. Appropriately for a model that is experiential by design, each author invites you into clinical sessions, offering a direct glimpse into the internal experience of the client, and often the therapist as well. Some chapters describe using IFS with specific client populations: trauma and dissociative disorders, pornography addiction, children and adolescents, chronic pain and disease. Others describe the use of IFS in different therapeutic modalities: couple therapy, psychopharmacology and health coaching. And others illustrate using IFS in relation to sexuality and shame.

The work of these authors makes it clear that IFS is continuing to evolve as a system of healing and a theory of mind. As Dr. Schwartz spells out in his pivotal chapter on the therapist–client relationship, IFS is not only finding new applications, but is discovering new dimensions of the model itself. He acknowledges he emphasized the relationship between the client's Self and parts as the primary mode of healing at the outset of developing IFS, giving much less attention to the relationship between therapist and client. As a result, though relational in multiple dimensions, IFS has sometimes been perceived as a nonrelational therapy. He describes himself as now having come full circle: from minimizing the role of the therapeutic relationship to appreciating the ways in which it is foundational.

In conclusion, each contributor to this volume hopes to stimulate your curiosity, broaden your options and perhaps inform your own internal family.

NOTE

1. This is reminiscent of what Buddhist psychology calls *asangkarikachitta*, unmotivated or spontaneous action that is appropriate and commensurate with the needs of the situation that prompted it, and that is not attached to a particular outcome.

REFERENCES

Assagioli, Roberto. 1976. *Psychosynthesis*. New York, NY: Penguin.
Engler, Jack. 2003. "On Being Somebody and Being Nobody." In *Buddhism and Psychoanalysis: An Unfolding Dialogue*, edited by Jeremy Safran, pp. 35–100. Somerville, MA: Wisdom Publications.
Engler, Jack, & Paul Fulton. 2012. "Self and No-Self in Psychotherapy." In *Wisdom and Compassion in Psychotherapy: Deepening Mindfulness in Clinical Practice*, edited by Christopher Germer & Ronald Siegel, pp. 176–188. New York, NY: Guilford Press.
Jung, Carl. 1969. "The Structure and Dynamics of the Psyche." *Collected Works*. Vol. 8. Princeton, NJ: Princeton University Press.
Mitchell, Stephen. 1993. *Hope and Dread in Psychoanalysis*. New York, NY: Basic Books.
Perls, Fritz. 1969. *The Gestalt Approach and Eyewitness to Therapy*. New York, NY: Bantam Books.

Schwartz, Richard. 1995. *Internal Family Systems Therapy*. New York, NY: Guilford Press.

Schwartz, Richard. 2001. *Introduction to the Internal Family Systems Model*. Oak Park, IL: Trailheads Publications.

Taylor, Charles. 1989. *Sources of the Self: The Making of the Modern Identity*. Cambridge, MA: Harvard University Press.

THE THERAPIST–CLIENT RELATIONSHIP AND THE TRANSFORMATIVE POWER OF SELF

Richard C. Schwartz

The primary healing relationship in internal family systems (IFS) therapy is between the client's Self and her young, injured parts. Because I have emphasized this aspect of IFS for many years while giving far less attention to the relationship surrounding it between therapist and client, I have contributed to the perception that IFS is not a relational therapy. This perception, however, is mistaken. IFS is designed to develop the relational field within and between each participant in a parallel process. In this chapter I spotlight the ways in which IFS is a relational treatment on multiple levels and I explain why the therapist–client relationship is as important in IFS as it is in any other therapy.

NURTURANCE IN THERAPY

Due to the influence of humanist therapists such as Carl Rogers (1951) and, more recently, of attachment theory, therapists have learned to emphasize nurturance in relationships with clients. Regardless of theoretical bent, therapists in training are now taught to attune to the emotions of their clients and respond genuinely. The importance of transference is also broadly accepted. Most clinicians are aware that the therapeutic relationship can evoke the client's extreme beliefs and feelings, and that these can be transformed through a safe, correctively healthy experience with the therapist.

1

SHIFT TO SELF/PART AS THE PRIMARY HEALING RELATIONSHIP

Nevertheless, the way IFS prioritizes the relationship between the client's Self and parts distinguishes it from most contemporary psychotherapies. Although the therapist–client relationship is key in IFS, much of the healing happens when the Self rather than the therapist becomes the primary, loving attachment figure for a client's injured young parts. This is a conceptual shift on the roles of therapist and client, which has partly obscured the importance of the therapeutic relationship. But I also contributed to the problem initially by minimizing the importance of the therapist–client relationship in response to my own experience.

While I was in college I worked summers as an aide on a psychoanalytically oriented psychiatric unit in Chicago, and I was disturbed by how much the patients there came to depend on their therapists. I got close to several adolescents on the ward who repeated some bizarre interpretations offered by their analysts and told me how, if they did not initiate speaking, whole sessions could go on in silence. I listened to them wonder obsessively whether their analysts cared about them and I watched them seek their analyst's approval before making even minor decisions. As a result, I decided that when I grew up professionally I would find a way to avoid making my clients dependent.

When I realized in the early 1980s that everyone has a Self, I felt tremendous relief. I knew it was possible to do deep healing work without fostering the kind of intensely dependent relationships that I viewed as disempowering and iatrogenic. I thought people would walk away from therapy feeling they had healed themselves. The focus would be the client's relationship with his or her parts rather than with me. When clients had transferential feelings toward me, casting me in the role of someone from their past, we would find the part who saw me that way and work with it rather than working through the issue between us. In turn, when parts of me came up, I would try to get them to step back and not interfere so I could hold Self-leadership for my client rather than bringing my countertransference into our relationship.

Although some of my desire to rely on the Self of the client rather than on the therapist–client relationship was based on solid observations and principles, some of it was based on extreme beliefs that came from my own parts. Like many men, I had a part who hated being clung to and recoiled from neediness with its implicit demand that I fix things. When I disappointed clients and sensed their anger, I had parts who felt imposed on and shamed, and my reactions were intense. As a result, as I developed the model I downplayed the importance of the relationship and did not fully consider the impact of therapists who were not able to maintain Self-leadership. Since those early days, I have learned from my clients, and from the experience of being a client, that the therapy relationship is crucial. This chapter is an attempt to remedy my early mistake.

THE IFS VERSION OF SAFE CONTAINMENT

Many clients enter therapy with their protectors on high alert. They know that therapy involves being vulnerable and trusting the therapist, and they have had terrible experiences with people (including former therapists) they trusted. If the therapist can hold Self-leadership from the first session, the client's protectors will immediately sense the safety. As Ann entered Larry's office for her first session she heard a familiar inner voice critiquing his taste in furniture and clothes. This part of her also said his handshake was weak and he looked like an old hippie. In her head she heard, "He won't be able to handle you—you should leave right now."

At the same time, Ann could not help noticing that he had friendly eyes and an easy, calm demeanor that felt different from the previous two therapists she had fired. As she described her dreadful history to him—the shameful suicide attempt and nightmarish hospitalization, the past bouts of depression and current emptiness—she scanned his face for signs of disdain or fear but found none. Instead, he asked questions about the "parts of her" who had made her depressed, empty and suicidal—what types of things had they said to her or made her feel—and how did they seem now? His voice betrayed no anxiety or judgment. Instead, Larry seemed genuinely curious about these parts.

Her protector decided to test him. "What do you mean parts?" she said with no little contempt. "Are you implying that I'm DID?" She knew all the psychiatric terms. He explained calmly that he was using a therapy model that believed we all have parts and there are no bad ones—just ones who are hurt or protective. He also said the model was effective in helping all parts to unload any pain, fear and shame they carry and, once they have unloaded it, to return to their naturally valuable states.

Her contempt did not seem to intimidate or provoke him and although this confidence raised hope in some of her parts, it scared others. The hope came from a sense that he understood. Ann knew that her tormenting inner voices and urges had a life of their own, which had always made her feel crazy. If he could deliver on the promise that these parts were not what they seemed—and they could change—it would mean liberation from constant torment.

On the other hand, if he could not deliver she would be devastatingly disappointed and would likely become suicidal again. After all, he had not yet met her incredible neediness and he did not know about the shameful things that had happened to her or why she deserved them. Maybe she was the defective exception, or maybe he was not as good at therapy as he was implying. While this debate raged inside her, Larry said something startling: "It looks like you have a part who's skeptical about what I'm saying and I want you to know, if that's true, I honor that part and won't go any further without its permission. I know I have to earn its trust and I'm happy to discuss all its fears."

In this brief exchange, Larry not only communicated curiosity, calm and confidence (three of the 8 Cs of Self-leadership), but also unflappable equanimity despite the severity of her history, symptoms and provocative challenges. He was a hope merchant, presenting a vision of new possibility to her pessimistic system. In addition, he was solicitous of her protector and respectful of its need to make sure that his approach would be safe.

Safety in IFS derives from a combination of potent ingredients. First, the therapist's unaffected warm, steady, accepting *presence*, fortified by the IFS *perspective* that allowed Larry to exude hope and confidence because he trusted that her severe symptoms were a product of extreme parts carrying pain that could be unloaded, rather than being evidence of scary pathology. Next, he showed *patience* and respect for what might be considered her resistance, which he viewed as the understandable need of her protectors to ensure that he was safe. These qualities instilled seeds of hope in Ann, while reducing her fear and frustration with her own parts. Because the therapist and client are in a parallel process, clients such as Ann increasingly demonstrate patience, perspective and presence with their own parts—they come to relate to their parts just as the therapist's Self relates to them.

THE 5 PS

In other words, Larry's Self-energy elicited Ann's, as one tuning fork wakens another. Ann's protectors sensed this safety and relaxed, allowing her Self to surface. As the therapy continued, she increasingly manifested more of the core qualities of Self-leadership, which I call the "8 Cs." In addition to curiosity, confidence and compassion (mentioned above), the others are *courage, clarity, creativity, calm* and *connectedness*. Over time, Ann displayed more of these signs of Self-leadership both in her relationship with Larry and with her parts.

The ability of the therapist to manifest those 8 Cs—to maintain Self-leadership—is also central in creating the safety and acceptance that characterizes the therapeutic relationship in IFS. In addition, we highlight five other qualities of the Self-led therapist, called the "5 Ps," which are the foundation of the therapeutic relationship in IFS. I just introduced the first three: patience, presence and perspective. In later sessions Larry will demonstrate the other two: *persistence* and *playfulness*.

Ann came to the fifth session determined to talk rather than turning her attention inside. In the previous two sessions, Larry had persuaded her to begin getting to know her parts and they had started with the skeptic. As Larry talked to this primary guardian directly, Ann was surprised at how quickly it was disarmed. Larry convinced the skeptic that Ann could witness and heal her sad part, whom the skeptic protected, without being overwhelmed, which would free the skeptic to take another role in her internal system. Immediately following this discussion, Ann saw herself as a little girl being sexually abused by the son of a neighbor—a memory she had vowed many years earlier never to revisit. While Larry was able to help Ann enter the scene and take the girl to a safe place, Ann had not checked on the girl during the ensuing week as she had promised. Indeed, she remembered nothing about the previous session until she arrived for the current one. She had no idea how the girl was doing and did not want to feel guilty about having abandoned her.

She told Larry that she felt much better since their last piece of work. She was very grateful for his help and thought she could take it from here. Larry asked permission to speak directly to the part talking, and then asked the part to be honest about why it wanted to stop. It replied, "I've had enough mucking around in the past! This is dangerous and scary. The suicide thoughts came up again for the first time in years."

Demonstrating perspective, Larry said, "I'm not surprised. Many clients have some kind of backlash after their first encounter with an exile." He did not seem flustered by the return of her suicidality, and he demonstrated presence by saying, "We just need to find the parts who made you forget about the girl." This felt strange to Ann, who was used to being attacked and shamed. Her protectors kept waiting for the other shoe to drop—for Larry to suddenly turn on her.

THE IFS VERSION OF THE CORRECTIVE EXPERIENCE

Many psychotherapies know that deep healing takes place when a client who expects to be humiliated or rejected experiences the therapist's acceptance and love instead. The IFS therapist's tenacious caring helps clients take the slogan *all parts are welcome* seriously and trust that no parts are bad. In this way IFS involves more of a corrective experience than I have discussed in the past. After disclosing or manifesting their most shameful parts, clients are profoundly relieved to be met with compassion and the words "It's just a part of you—not who you are—and even that part isn't what it seems to be." This is the parallel process. When the therapist responds to the client's extreme parts from Self, the client does also. Compassion and acceptance are contagious and can seep through the cracks into all levels of the internal system.

Even better, clients learn Self-leadership is not an exercise in becoming one's own cheerleader through affirmations (e.g., "I am a good person"), which inner critics can deconstruct seconds later. Instead, during inner work clients have an in-the-bones experience that who they really are is pure goodness and strength (the Self). After these experiences, clients who had no inkling of such internal capacities are often shocked when I point out how strong and caring they became once their parts opened space for their Self to emerge.

THERAPIST'S TRUST IN THE CLIENT'S SELF

In IFS, the client is empowered by the therapist's complete trust that she will know what to do once she has accessed her Self. However, until the moment when the critical mass of Self manifests (which can be seen in the client's shift in tone of voice, facial expression and word content), I am often reflecting back empathically what the client reports her parts saying, and offering suggestions for what the client might say or do with a part. This stage is quite similar to reflective listening, which most therapists learn in graduate school. Reflective listening helps the target part feel accepted by me before more of the client's Self emerges, and it also helps her protectors trust that we are on the right path so they can relax their grip. Once a client manifests a critical mass of Self, IFS therapists learn to get out of the way, just to keep an eye out for parts of the client who might interfere, making occasional empathic comments, or sometimes asking questions like, "What do you say to the part about that?" or "Where do you want to go now?" or "What feels like the right next step?" As well as the ubiquitous Self-detecting question "How do you feel toward the part now?"

As the therapist continues to be a curious, empathic partner in exploration with the client rather than an expert who is figuring it out for the client and giving her the missing direction, the client's Self is allowed to demonstrate its abilities and increasingly her parts come to trust her own leadership rather than looking to the therapist. The restoration of trust in Self-leadership is a major goal of IFS, a goal that can be impeded by the therapist's need to be useful or in control.

Suggesting that they get to know the suicidal part before returning to the girl, Larry said, "Until we befriend that part, it will be hard for your system to relax and let you be with your exiles because they will constantly be afraid of suicide." Although Ann could understand this logic, the thought of approaching her most lethal part seemed crazy. She had worked hard to keep it locked away and he wanted her to throw the gates wide open! Larry reassured her that the process would not give the suicidal one more power. Instead the goal was to get to know the part and help it realize that there was a different way to relieve her misery. To calm all fears about approaching the suicide part, Larry had to help Ann reassure six different parts. And although several initially separated, they returned when she got closer to the suicide part. Ann expected Larry to become frustrated with the seemingly endless stream of obstacles presented by her system. A part of her was listening carefully, prepared to shut everything down at any hint of impatience.

PATIENT PERSISTENCE

In our trainings, IFS therapists learn to be patiently *persistent*. Until there is a clear message from the client's protectors to stop, they learn to consistently offer the opportunity to keep going, knowing that, in many cases, the client is being invited to do the scariest thing she has ever done. When a therapist leads from Self, she can be doggedly persistent without coming across as pushy or insistent because she is not emotionally attached to achieving the goal. Instead she is calmly holding up a hopeful possibility and inviting the client to try it out. She also conveys such respect for the client's protectors and their right to refuse entrance that they do not feel threatened by her persistence. Protectors may feel frightened about opening the door to exiles but not feel additional pressure from the therapist's need for them to do it. Instead, protectors appreciate the therapist's concern along with her recognition that their fears must be addressed before entrance is permitted.

IFS therapists persist in many other ways as well. For example, the session after an exile is unburdened, the therapist remembers to follow up and see if the part is still doing well, even if the client wants to start with something else. In addition, in the face of provocative testing from the client's protectors, the therapist persists in responding with Self-energy or, if triggered, works to find her own upset part, speak for it, and return to Self-leadership. We call this tenacious caring.

PLAYFULNESS

The final P, *playfulness*, is an attitude; a lightness of being that accompanies Self-leadership. To paraphrase Oscar Wilde (1893), life is too important to be taken seriously. The Self-led therapist feels compassion for the client's suffering and therefore takes it seriously but, at another level, knows that her suffering will be lifted by the work and is often amused by the dance of the client's protectors as they try to distract, deter, dominate and divert both client and therapist. Despite how wise, dangerous or powerful they seem, most protectors are young. Like children who do not think they will be heard if they are direct, protectors believe they have to manipulate. From the position of Self, those manipulations often seem more funny or cute than threatening.

The therapist's amusement with protectors can help the client take them less seriously, too. I often remind clients that these parts are really scared, desperate children who need reassurance and firmness. Once separated from the fear of protectors, clients can often relate to them playfully. Of course, the therapist is not always playful. If the therapist's amusement is interpreted as mocking or trivializing, clients can lose trust. Therefore a therapist finds a balance between serious intensity and a bit of comic relief that fosters connection and perspective. And with some clients, the risk that they will misinterpret humor is so high that one only chuckles inside, privately.

CONNECTION TO AND TRUST IN CLIENT'S SELF

Playfulness requires a level of safety and connectedness in a relationship such that each person feels free to have fun with the other. There is something beautiful about being present when clients' Selves emerge and I witness their courage, grace and vulnerability. When my Self is fully embodied during those sessions, I feel a deep, pure loving connection to my clients and many clients report feeling the same. We do not have to talk about it to feel it. The Self-to-Self connection is wordless, joyful and often brings tears to my eyes.

I am convinced that this transcendent sense of connection is a key to the healing process. The more my client feels it with me, the more she can feel it with her parts, which is what they long for (what we all long for, for that matter). The more the client feels it, the more emboldened she is to enter terrifying inner chasms and abysses, knowing she's not alone. And the more she trusts that we are energetically connected even when not together, the more she can take risks in the outside world.

There is one more aspect of IFS that therapists trained in other therapeutic approaches say they have trouble trusting. Therapists who do not believe that the client feels their presence when they are silent will tend to keep talking while the client is working inside, asking how things are going or giving frequent direction. A high level of therapist activity such as this is generally unnecessary and can have a couple of negative consequences. First, while exploring inside, many clients have trouble remaining focused when they are interrupted. I often suggest to therapists in our trainings that they use the acronym WAIT, which stands for "Why am I talking?" Second, the more the therapist checks to see how clients are doing or tells them what to do, the less their parts trust that their Self is capable of leading. In other words, many clients' parts have little or no trust (or even awareness of) their Self and as long as they can look to the therapist for guidance, they will never learn how wise, strong and caring their own Self is.

In some of my sessions there are either long periods of silence while clients work inside or times when only the client is talking, describing what she is doing in the inner world. As long as I trust that the client's Self is actively present and she is not being distracted or sent on a wild goose chase with protectors, I remain a quiet witness, extending loving energy silently. For many clients, however, I am not entirely quiet and make frequent brief empathic comments like: "yes," "that's right," "I get it too" or "of course" to let them know I am with them, and I understand what happened and how bad it was. Although I can be quiet for long intervals, as long as I am fully present and openhearted clients often report sensing my presence powerfully while they explore inside. I also find that the silent presence of a group of Self-led observers, such as a training context or group therapy, bolsters clients' access to Self-energy. However, if a client has parts who are bothered by long silences and the client wants me to be verbally present on the journey, I accommodate.

Ann focused on her suicide part and said warily, "It's a dark, menacing presence." The parts who feared this impulse toward suicide kept jumping in like a tag team, making Ann either terrified of the part, furious with it, thinking about why it was there or confused and blanking out. With each of these appearances, Larry chuckled and said things like, "Oh, I see! The part who takes your brain is back. See if it's willing to step back and trust us just to get to know this suicidal one." Larry finally suggested that she put the suicide part in a contained room in her mind. Once it was contained, her other parts relaxed and, when Larry asked how she felt toward the part, Ann replied, "It looks so sad. I feel sorry for it."

Larry said, "Now it's safe to begin to get to know the suicide part. Ask through the walls of the room what it wants you to know."

Ann reported that the part, who now looked like a keening woman, was tired of being in pain and wanted out. In response Ann wanted to enter the room and comfort the woman, so Larry told her to go ahead. From that point on, Larry simply listened to Ann describe her loving interactions with the woman, who was grateful to be heard finally rather than pushed away, and was welcoming Ann's attention and hugs.

With about 10 minutes left in the session, Larry let Ann know that they would have to stop soon and had her ask the woman what she would need from Ann until their next session. The woman said she just needed to know that Ann would return. After closing with the woman, Larry asked Ann if she had noticed how much she had taken over during the last half of the session and how she knew just what the woman needed. Ann had noticed and was shocked by how well the session went. But she also had parts telling her that it was not real—that she had faked it all to comply with what Larry wanted. "I'm not sure what happened," she said.

THERAPIST AS LOVING COMPANION

I have been emphasizing how the therapist in IFS moves as quickly as possible to be maximally present but minimally directive. I also want to discuss the other, more active side of the therapist–client relationship. With some clients we go inside almost every session but with others there is a balance between sessions where we talk about the client's life or problems and sessions where the client is inside most of the time. Or the focus may shift fluidly from the outside (i.e., discussing a dilemma in a relationship with a boyfriend and giving some advice) to having the client find the parts who come up as she thinks about the dilemma, shifting the focus inside to work with them. The session may end with the client thinking about the dilemma again seeing how her perception or plan-of-action changed. In a few rare cases where inner work is too threatening, we go inside infrequently and talk, though this balance between talking and inner work may shift at different points in the therapy.

Many therapists believe that they are only doing IFS when the client is focused internally, but I believe that anytime you relate to the client from your Self, and you keep in mind her system of parts, with or without using parts language, you are doing IFS. As with other therapies, the healing connection between you and your client is also fostered by a high level of interest in the details of her life and how you remember those details. It is fostered by your explicit support for the risks she starts taking, by your acceptance of her perceived failures and the parts she's ashamed of. It is also fostered by collaborative strategizing to handle difficult relationships or predicaments, by your excitement about her successes and, when appropriate, by your openness about your own parts, including apologizing when your parts get in the way. In other words, the IFS therapist forms a collaborative relationship with the client so that the client senses she is truly cared for and is not alone in her inner or outer journeys. The more clients sense that you care about their lives; the more their protectors relax when you do go inside. This way of being with clients is, in my view, key to the success of any therapy.

Another important therapist role is helping clients achieve clarity. When a client views the world through a distorted lens because she is blended with an extreme part, she often cannot access a realistic perspective on events in her life. For example, when she gets into conflict with someone, she automatically assumes she was wrong, or the opposite—that the other person was wrong. If the therapist can maintain Self-leadership and view the client's predicaments clearly and compassionately, then, by simply sharing a less distorted perspective, he can help the client separate from her parts and see the events from her Self. Once the client has access to her Self, she can reassure her parts instead of blending with them. Bateman and Fonagy (2004) called this ability to step out of one's emotions and gain perspective *mentalizing*; Main (as cited in Fonagy, 1996) called it *meta-cognition*. It is now widely accepted as an important quality of secure attachment. Siegel (2011) described the same ability in the practice of mindfulness, a skill taught in many modalities of psychotherapy.

There is, however, a risk in this kind of perspective sharing. When a client's parts are highly attached to their burdened viewpoint, they can become polarized with the therapist. The goal for the IFS therapist is to share his own perspective from Self, without being attached to the client's agreement and with respect for the parts who need to disagree. And then the therapist helps the client get to know and heal the parts who disagree. The challenge in this process is for the therapist to remain humble with her perspective, knowing that sometimes the client's seemingly extreme view contains some reality.

As I write this, however, parts of me worry that beginning IFS therapists will be more comfortable talking with clients rather than leading them inside and will use these paragraphs to justify avoidance of parts work. So I do want to stress that the balance between an inner and outer focus should be determined by what seems best for the client rather than by collusions between scared protectors in both client and therapist. It is tempting for therapists who are insecure in their inner skills to be relieved when the client does not want to go inside. They can both retreat to the safety of a familiar external focus.

THE EMERGENCE OF EXTREME PARTS

As clients feel a growing connection with their therapists, parts who do not ordinarily show up with other people will be drawn to make an appearance by the safety and acceptance of the relationship. Clients do not usually expose those parts to the world because they offend, scare or enrage other people. Some of these hidden parts are clearly related to what most of the field calls transference. They are frozen in hurtful times from the client's past and are concerned by the growing intimacy of the therapeutic relationship or by certain similarities between interactions with the therapist and a hurtful caretaker.

Other appearances by extreme parts are not necessarily related to transference. These parts come out just because it feels safe and they yearn for external contact or expression. The Self-led therapist is implicitly issuing an invitation to the client: "All parts are welcome!" And from the darkest corners of their psyches come the hidden aspects of clients in all their crazy glory. And that's a good thing. The inescapable reality of therapy is that if we do our job well some clients will do all kinds of provocative things and will repeatedly test us. They will resist, get angry and critical; become hugely dependent; talk incessantly; behave dangerously between sessions; show intense vulnerability; idealize us; attack themselves and display astounding narcissism and self-centeredness.

Therapists must learn to be mindful of their own parts as they work with clients, recognizing that transference and countertransference form a continuing behind-the-scenes interaction as therapists and clients inevitably evoke each other's protectors and exiles. When therapists are not overwhelmed by their own parts and remain Self-led, the client's parts feel acceptance despite their extremes and can relax, allowing the client's Self to return and help.

Remaining Self-led, however, is not easy. When you encourage clients to work with their exiles, you invite them to be extremely vulnerable. These exiles become hopeful that they will finally be healed, and they can become very attached to you as their redeemer. You may be idealized in ways that feel uncomfortable to some parts of you but great to other parts. Protectors will watch your every move, waiting for a sign that you are not safe and are looking for an excuse to shut down the process or attack you.

PARTS OF THE THERAPIST

For all these reasons, IFS therapists will be the targets of the extreme parts of their clients. Regardless of why these parts appear, sudden and extreme shifts in clients can be startling and can trigger therapists' protectors. During this stage of client vulnerability, the clients' firefighters are most protective and it is during this stage that therapists can do the most harm if they lose Self-leadership. Vicious cycles can easily escalate between the protectors of the therapist and client, which result in at least temporary breaks in connection. Sometimes this disconnect is obvious to the mindful therapist, who notices negative thoughts about the client or a judgmental tone in his voice. When this occurs and the therapist is able to ask his protectors to relax and step back, his return to Self-leadership may be enough to also help the client's protectors relax. On the other hand, I often try to take advantage of these moments to model speaking for parts. I might say, "I just noticed one of my judgmental protectors reacting to what you just said and I was able to help it relax. I apologize if it triggered you. I wonder if you noticed it and, if so, how you reacted?"

This type of meta-communication validating the dance of parts between intimates can be healing in any relationship and especially so for clients who have had little validation in their lives. Many clients have never experienced conflict with someone after which the other person owned their role and apologized. Instead, they are used to being shamed and then rejected for being so sensitive, emotional or impulsive. Many of my clients have histories of severe abuse, betrayal and neglect, so their protectors do sometimes overreact and view their partners (or therapists) as perpetrators. As a result, they often carry the sense that they are too difficult and are doomed to be alone. It is one of life's great inequities that so many people who get hurt as children are reinjured throughout their lives because the original hurt left them so raw and reactive. They deserve to be close to someone who, after initially being triggered, can regain *perspective* and see behind the client's explosive rage, icy withdrawal or manipulative controlling, to the pain that drives those behaviors. The ability to regain compassionate *presence* in the face of a client's extreme protectors or exiles is the *sine qua non* of a good IFS therapist.

After the fifth session in which Larry had acknowledged the suicidal part, Ann seriously considered not returning. She had left that session with an unfamiliar sense of hope—feeling that maybe some things in her life really could change and maybe she was not as inept as she had always thought. But within a day or two a coalition of self-hating critics tore apart her momentary sense of pride and ridiculed her for daring to think she was good at anything. The suicidal part, feeling duped into believing that it might get some attention before being abandoned by her, was stronger than ever. She felt bereft, worse than if she had never tried therapy.

When she arrived at the sixth session, she was distant and shut down, not looking at Larry and answering all his questions with "I don't know." At some point, Larry decided to stop trying so hard and quit talking, too. They sat together in an icy silence until Ann finally said that she was going to leave.

As she got up, Larry asked her to sit down again. He told her that during the silence he had found a part of his own who was feeling discouraged by how distant she seemed and was taking it personally. He had been moved and excited by the last session and his part felt disappointed that the change in her had not lasted but, instead, she seemed hostile. He had worked with this part and gotten it to step back. Once it did, he could immediately sense that she was hurting and disappointed.

Larry apologized to Ann for letting that part take over and Ann appreciated the apology. It was true, she said, that when she arrived she was scared by how bad she felt and was afraid to let him in again. His reaction had only compounded her shame and hopelessness because she sensed he was abandoning her. It meant a lot that he cared enough to work on himself and come back to her. She confessed that she was more suicidal than ever and that her critics had started working overtime soon after their last session.

Larry said, "If I wasn't triggered, I would have realized that the reaction in your system to the hope we both felt last time was very predictable. Your protectors probably knew that you couldn't afford to get hopeful and then feel disappointed again, so they sabotaged the work and attacked your confidence."

They agreed to work with her critical protectors in the next session, but until then Larry asked her to try to realize what her protectors were really about and not to take their rants so seriously. She said she thought she could do that. He also told her suicide part to not despair—that they were coming back to it as soon as possible.

BURDENED THERAPISTS

Remaining Self-led in the presence of extreme protectors is not easy because the client is not the only one in the room who has them. Most therapists I know are like me, wounded healers who are heavily burdened from their families and peers. We enter the therapeutic arena full of polarizations among our parts. For example, many of us have our own inner critics who attack us for making mistakes and hate the weakness and neediness of our exiles. These critics are polarized with angry parts who defend our exiles from inside and attack anyone else who judges us. When a client is weak or needy, tells us that we are mistaken or challenges our competence, she inadvertently stumbles into the middle of our internal wars. Some of us were led to be therapists by extreme caretaker parts who developed their self-sacrificial, overly responsible roles as children. These caretaker parts are often polarized with parts who are tired of worrying about everyone else and want people to quit sniveling and leave us alone. This was the case with Larry's inner system.

Sometimes it does not take much for clients to trigger a part who makes us try too hard or one who gives our clients the message that they want too much from us, that we are frustrated with their demands. Often clients will get these contradictory messages back-to-back, which can be very confusing. There are a myriad of other vulnerabilities and common polarizations inside of therapists that clients can innocently activate. Some clients look or act like dreaded members of the therapist's family-of-origin, or complain about the things that his or her spouse complains about. Many of my clients have suffered by unwittingly stepping on my internal landmines or wandering into my inner crossfire.

In the book *Love's Executioner and Other Tales of Psychotherapy*, Yalom (1989) was brutally transparent about his reaction to his first encounter with a client named Betty.

> The day Betty entered my office, the instant I saw her steering her ponderous two-hundred fifty pound, five-foot-two-inch frame toward my trim high-tech office chair, I knew that a great trial of countertransference was in store for me.
>
> I have always been repelled by fat women. I find them disgusting: their absurd sidewise waddle, their absence of body contour—breasts, hips, buttocks, shoulders, jaw lines, cheekbones, everything, everything I like to see in a woman, obscured in an avalanche of flesh. . . . How dare they impose that body on the rest of us? (pp. 107–108)

Yalom was courageous in acknowledging the prejudice clients can stir in us simply by the way they look or because of their history or diagnosis. But as he noticed one judgmental thought about Betty after another, his solution was to try to eliminate them from his mind.

And so it went: the entire hour with her was an exercise of my sweeping from my mind one derogatory thought after another in order to offer her my full attention. I fantasized Mickey Mouse, the sorcerers apprentice in Fantasia, sweeping away my distracting thoughts until I had to sweep away that image, too, in order to attend to Betty. (p. 109)

Although it may be instinctively tempting to sweep away a disturbing thought that is interfering in the relationship with the client, it is now widely accepted that countertransference feelings require attention and that attending to them is important for the therapy process as well as for the therapist. In my view, IFS offers a practical and highly effective way of working in the moment with countertransference.

I have had to work with many parts who were triggered by clients. Because I have specialized in the treatment of survivors of severe sexual abuse for years, many of my clients have, at times, been highly suicidal, cut their arms or torsos, binged on alcohol or stolen things. At times they also formed a childlike dependence on me, wanting, and sometimes demanding, lots of decision making, reassurance, contact between sessions, information about my feelings for them or about my personal life, and having tantrums when I left town. Or, at other times, they let me know that I was a terrible therapist, that they had received no help from me, that I did not care about them and had a defective character or that I had hurt them in an extreme way. In addition, they sometimes tried to control how I acted and used the threat of suicide or cutting to manipulate me. Some of them suddenly shifted to thought processes that seemed paranoid or schizophrenic, regressed or deluded. For others, a seemingly small provocation would result in almost murderous rage. Some alternately idealized and devalued me with an unpredictability that made my head spin, and they constantly tried to stretch my boundaries by demanding special treatment or violating my privacy. With some, any progress in therapy was always followed by various kinds of self-sabotage or backlash that made treatment with them seem like a Sisyphean nightmare. All of those behaviors evoked parts of me who could be as extreme as Yalom's. Before I was sensitized to the importance of noticing my reactive protectors, I tortured many clients. My Self would disappear and they were left in a face-off with one of my protectors, which would make their own protectors more extreme.

Of course I am not alone in this. Many therapists are triggered by extreme parts in their clients and interpret the emergence of these protectors as signs of pathology. Those therapists become clinical, detached, defensive and controlling. Others react by trying harder to care take, becoming obsessed with the client and expanding their boundaries beyond their comfort level but finally feeling resentful. I have witnessed therapists resenting clients who test competence and boundaries and who accuse challenging clients of being manipulative. Being around all of that expressed pain can traumatize therapists vicariously and cause them to dissociate. Finally, clients in IFS therapy sometimes find themselves on a roller coaster of highs and lows and many therapists climb on board, getting excited by apparent improvements and equally discouraged by the inevitable backlash reactions they view as setbacks.

In these reactions the therapist winds up closing her heart to her client. The client will sense abandonment and become increasingly protective, either withdrawing or escalating the provocative activity. I have consulted on any number of cases where the therapists' reactions started a vicious cycle that resulted in the client's rapid disintegration, impaired functioning, serial hospitalizations or overmedication. The therapists involved were generally convinced that their actions were justified by the pathology of the client and were often oblivious to their role in creating it. For some clients, just being with a compassionate, confident therapist who could put an IFS perspective on what happened could reverse the cycle and they improved quickly. Others were left so distrusting of therapists that it took a long time to earn their trust. So, as others have written using different language (Herman, 1992; Linehan, 1993), we play a dangerous game when we subscribe to views of clients that emphasize their pathological or manipulative nature, and ignore, minimize or deny the influence of our own parts.

It is not possible to do therapy without having parts take over at times. The level of intimacy required for clients to feel safe in going to their exiles will result in the emergence of all kinds of parts in both the client and therapist. Ideally, when that happens I notice that I have lost Self-leadership and quickly get my parts to step back during the session, as Larry did. Often I will apologize to the client for the intrusion. In this way it's possible to quickly repair breaks in Self-to-Self connections with clients. After the session I try to use the experience to find out why the part felt the need to take over and what it needs to trust my Self in the future. This often leads me to care for exiled parts whom I might not have found otherwise. So therapists can use their countertransference reactions as trailheads for their own healing. This, in turn, makes for one less landmine or crossfire for clients to deal with.

THERAPIST: MONITOR THYSELF

To catch oneself in a part, one needs to have an exquisitely sensitive parts' detector focused on one's own inner family. I am frequently asking myself how I feel toward certain clients and checking the openness of my heart or the energy in my body as I visualize those clients. Different IFS therapists have different ways of noticing the degree to which their Self is present and the reader is encouraged to develop rituals for doing so as well.

Unfortunately we are not always the best detectors of our own parts. We all have blind spots—protectors with whom we are so closely identified or who are so clever that they seem like our Selves. These pseudo-Selves (aka Self-like parts) are extremely difficult for us to detect, even though they may be quite apparent to others, including our clients. Clients often detect these parts and, if they have the courage to mention it, we should heed their warning and take a careful look. Of course it's hard to totally trust a client's parts detector because of their transference, but I have found more often than not that clients correctly note the absence of my Self even if sometimes they misinterpret the reasons and overreact.

So, we therapists are not Buddhas and whether we notice it or not we are regularly triggered by the intense interplay with our clients. Therefore, we must keep honing our parts detectors regarding ourselves. Fortunately, as we become increasingly familiar with the physical experience of embodying the Self (McConnell, this volume), we are also better able to notice the somatic and mental shifts when a troubled part hijacks us (we have a "part attack"). With this awareness—and lots of experience doing this type of clinical work—comes the ability to calm the part in the moment and ask it to separate so that Self can return.

GETTING PARTS TO STEP BACK IN THE MOMENT

To illustrate how the therapist works with her own parts, I will return for a moment to the session in which Larry sat in silence with Ann because he was triggered. He scanned his body and found a tension in his face, noting that his heart felt closed. As he focused on those sensations, he found an angry part and asked it to step back. Immediately he felt his heart open. He had compassion rather than resentment for Ann and was free to apologize.

If I had a microphone in my head when I was treating certain challenging clients, you would hear me saying to myself repeatedly something like: "I know you're upset, but just let me stay and handle this. Remember it always goes better if you let me keep my mind open. Just relax and trust me, and I'll talk to you after the session." On good days, those words produce an immediate shift in my level of Self-embodiment—my heart opens, my shoulder muscles release or the crowd of negative thoughts in my head disperses. My client suddenly looks different—less menacing or hopeless and more vulnerable. Between sessions, I will follow up by bringing the parts who my client aroused to my own therapy to give them attention. In this way, our clients become our *tor-mentors*—by tormenting us, they mentor us, making us aware of who in us needs our loving attention.

During the ensuing week, Larry asked his therapist to help him with the angry part who had reacted to Ann's shut down. As he focused on that part, it showed scenes of himself as a 10-year-old futilely trying to cheer up his depressed mother, and he was able to retrieve and unburden that boy. In the next session, he told Ann that he had healed that part so he hoped she would not have to worry about it interfering any more. But he added that if she did sense it, she should tell him.

BEING A SENSITIVE DETECTOR OF CLIENT PARTS

Although therapists are often unaware of their parts, clients, who have not studied IFS, are often even less aware of their parts. As therapists detect client parts, it is tempting to point them out and educate the client regarding their appearance or impact. There are often telltale signs like shifts in tone of voice, content of conversation, body movement or facial expression. And many therapists come to IFS from traditions in which they were trained to help clients notice those shifts or interpret what they mean.

There are times in IFS therapy where this kind of confronting is necessary and helpful in bringing Self-energy to key parts. There are other times, however, when it will activate the client's protectors in a way that sets the therapy back unnecessarily. You may expose parts whom the system was not yet ready to handle or is not even aware of. Many clients' systems have a wisdom about what to reveal to them and when. Therapists who point out evidence of parts in a well-meaning attempt to move the therapy along, or to bypass resistance, can violate this wise pace. My experience, more often than not, is that if I remain Self-led and keep things safe, the client will find those parts on her own when the time is right. Ironically when resistant protectors are treated with respect rather than as the enemy, the doors often open with surprising speed.

On the other hand, IFS therapists do often operate as parts detectors for clients by helping them remain Self-led while they work inside. For example, when a client is trying to get to know a part, I am constantly pointing out if she is blended with a polarized part, and I ask her to get the second part to step back. I do the same with couples—I catch the parts of each as they pop up. My point is that it is one thing to help a client become aware that she is blended with a protector when you have an explicit contract to keep her in Self, but quite another to point out a movement or body posture that may well be a manifestation of an exile whom the system wants to keep hidden. By having the client focus prematurely on a feared trailhead, you show her protectors that you are not safe and should be resisted in the future. Or, worse, protectors punish the client because you encouraged her to violate their rules.

Nevertheless, there are situations where, to expedite things, I will point to evidence of parts. As I said earlier, I rarely hesitate to identify signs of a client's protector and I also will help clients notice potential exiles when

I already have a strong relationship with the client's protectors, or when I believe the client's system could handle the consequences even if some protectors do not agree. When I do spotlight a trailhead that could lead to an exile, I do so in the form of a question, for example, "I noticed that you just flinched. Could you focus on that sensation and see what that's about?" In this way, I have no need to make an interpretation and the client remains the expert on her experience. My choice of whether to focus on such evidence is intuitive and based on knowing the client. The main point is that in IFS we try to be ecologically sensitive and we do not feel compelled to point out signs of parts just because we notice them.

CHALLENGING

Having said all this, therapists are often struck when watching tapes of me working by how strongly I challenge some clients and their parts. These therapists were assuming that being Self-led meant never having to challenge but instead always remaining receptive and empathic. They forget that courage, clarity and confidence are important qualities of Self-energy. When I sense it would be helpful, I do not hesitate to be forceful. The key is to be forceful from Self rather than from your assertive, judgmental manager or pseudo-Self.

I might tell a protector that I do not believe what it is saying and I want it to be direct and honest. Or I might insist that the client get certain protectors to go to a waiting room and remember that they are just scared children. My goal in these instances is to demonstrate to the client that regardless of how imposing, adult-like or convincing their protectors seem, these parts respond to firmness and strong leadership just as out-of-control children do. You can tell whether you are Self-led in these instances by checking on how attached you are to winning any power struggle that might ensue. When in Self, you can be forceful without being attached to the outcome, remembering that it is the protector's right to resist and that they often know better than you about the negative consequences that could arise if the client goes further.

Although most of us do not have a lot of practice, there is an art to being forceful while remaining Self-led. We grow up relying on various protectors to handle the moments of conflict or assertiveness. When you can be assertive from Self, clients not only experience your confidence that they can handle whatever comes, they also sense that you care and that you remain connected even as you challenge them. For many clients such experiences represent the first time anyone has believed in their ability to handle something (i.e., dreaded memories, strong affect, standing up for themselves with someone), and the first time they have been pushed without feeling criticized or disconnected.

Larry's invitation to Ann to speak about his part when she sensed it, made several of her protectors relax. They felt more in control of the therapy and less as if he were the big expert and she were the crazy patient. Instead he was saying they both had parts who could interfere—they were both human. The fact that Larry was committed enough to spend time on what had happened between them in his own therapy reinforced Ann's burgeoning belief that he actually did care. The problem, however, was that if she really believed he cared, he would have a level of power to hurt her that her protectors had vowed never to give another person. So they remained on high alert while agreeing to let her return to her suicidal part. Her protectors all wanted it to work even though they were terrified that it would result in another disappointment.

At first the suicidal part (the keening woman) ignored Ann's attempts to reengage. Larry helped Ann remain persistently caring until she fell back into Ann's arms. Ann asked her what had happened in the past to make her want to leave this world so badly and the woman showed Ann scenes of her mother's funeral when she was 12-years-old. With her mother gone, the girl was totally dependent on her violent father—there was no more escape from him. Ann was able to enter the scene, stand up to the father for the girl, take the girl out of that time to a safe place and help her unburden the terror and despair. Larry was moved to tears while witnessing this work. He felt so much for the 12-year-old and also was proud of how courageously Ann helped her. He did not hide his reaction and, on seeing it, Ann once again could not deny that he cared for her. Their connection was solidifying. When Ann's protectors saw that the girl was now OK and they no longer had to prevent disappointments that could lead to suicide, they became interested in unburdening and taking on new roles.

In a later session, Ann talked about the man she visited periodically for sex. She said she enjoyed being with him even though he only wanted to be serviced by her and would not do anything to take care of her sexually. Larry replied, "Are you sure all of you enjoys it?" Despite Ann's assurances that she was happy spending time with this guy, he kept challenging her. Finally he said, "Why don't we just check inside and see if what you're saying is true?"

Ann agreed reluctantly, and Larry had her start by finding the part who had been talking up to that point in the session. Ann saw a tough teenager and asked her why she liked servicing this man sexually. She replied that she liked being in control of him—he was totally under her power for a period of time and she could do whatever she wanted. After considerable negotiating, the teenager agreed to let Ann get to know the vulnerable parts whom she had to lock up to be with the man. Ann found several younger ones who let her know how humiliated they felt every time she was with him. Ann returned to the tough teenager and told her that it was not OK to incarcerate the young ones so she could have fun. The teenager dropped her guard and showed Ann more scenes of abuse by the neighbor's son and how much she had wanted to be in control with him. After retrieving that girl, the teenager was softer and Ann stopped seeing the man.

Then Ann's self-hating part began to attack her for having serviced this man for so many years, saying, "You are worse than a whore because you didn't even get paid." Larry had Ann ask this part the standard question, "What are you afraid would happen if you didn't call her those names?" It replied that it did not fear anything—it was just speaking the sorry truth. Larry decided he would challenge the self-hating part and asked to talk to it directly. The following conversation ensued:

"Where did you get the idea that Ann is a whore?"

"It's not an idea—it's who she is and she proved that for years."

"I get that doing that with him really bothered you, but Ann is not a whore, so let me ask you again. Where did you get that belief?"

"From her mother."

"OK, I appreciate your being honest about that. Can you let us know how the mother gave you that idea about Ann?"

The self-hating part then showed Ann a scene from the period of time when she was being abused by the neighbor in which her mother found her masturbating and called her a whore. After Ann was able to retrieve and unburden that shamed girl, the self-hating part gave up the belief that Ann was a whore.

I use this form of challenging frequently when a protector attacks a client repeatedly for reasons that do not seem to be protective but instead seem to reflect a core belief. Just as postmodernists deconstruct truths that seem god given, asking parts where they got beliefs that just seem to be true can help them realize that those beliefs actually came from a person or event and this helps the part let the belief go.

THE TRANSFORMATIVE POWER OF SELF

While I have discussed many different aspects of the relationship between the IFS therapist and client in this chapter, the main theme can be summarized simply. Self-energy has tremendous transformative power. When the client experiences the compassion and acceptance of the therapist's Self, she heals. When the clients' parts experience the compassion and love of the client's Self, they heal. When the client and therapist connect Self-to-Self, they both heal. There is a transpersonal dimension to all of this that I sense strongly but do not often articulate. Others have also recognized this aspect of healing and describe it similarly and eloquently. Consider, for example, these words from Pendergast, Fenner, and Krystal (2003) regarding what happens when therapists can access this state:

The result is the emergence of a natural simplicity, transparency, clarity, and warm acceptance of whatever arises within themselves and their clients (p. 3) . . . Attention drops from the head to the heart. Without any conscious intention on the part of the therapist, an optimal field of loving acceptance arises that facilitates transformation. What has been unmet is waiting to be fully embraced before it can transform. . . . We are no longer problem solvers facing problem holders. Instead, we are Being meeting itself in one of its infinite and intriguing disguises. (pp. 7–8)

Toward the end of his career, Rogers (as cited in Pendergast et al., 2003) also put it beautifully and succinctly:

I find that when I am closest to my inner, intuitive self, when I am some-how in touch with the unknown in me . . . whatever I do seems to be full of healing. Then, simply my *presence* is releasing and helpful to the other. There is nothing I can do to force this experience, but when I can relax and be close to the transcendental core of me . . . it seems that my inner spirit has reached out and touched the inner spirit of the other. Our relationship transcends itself and becomes a part of something larger. Profound growth and healing and energy are present. (p. 93)

So the IFS bumper sticker could be: "Self Heals." The essence of the therapeutic relationship is in this ineffable touching of spirits, Being meeting itself, the Self-to-Self connection. Humanists, transpersonalists, Buddhists and some current analysts use different words to describe it, but we are all getting at the same essence. IFS is but one map to that sacred place. It is, however, a clear, nonpathologizing, empowering user-friendly map. It is rela-tional in multiple dimensions and promotes healing connections at all levels of the client's system, most crucially between the client's Self and parts but also between the therapist's Self and the client's whole system.

Thus I have come full circle on the importance of the therapeutic relationship, from minimizing its role to making it a foundational element of IFS therapy. As I mentioned earlier, psychotherapy research has shown that the therapeutic relationship is key. Through IFS, therapists are given clear-cut ways to ensure that the relationship is filled with Self-energy. The loving, re-spectful, supportive, challenging and accepting manner in which the therapist relates to the client accesses her Self, who then relates that way to her parts. When the therapist notices, listens to and speaks for her own parts from Self, the client opens to this new way of being in the inner and outer world. The sacred connection they form transcends the therapy hour. It facilitates unbur-dening and bolsters a lifelong practice of learning to trust Self-leadership for both client and therapist.

REFERENCES

Bateman, A., & Fonagy, P. (2004). *Psychotherapy for borderline personality disorder: Mentalization based treatment.* New York, NY: Oxford University Press.

Fonagy, P. (1996). The significance of the development of metacognitive control over mental representations in parenting and infant development. *Journal of Clinical Psychoanalysis, 5*, 67–86.

Herman, J.L. (1992). *Trauma and recovery.* New York, NY: Basic Books.

Linehan, M.M. (1993). *Cognitive behavioral treatment of borderline personality disorder.* New York, NY: Guilford Press.

Pendergast, J., Fenner, P., & Krystal, S. (2003). *Sacred mirror: Nondual wisdom and psychotherapy.* St. Paul, MN: Paragon House.

Rogers, C. (1951). *Client-centered therapy: Its current practice, implications and theory.* London, England: Constable.

Siegel, D. J. (2011). *Mindsight: The new science of personal transformation.* New York, NY: Bantam Books.

Wilde, O. (1893). *Lady Windermere's Fan.* London, England: Nick Hern Books, 2005.

Yalom, I.D. (1989). *Love's executioner and other tales of psychotherapy.* New York, NY: Basic Books.

EMOTIONAL CANNIBALISM: SHAME IN ACTION

Martha Sweezy

INTRODUCTION

When Sami, the 21-year-old client described in this chapter, walked into my office there was a noteworthy discrepancy between what I saw—a young woman whose fashionable but conservative style conveyed her concern with propriety and appearances—and the referral notes I had just read, which included a laundry list of psychiatric diagnoses involving a high pitch of dys-regulated emotion. These included borderline personality disorder (due to self-cutting, intermittent suicidality and intense unstable relationships), major depression with psychotic features, binge eating disorder, body dysmorphic disorder and polysubstance abuse.

Sami's diagnoses indicated a whirl of conflict under her polished veneer and alerted me to the possibility that she had been traumatically shamed, probably in childhood. This chapter explores how interpersonal trauma can unleash the destructive force of shame into both external and internal relationships, morphing a dangerous event into a dangerous identity, which psychiatric symptoms—the behaviors of parts—are attempting to handle.

CHAPTER OVERVIEW

This chapter charts the movement of shame through external and internal relational systems, exploring motivations for shaming along with the consequences

---

I thank Patty Collinge, Matt Leeds, Janna Smith and Ellen Ziskind for reading this chapter and helping with my process of rewriting.

of feeling shamed. Because shaming can be intentional or unintentional, and the relational impact varies, I differentiate between the two. As Schore (2003) pointed out, unintentional shaming is an inevitable part of the relationship between children and any adult in the role of "socializing agent." Differences in temperament between parent and child also can give rise to unintentional shaming (Linehan, 1993). I focus here only on intentional shaming, either of oneself or someone else, and view it as an expeditious means of regulating shame in the short, though not the long run. The frame for exploring shaming is psychic multiplicity, or *parts*, and internal family systems therapy (IFS).

Intentional shaming, external or internal, has a damning message that feels highly personal and true to the recipient, as if something deplorable and permanent has been revealed. The ballpark message of shaming is that imperfection makes you bad, unacceptable and alone. Shaming someone else intentionally and cultivating a feeling of power in comparison to that belittled other can be quite effective in the short run at regulating shame. In contrast, self-directed shaming evokes shame and often precipitates symptomatic behavior like binge drinking and binge eating. But in either case, it is the thesis of this chapter that intentional shaming is commonly motivated by the urge to regulate the feeling of shame and that the target of attack will be determined by vulnerability and not (as it feels to the victim) worth.

The case example below illustrates Sami's chronic self-shaming, which followed from her father shaming her. In this session, the IFS protocol regulated Sami's shame with its generic evocation of compassion, calming a critical manager and several firefighters and laying the groundwork for healing her attachment injuries. But before illustrating Sami's experience in therapy I review the relationship between shame and psychopathology, note how researchers have decoded shame and look at how victim and perpetrator can become inextricable in the shame dynamic.

SHAME IN PSYCHOTHERAPY

Because the exquisite pain of feeling unacceptable, excluded and alone that typifies shame can be so toxic to current functioning, parts who experience it are often sealed off and left behind in time, with their management becoming a systemic enterprise that can last a lifetime. Therefore, with or without awareness, psychotherapists routinely navigate a host of symptoms associated with shame. The urges to withdraw, hide and avoid (the action tendencies of shame) show up in a wide variety of behaviors, including addiction, depression, anxiety, psychic numbing, cognitive attempts to undo reality, insensitivity to emotional and physical pain (both one's own and that of others) and dissociation (Dearing & Tangney, 2011; Lewis, 1971; Tangney & Dearing, 2002; Tracy, Robins, & Tangney, 2007). In converse to that the urge to regulate shame through attacking and blaming the self or others is also commonplace (Dearing & Tangney, 2011; Herbine-Blank, this volume; Tangney & Dearing, 2002; Tracy et al., 2007). Visible modes of self-attack that are often seen in mental health treatment include starving, cutting, burning, risk taking and suicide. More invisible forms include chronic self-criticism and self-loathing. Attacking others can involve a threatening tone and attitude, ostensible humor, contempt, being dismissive, entitled, disgusted or enraged; or it can involve actual assault up to the extremity of homicide (Gilligan, 1997). Shame is thus a force in much human conduct that is puzzling, alienating, dangerous and assigned either to the law or mental health professionals. We need effective strategies for treating it and, as this chapter illustrates, IFS is well designed to meet that need.

THE FUNCTION OF SHAME

Each human emotion is a directional compass with a true north derived from evolution, and true north for shame is conformity. Although conforming to the group norm has advantages, shame is a costly enforcer. Researchers agree that shame, like guilt, involves an internal audience giving a mental thumbs down to the self. In guilt this judgment is focused on behavior (I *did* wrong) while in shame it is global (I *am* bad) (Lewis, 1971; Tangney & Dearing, 2002; Tracy et al., 2007). The belief that one is being judged and that personal defects are being exposed launches the physical, emotional and cognitive cascade of the shame experience. This can include feeling queasy, heavy, shrunken, child-like, foolish, stupid, different, singular, alone, unwanted, unlovable and worthless (Mills, 2005; Tangney & Dearing, 2002; Tracy et al., 2007). Relationally guilt and shame are opposites. Pure guilt promotes concern for others and a desire to repair (Tangney & Dearing, 2002; Tracy et al., 2007) whereas shame, along with guilt linked to shame (e.g., I *did* wrong so I *am* bad), promotes intense, negative self-focus, which is often followed by symptomatic behavior.

HISTORICAL VERSUS INSTRUMENTAL SHAME

Although the cyclical nature of the shame dynamic described in this chapter can make it appear that shame originates internally, children are not born ashamed. Therefore, this chapter takes the view that children are born with the capacity to feel shame but actually feel it due to experience. That is, shame is precipitated interpersonally, by shaming, and abuse or neglect can be intensely shaming.

In the description that follows, I call the range of intentional, interpersonal insults—from prejudice about physical, cultural and class differences to peer bullying, beatings and molestation—*historical shame*. Although historical shame is a passive, interpersonal experience, the internal dynamic that follows, *instrumental shaming* is active, self-generated and self-directed. Although the perspectives of victim and perpetrator are easily distinguished between historical shame and instrumental shaming, this distinction is soon lost once the victim incorporates the behavior of the perpetrator and transforms *a bad thing happened to me* into *I am bad*. The treatment goal of IFS is to help the client access enough Self-energy to reverse this sentence, returning *I am* to *it happened*.

Using the IFS lens, and looking at the motivation of parts, we can understand how a shamed individual turns to shaming someone else, or else picks up the habit of self-attack. In both cases, the victim becomes a perpetrator. The interpersonal perpetrator is generally a firefighter (a reactive protector) who is trying to regulate shame with externally focused anger, while the intrapsychic perpetrator is usually a manager (a proactive protector) trying to regulate shame with internally focused anger. Because self-criticism and self-attack evoke rather than suppress shame, critical managers tend to stimulate a wide variety of firefighter responses that involve either passive avoidance (like dissociation and denial) or the high-risk behaviors more likely to begin in adolescence (addictions, eating disorders, self-harm, suicide, rage). Extreme firefighter behaviors torment the manager who, in turn, intensifies efforts to exert control with more internal shaming. Like an overactive immune system, this typical, escalating polarity between managers and firefighters can be very hazardous for the client's health.

THE CASE OF SAMI

Sami was born in California and had a pleasant childhood until the age of 5 years when her father, a prominent businessman, was arrested and put on trial for financial fraud. In response, he became violent at home—but only toward Sami. Her two older brothers were maintained in private boarding schools and her mother, an aloof woman with an active social life who spent little time at home, became even more distant during this crisis.

Thus Sami took the brunt of her father's rage. Although his behavior was morally reprehensible and traumatic for her, it was likely to have been instrumental for him. We can surmise that as he succumbed to self-loathing due to public humiliation, a firefighter stepped in to reboot his self-worth at the expense of the most vulnerable target in his vicinity. Once his equilibrium was restored, he did try to repair the relationship with Sami but by then she was a self-destructive teenager who used her mother's diet pills, restricted her calorie intake, purged after meals, had a violent boyfriend, binge drank with friends on weekends to the point of blacking out and destroyed her first car in a crash. In addition, when she was 17 she got pregnant. Her father and brothers insisted on an abortion while her mother, a devout Catholic, looked the other way.

Although Sami was a complete novice to the idea of psychic multiplicity, she took easily to *going inside*, Schwartz's (1995) term for paying attention to the subjective experience of having parts. In this session, a couple of months into treatment, she was just out of the hospital where she had gone after feeling suicidal about her performance in college and a planned holiday with her eldest brother, a graduate student at a prestigious business school. At the outset of the session she announced that she might need to return to the hospital.

"Why?" I asked.

"I have a part that wants me to believe my son is alive," she replied.

"How do you know?" I asked.

"It shows him to me," she said. "It wants me to take care of him. He's four now. But if I go there, I'll be crazy again."

In the IFS protocol the central goal is to foster a relationship inside the client between her *parts* and the core presence that differs from parts that Schwartz calls *Self.* IFS asserts that this core presence is sentient, motivated by love, exists in everyone and can be accessed in the emotional octave where feelings range from curiosity to compassion. Once the client has located and learned to stay in this affective interval while also being in relationship with her other feelings, even strong, negative ones, she has cracked the formula for attending safely to her subjective experience. But at this point in therapy Sami was far from having the skill to accompany herself kindly, and my first goal, as she revealed a looming psychosis, was to help her access enough Self-energy to proceed safely to the second step of the IFS protocol, exploring the motivations of her activated parts.

So I asked Sami the key question for locating and helping parts to differentiate from the Self, "How do you feel toward the part who is showing the child to you?"

"Guilty," she replied.

In IFS we stay with the target part, if possible, and ask other parts with strong feelings not to interfere. So I said, "Would the guilty part be willing to relax and let you help the part who brings your child?"

"OK," Sami reported, "but it doesn't want us to forget."

"We may have to come back to it another week. If it's worried that we have forgotten, will it please remind you?" I asked. Sami nodded. "How do you feel now toward the part who brings your child?" I said.

"I wish it would stop," Sami said.

"Would the part who wants it to stop be willing to relax for a few minutes, too?"

"OK," Sami replied.

"How do you feel toward it now?" I asked.

"I feel angry," Sami said. "How can I live like this?"

"Would the angry part trust you and give you some space?" I said. After a pause, she nodded. "How do you feel now?" Because negotiating with protectors must continue in this way as long as they persist in doing whatever they do, the therapist must accommodate. However, once the client feels curious the action of the session can move to the next phase.

"I want to know why," Sami said.

"Can you see the part who brings the child?" I asked.

"No," Sami explained, "it stands behind, pushing."

"Behind what?"

"Him."

"What makes it decide to bring him to you?" I asked.

"It's when the yelling gets louder," she said.

"Who's yelling?" I asked

"The part who tells me I'm a failure," Sami said. "I'm not good enough. I'm ugly, fat, stupid. My brothers are the smart ones."

I nodded, "The critic." Critics are, as mentioned, marquee advertising for a historical, traumatic experience of being shamed, and they are extremely common. I went on, "If we could help this critic, would it be good for the part who wants you to believe your child is alive?"

"What do you mean, 'help this critic'?" Sami asked suspiciously.

"I mean if the critic didn't feel the need to criticize you anymore would this other part still feel a need to push him forward?"

"No," Sami said. "But it doesn't believe you can stop the critic."

"I understand," I said. "But will it let us try?"

Sami thought for a moment and then said, "OK."

With this permission we shifted our attention to the critic and back-tracked to the same basic questions that would help it differentiate from Sami's Self.

"Where do you notice the critic in your body?"

"It's not in my body," Sami replied. "It's around my body. It's like—you know the red Spider-Man suit with all the lines? It looks like that. My body dangles inside."

"How do you feel toward Spider-Man?" I asked.

"I'm glad he's there," Sami said.

"Ask the part who's glad he's there to give you room to be there too—just so you can get to know him," I said. Sami nodded. "How do you feel toward him now?"

"I understand him," she said.

"Let him know what you understand and see if you've got it right," I said.

"Yes," she said. "He protects me."

"Does he feel successful?" I asked.

"No," Sami observed. Then she frowned, "He's mad. He squeezes to punish me."

Reports of a part hurting the client's body illustrate that parts can and do affect physical experience and are an opportunity to negotiate more effective ways for the part to exert influence.

"Ask Spider-Man to stop doing that," I said. "He doesn't have to hurt you to get your attention. Tell him it's much more persuasive to be direct so you understand. Is he willing to stop?"

"For now," Sami reported.

Although managers such as Spider-Man are usually polarized with a firefighter, the part who is getting bullied (or, from the manager's point of view, protected) is a vulnerable, young exile. So I asked, "How old does Spider-Man think you are?"

"Five," Sami reported.

I said, "Let him know the five-year-old is another part and not you."

"He doesn't believe me," Sami said.

Because protective parts excel at escalating conflict but relax in response to curiosity, the best policy is to be curious. So I returned to the standard IFS question, "How do you feel toward him now?"

"Scared," Sami said.

"Is he still squeezing you?" I asked.

"No."

"Good. Then ask the scared part to relax and let you handle this."

"OK," she said.

"Now how do you feel toward him?"

"Interested," she said.

"Does he notice the difference?" I asked.

"Yes," she said. "He's puzzled."

"That you are not the five-year-old?"

"Yes."

"How old is he?"

"He won't tell."

Again, because opposition melts in the part's relationship to Self, I shift back to building this relationship. "Would you like to get to know Spider-Man better?"

"Yes," she said.

"Good. He has your attention, right? Remind him that he doesn't have to hurt you now," I said.

"He doesn't trust me."

"What does he want you to know about that?"

"He says where have I been?"

This question is a milestone in the relationship between the client's Self and her parts, so I repeated it. "He wants to know where you've been. What does he need to hear from you about that?"

"I didn't mean to leave him alone."

"Yes. Is he aware that when he or any other part takes you over, you can't be there with him?"

"He says why should he trust me now," Sami reported.

"He doesn't have to trust you without reason. Everybody has to earn trust," I said. "What does he want you to know about his job?"

"He protects me by saying those things to me."

Note that when Sami said, "He protects me," she had shifted back to the perspective of the 5-year-old girl.

"How's that going?" I asked.

"Not so good," Sami reported.

"He works hard but it's not going so good," I said.

"He's tired."

"No wonder."

"But he has to do it so he will."

"Really?" I asked. "Who is he responsible for?"

"Me," she said.

"The five-year-old?"

Sami paused before replying, "Yes actually. Her."

"Why does the five-year-old need help?" I asked.

"She's bad," Sami said.

"How did she get the idea that she's bad?" I asked.

"It happened to her," Sami said.

"Yes it did," I said.

"Yes it did," Sami repeated quietly.

"So of course she believed it," I said. "But tell Spider-Man that her father did all that to make himself feel better—she wasn't bad." Sami stopped speaking for more than a minute. "What's going on?" I finally asked.

"Spider-Man feels sad," she said. "He just wanted to make her good enough."

"By telling her she's not?"

"He's thinking," Sami reported.

"It's a puzzle, isn't it?" I said. "Shaming a little girl to protect her from feeling shame."

"He's confused," Sami reported.

"What's the most confusing thing for him?"

"He wants to save her."

"I can guess why he thought it might work. If I tell him, will he say if I'm right?"

"Yes."

"OK. Spider-Man learned to treat you this way when he watched your father yelling and hitting you and then heard him say that he was doing it for you. But when Spider-Man does the same thing it scares the little girl, which scares those other parts who do wild things. And then her father and brothers are disappointed. And then Spider-Man feels even more desperate. He squeezes and yells more insults to make her better—"

Sami interrupted, "He hits me inside with words."

"He hits you inside with words. And then what happens?"

"The little girl stands in the corner."

"Does he hear us now?"

"Yes he's listening."

"Can he see that shaming and squeezing and hitting the little girl with words to keep her from feeling shame will never work?"

"But what can he do?"

"How do you feel toward him now, Sami?"

"I love him."

"Does he know?" She nodded. I said, "Tell him there's nothing wrong with the little girl and there never was—and I will show you how to take care of her so that Spider-Man is free to be himself. Would he like that?"

"Yes. But he says who is he?"

"When he has time to explore, he'll find out."

"OK. He likes that."

We ended this session by checking back with the reactive part who was threatening to make Sami psychotic. It felt calmer and was, for the moment, willing to withdraw so Sami could stay out of the hospital and continue in therapy.

SUMMARY OF CASE EXAMPLE

Spider-Man's relentless criticisms stirred up the exiled little girl's fear and shame, which caused another protector to offer short-term comfort in the form of unreality, or psychosis. Although this part was reactive and came last in the chain of events, we noticed it first. In IFS we often work back from the most recent attempt at protection to an original injury. In this session, Sami noted an impending psychiatric emergency and from there we made our way to the shaming of Spider-Man before finally reaching the underlying cause, the shame and fear of the little girl.

Because this pattern of interactions between protectors is so characteristic and repetitive, I could predict that we would discover a manager provoking the behavior of the firefighter. Sami, however, was only aware that she was about to be in serious trouble again. If she became psychotic, she would be hospitalized and put on medication, which would cause weight gain—a major precipitant for shame in her system—and would cause other firefighters to begin restricting, purging and planning suicide. Although this prospect terrified most of her system, the part pushing psychosis had no concern for long-term consequences. Hospital stay? Antipsychotics? Weight gain? Bulimia? Suicidality? Dropped credits? Family upset? Friends disappearing? Not my problem!

When a manager such as Spider-Man stimulates a firefighter to step in with extreme solutions and neither part is capable of unilateral de-escalation, ever more drastic consequences ensue. Even so, once Spider-Man differentiated enough to experience Sami's Self, he realized that she could help the little girl and he relaxed. This, in turn, decommissioned the firefighters who were gearing up for restricting, bingeing and purging and suicide. And we could continue in therapy toward the goal of unburdening the little girl and other exiles.

DISCUSSION

In sessions we hear protective parts frantically trying to undo what has been done to the client and sometimes what the client has done to others. The client's attachment injuries, and the attempts of her parts to prevent further injury, are the bread and butter of psychotherapy. As we have seen, therapy can track this historical experience back to the point where shaming judgments were accepted as identity (I am *bad*, *defective* and *alone*—and this is *all* I am) and where protective parts, in an effort to reverse these judgments, defensively incorporated the attitude of the perpetrator.

Ironically, we are capable of feeling shame for the same reason we can feel compassion: because the mind has the capacity to shift perspectives and move between mental vantage points. Yet without a concept of psychic multiplicity, this mental act of stepping out and looking back can be hard to account for. For example, when one is feeling shame, who is judging whom, and why? The answer in IFS is that individuals contain many subjects, an interactive multitude. Although shame is evoked for this multitude interpersonally, they maintain it intrapsychically. As a result, clients often come to us feeling that something is being done to them over which they have no control. Lacking a concept of how this can be true without someone else being involved, a sense of persecution, social exile and hopelessness are common.

In IFS, clients learn to enter into their psychic multiplicity and discover who is doing what to whom and why. And in contrast to the negative valance of shame, IFS teaches clients to go inside like contemplatives and meditators, those practitioners of perspective shifting who cultivate curiosity and compassion, the feeling states of Self that truly oppose (and are mutually exclusive with) shame.

CONCLUSIONS

Shaming is an extraordinarily dynamic phenomenon that loops from external to internal relationships and back, gathering strength like a hurricane that can blow the message *I am flawed and alone* through generations. Yet the content of shaming is a motivated fiction, often a shame regulation strategy and not an accurate communication about the worth or singular (and therefore shameful) nature of the individual being shamed. We are born imperfect but not unacceptable, unique or alone. We spend our lives embedded in relational systems, usually external, always internal. Clients who are guided into rather than away from their Self and their multiplicity of mind have the opportunity to undo, experientially, this fiction at the heart of shame.

REFERENCES

Dearing, R.L., & Tangney, J.P. (Eds.). (2011). *Shame in the therapy hour.* Washington, DC: American Psychological Association.

Gilligan, J. (1997). *Violence: Reflections on a national epidemic.* New York, NY: Vintage Books.

Lewis, H. B. (1971). *Shame and guilt in neurosis.* New York, NY: International Universities Press.

Linehan, M.M. (1993). *Cognitive behavioral treatment of borderline personality disorder.* New York, NY: Guilford Press.

Mills, R.S.L. (2005). Taking stock of the developmental literature on shame. *Developmental Review, 25,* 26–63.

Schore, A.N. (2003). *Affect dysregulation and disorders of the self.* New York, NY: Norton.

Schwartz, R.C. (1995). *Internal family systems therapy.* New York, NY: Guilford Press.

Tangney, J.P., & Dearing, R.L. (2002). *Shame and guilt.* New York, NY: Guilford Press.

Tracy, J.L., Robins, R.W., & Tangney, J.P. (Eds.). (2007). *The self-conscious emotions: Theory and research.* New York, NY: Guilford Press.

IFS WITH CHILDREN AND ADOLESCENTS

Pamela K. Krause

In working with children and adolescents who are dependent on their families, the internal family systems (IFS) therapist must consider how this vulnerable population is embedded in an external as well as internal family system. This chapter illustrates ways in which parts of children get injured in relationships and become burdened; how those polarizations in the external family can impact the child's injured parts and seriously impinge on the child's capacity for Self-leadership; and how healing the external family helps facilitate the child's internal healing. Finally, I discuss some specific clinical techniques for using IFS with very young children and adolescents.

BASIC ASSUMPTIONS OF THE IFS MODEL

IFS posits that the natural state of human beings is to be subdivided into parts. It maintains that everyone is born with a Self who contains desirable qualities such as calmness, curiosity and compassion as well as perseverance and patience. IFS assumes that we are born with this Self-energy as well as with parts and the ability to produce more parts, and asserts that internal balance and harmony are fostered as parts develop a relationship with, and act as a resource for, the Self.

As burdens are transmitted from adults to children, the child's Self-leadership is blocked. When vulnerable, wounded parts of the child are pushed into exile, protective parts who are searching for solutions often become polarized. For example, one part may urge compliance whereas another urges rebellion. And, as protectors jostle for influence in the internal system, they tend to become more extreme.

HOW CHILDREN ARE BURDENED

When a child feels ignored, dismissed, embarrassed, humiliated, terrified or ashamed and develops the belief that she is unloved, unlovable or worthless she can develop what IFS calls a burden. Parts acquire burdens due to attachment disruptions that range from milder traumas (illustrated later) to neglect, physical and sexual abuse, the extremes of interpersonal trauma.

Beliefs about self-worth and lovability that children develop in extreme types of abuse can be predictable and straightforward. Protectors will exile the parts who hold these beliefs to minimize the child's vulnerability. But more subtle and elusive avenues of burdening are equally important to understand when working with children. Let's take the example of a 2-year-old who is running along a sidewalk and falls, scraping his knee. He gets up, looks at his knee, sees blood and cries. He has ventured into the world and been injured. His parts will look for a Self-led response of welcome for his feelings and permission to feel them for as long as he needs, signaling that both he and his feelings are acceptable. This response will comfort and reassure. If, however, he is told, "Boys don't cry, brush it off, you're fine," he will begin to see that this feeling and his behavior are unacceptable.

Clearly, he has run into a part of his parent who does not welcome his fear and sadness and literally advises him to brush off the tearful part. Some parts of the child may feel hurt by the parent's rebuke whereas others feel angry. However, parts seeking to protect the child's connection with the parent may pursue various options for suppressing his feelings, reasoning, "If he doesn't cry, he won't be criticized and he won't feel this pain and anger. I'll never let him cry again," and/or "I'll tell him that he's bad for being angry so he won't make dad angry."

Or suppose a parent were to respond by scooping up the child and exclaiming, "Are you OK? Please don't cry, don't cry! Don't let go of my hand again." This more attentive response still teaches the child that his tearfulness is unwelcome and once again he is offered no real comfort. Instead he might feel wrong for having run ahead alone or for crying. His parts could decide, "He should never let go of mom's hand again because if he's safe, he won't feel scared and cry, and then he won't feel wrong."

In sum, although it may be easier to understand that a parent's angry, critical, judging parts create burdens, caretaking parts with an agenda of soothing parental anxiety can also produce burdens. When any part blends it eliminates Self-leadership. I'll call this being parts-led rather than Self-led. Parenting that is parts-led inevitably burdens. The degree of burdening is dependent on the agendas of the parent's parts, how extreme they get and to what degree they are polarized with the child's parts.

POLARIZATIONS

The parent/child system is not one of equality. Adults have more power and more choices. A dependent child relies on her parents for food, shelter, clothing, education and nurturing. Children are almost universally powerless to change the nature of their relationships with their parents without some support from a parent. The child can only attempt to drive change in the external family system indirectly and symptomatically, and this is notoriously ineffective. Change comes when those who hold power in the family shift behavior, allowing less powerful family members to shift as well. Children must look to their parents and other important adults (caretakers, relatives, teachers) to gain a sense of identity and be loved. In the course of parts-led parenting they also discover what will not be accepted. This can be a sorrowful shock to a child but it will also become part of her reality—a problem that requires immediate internal attention and problem solving. Symptoms are markers for that internal problem-solving process.

In a perfect world, children would have Self-led caregivers who would welcome all of their parts with compassion, loving all equally, allowing the child's Self to emerge so that she would grow into a Self-led adult. However real parents are, almost inevitably, somewhat or totally parts led. IFS theory asserts that how we react to our own parts will govern how we react to similar parts in other people: parts who have been exiled by our protectors will be equally unacceptable in other people.

For example, suppose I have a clingy, needy exile who wants to be cared for by others and a protector who feels irritated with it and, believing it's too much and will drive people away, tells it to grow up. This intolerant protector will react to all needy, dependent parts the same way, whether it is mine or someone else's. If I have children this protector will also be intolerant of my child's needy, clinging part. Given this chain of negative influence, attending to parent/child polarizations must be a major focus of IFS therapy. Polarizations are addressed in two ways: first by helping the parents identify and lessen the impact of their own parts and, second, by helping the child to unburden his parts. Because parents have more power, they authorize change in family relationships when they are willing to heal their own parts. When parental unburdening occurs, the parent's protectors relax both internally and externally with the child's parts. As the child has less to defend against from the outside, her protectors are more likely step back and allow exiles to be healed. Therefore, the best therapeutic results are achieved when parents attend to their own burdened parts and become more Self-led.

When parents will not actively engage in therapy it is likely that parts of the parent/child system will continue to be polarized. In this case, the child will feel less safe, her protectors must continue to defend, and she may be in too much pain for the therapy to access exiles, all of which hinders unburdening. For these children, the therapy will focus on facilitating relationships between the child's Self and her protective parts. In the course of developing a relationship with the Self, protectors unblend and Self-energy is released. More Self-energy facilitates stability and calm. Therefore working with protectors can be highly effective and is worthwhile even when access to exiles is limited.

COMMON POLARIZATIONS BETWEEN PARENTS AND CHILDREN

Polarizations typically occur between parent and child in a number of ways. A parent's manager(s) or firefighter(s) can become polarized with a child's exile(s). For example, an adult has a manager who does not want to "spoil" a baby by picking it up when it cries; or an adult has a firefighter who gets irritated or angry when the child needs help or clings. Or a parent's exile(s) and a child's manager(s) or firefighter(s) can become polarized. For example, a parent has an exile who feels worthless when her child becomes more independent, or a parent has an exile who feels unloved when his child's firefighter gets angry and lashes out.

A parent's firefighter(s) and a child's managers can get polarized. For example, an adolescent's manager throws out all the alcohol so that his alcohol-dependent mother cannot drink, or a child's manager tries to make her behave "perfectly" in an attempt to keep her father from becoming rageful. We also see polarizations between a parent's manager(s) and a child's firefighter(s). This is especially common during adolescence when firefighters can step up with force. Common adolescent firefighter behaviors include excessive body piercing and tattooing; unconventional hair colors and styles; impulsive anger; risk-taking behaviors such as fast driving, hazardous sports and perilous sexual activity; eating disorders and use of alcohol and drugs. An example of a polarization between a parent's manager(s) and a child's firefighter(s) would be a parent forbidding an adolescent girl from dating for fear that she would become sexually active.

DIRECT ACCESS AND INSIGHT

The techniques called direct access and insight are the foundation of IFS therapy with both children and adults. When the therapist uses direct access she centers in Self-energy and then speaks directly to one or more parts of the client. This is not a conversation between a part of the therapist and a part of the client; rather it is a Self-to-part relationship. Insight also involves the Self-to-part relationship but the relationship is between the Self of the client and a part of the client. When using insight we guide the

Table 3.1 Accessing Parts in Therapy

Insight	Client's parts	Client's Self	Therapist's Self
Direct access	Client's parts		Therapist's Self
A problem	Client's parts	Therapist's parts	No Self

client to "go inside" and get to know parts. Both modalities, then, require a Self-to-part relationship, one between the Self of the therapist and a part of the client (direct access) and one between the Self and a part of the client (insight). In either Self-to-part relationship, Self-energy, that feeling state that lies along the continuum from curiosity to compassion, is available to the client's parts. Table 3.1 illustrates the difference between insight and direct access.

For those children who can use insight, IFS therapy looks much the same as it does for older adolescents and adults. However, a significant number of children have difficulty going inside. For them, the therapist can gain all the benefits of insight with the following externalizing techniques.

INSIGHT AND EXTERNALIZING PARTS

In some children, parts are externalized (and therefore unblended) naturally in play. For other children, the therapist will want to facilitate unblending with externalization. Once parts unblend, the therapist can engage the child with insight. Two examples follow: the first illustrates natural unblending during play; the second illustrates how parts can be externalized to facilitate unblending.

PARTS WHO ARE NATURALLY EXTERNALIZED IN PLAY

The child whose parts are naturally externalized into objects will engage with those objects as motivated beings. For example, she might pick up two dolls and have the dolls converse. In IFS we think of each doll as a part. Here is a case example. Ellie came to me at age 7 years because of her "uncontrollable" anger. Ellie's parents were divorced and she lived with her mother and siblings but stayed with her biological father every other weekend. Ellie's biological father had some intimidating parts whose anger was often directed at Ellie. In consequence she was angry in both homes and in school and because her peers were afraid of her, she had no friends. Ellie loved to play with figures in my office, especially a brown horse and a velociraptor (raptor). The raptor was angry and aggressive and dominated the horse. It would knock the horse over, jump up and down on it and refuse to let it speak.

I asked the raptor, "What are you afraid would happen if you let the horse stand up and talk?"

It replied, "The horse is so weak it gets hurt. I have to keep it down and quiet so it's safe."

In other words, the raptor was a protector trying to keep the horse (an exile) from being hurt again. Over the next several sessions I continued to talk with the raptor and heard that the raptor was actually sad. It did not want to be angry but felt that no one else was keeping Ellie and the brown horse safe when she visited her father.

The raptor explained, "When Ellie's father yells at her, the brown horse gets scared and feels like no one is going to help and no one loves her. This is how I have to protect the brown horse."

Once the raptor revealed more of its purpose, I asked Ellie how she felt toward the raptor. This fundamental question in the IFS model reveals how much Self-energy is available.

Ellie said, "I like the raptor. I know what it wants to do." Her answer showed me that she now had access to Self-energy so I could begin to facilitate the relationship between Ellie's Self and her parts with the eventual goal of the horse releasing her burdens.

During the next several sessions Ellie listened to the raptor talk about what made it angry. Some of the events were current and some were in the past. As the raptor felt more understood and less criticized we told it that Ellie herself could help the horse not be as vulnerable to feeling hurt. However, to do that we needed the raptor to step back and let us talk directly with the horse. When we promised to make sure the horse was safely tucked away before we ended each session, the raptor agreed to let the horse talk.

As Ellie developed a relationship with the raptor both her mother and teacher reported Ellie was less angry. I asked Ellie if she noticed the change in her behavior; she confirmed she had not felt so angry lately. We were both curious about the reason for the difference and Ellie suggested we ask the raptor.

When asked, the raptor replied, "Before I met you everybody told me I was bad and yelled at me all the time. Nobody liked me. But you like me and want to help me and that makes me feel better."

It is important to note that Ellie's behavior began to change as soon as Ellie's Self developed a relationship with the protector (raptor) even though she had not witnessed or unburdened her exile (the horse). This illustrates the importance of the Self-to-part relationship with protectors and how changes can begin early in the therapeutic process.

Subsequently, Ellie developed a relationship with the horse in the same way she had with the raptor. As Ellie witnessed and unburdened the horse her anger regulated in most environments. But the raptor continued to feel unsafe with Ellie's father and so continued to be more active when Ellie was visiting him. Nevertheless, even with Ellie's father the raptor was less angry and reactive than it had been before she witnessed and unburdened the horse.

INVITING PARTS TO EXTERNALIZE

When a child's parts do not naturally unblend, the therapist can invite the child to choose an object that represents his feeling state. For example, when a child arrives at a session visibly feeling an emotion such as anger, sadness, or anxiety the therapist can ask her to let that feeling pick an object to represent itself. Parts can be externalized in this way into a wide variety of objects, including puppets, dolls, drawings, stones, seashells and clay. Feel free to use whatever mode or object is most comfortable for the child and you. In the following example Simon used animal figures.

Simon entered therapy with me at the age of 9 years because he was breaking things in his bedroom during episodes of anger. Before starting with Simon, I met with his parents to discuss their concerns and hopes. I introduced them to IFS and explained that I would initially meet separately with Simon and with them but eventually we would have family sessions. In my first session with Simon, I introduced myself and invited him to explore my office. In general, the early stages of IFS play therapy are nondirective so that the child can become comfortable and feel safe. I told Simon that he was free to talk with me or not, and to play with any toys and games or not.

Initially, Simon was agreeable and easy going. He liked to play games and often brought his own game to our sessions and showed little affect whether he won or lost. During this phase of treatment I saw only this part of Simon. There was no sign of the angry part who continued to rail at home. Naturally, Simon's parents were concerned that he was not "dealing with" his anger. I assured them that the anger would emerge when he felt comfortable enough with me. As an IFS therapist I know that parts emerge when they feel safe and, indeed, several weeks into our work Simon's behavior changed, indicating that other parts were emerging. He was now reluctant to leave his mother's car to come into my office. I encouraged his parents to continue bringing him.

Now Simon began to get angry about coming to our sessions. His mother frequently had to take his hand and lead him to my office and once even carried him in. I helped her work with her parts to stay calm and determined when she brought Simon. Now he refused to play when he met with me. He sometimes sat in silence and other times spoke loudly and angrily about how much he hated therapy. During these sessions, I remained curious about Simon and welcoming of his anger. I asked Simon, "Are you interested in knowing more about your anger since it gets you in trouble at home?"

The first four times I made this invitation Simon refused. However, the fifth time he said, "Yes, I would like to know my anger because I hate feeling angry all the time!" Simon loved animals so I asked him to pick one of the animals on my shelf to be his anger. He chose a large gorilla and put it on my table. To begin the unblending process, I asked Simon, "How do you feel toward the gorilla?" In my mind, the gorilla was, of course, a part.

He said, "I hate it."

Clearly this was another part speaking and I knew that the gorilla could not reveal itself as long as this highly critical part was blended with Simon.

So I said, "Can you find an animal who looks like this feeling of 'hate' toward the gorilla and put it on the table too?"

He selected a black panther and placed it face-to-face with the gorilla. When I asked if he wanted to know more about the gorilla and the panther, Simon said, "Yes." This curiosity indicated Simon had some Self-energy.

I said, "Why don't you ask them what they want to say to each other?"

Simon explained, "The panther doesn't like the gorilla because it gets him in so much trouble. The panther says Simon's mother, father and sister are always angry or afraid of him and don't want to be around him."

I said to Simon, "Ask the panther what is so bad about people not wanting to be around him?"

The panther replied, "Then Simon feels empty and alone. If he could just be a little nicer and do what people want him to then everyone would like him and he would feel better. But," the panther added sadly, "even though I've tried and tried to get the gorilla to stop being so angry he never listens."

I asked, "How do you feel toward the panther now?"

Simon said, "I feel sad for him. He's doing his best."

I asked Simon to tell this to the panther, who listened and felt reassured. Then I said, "Shall we offer the panther some hope by saying that we can talk with the gorilla and find out what makes him so angry? Once we know why, we can heal the gorilla. All we need is for the panther to move aside so that we can talk to the gorilla directly." The panther agreed and Simon moved the panther to the far edge of the table.

Then Simon turned his attention to the gorilla. This time when I asked Simon how he felt toward the gorilla, he responded, "I want to get to know it." I invited Simon to ask the gorilla what it wanted Simon to know about himself.

The gorilla told Simon, "I am trying to help you, not get you in trouble. I want you to feel strong and have people listen to you because no one ever does. No one ever asks what you want, they just tell you what to do."

We asked the gorilla what was so bad about not being asked and he replied, "Then Simon feels like he's invisible and no one cares about him. He feels like he has nothing inside. He hates that. I don't like having to get so angry but I don't know any other way to help Simon feel strong."

Simon listened and then said, "I understand. I feel sad that the gorilla has to get angry for me."

"How about if we find and heal the part in you who feels weak and invisible?" I asked. Simon repeated this question to the gorilla, who agreed that if Simon could do this it would not need to get so angry.

And so Simon finally had permission to contact his weak, invisible part. Our work with the panther and gorilla had unfolded over several sessions. We had been careful to allow as much time as they needed to trust Simon's Self so they would feel confident that he could take care of this most vulnerable part.

With this permission, Simon moved the gorilla to the back of the table and almost immediately began to feel the weak, invisible part. I asked Simon to pick an animal who looked like this feeling and he selected a wolf whose head was raised in a howl. He placed the howling wolf on the table in front of him.

"How do you feel toward the wolf?" I asked.

"I feel kinda mad at him," Simon said.

"Is it the gorilla who's mad?" I asked.

"Yeah," Simon nodded. "He doesn't like when the wolf feels this way." Simon picked up the gorilla and looked it in the eye. He said, "It's OK. The wolf won't hurt me." Simon listened to the gorilla for a moment and then placed him at the back of the table again. "He says he'll watch," Simon reported.

"How do you feel toward the wolf now?" I asked.

"I want to know more," Simon said.

"What's going on?" I asked.

"I feel smaller," Simon reported.

When a part begins to blend like this, I do not want it to blend fully and overwhelm the client. My goal is to maintain enough of the Self-to-part relationship that the Self is still the part's witness. So I said to the wolf, "If you take Simon over, he won't be there to help you feel better. It's good to show him what you feel but check to be sure he's still with you."

Because parts long for help, they generally agree to this invitation, as the wolf did. And Simon immediately began to have memories of feeling invisible, including the day his younger sister was born. He saw images of his mother attending to the baby and not him, and then images of times in kindergarten and elementary school when he felt unheard or unimportant. He told me what he was remembering and said he was feeling sad, lonely, scared, unlovable and worthless.

"I have a pit in my stomach," he said. "It feels empty."

"How do you feel toward the wolf?" I asked, monitoring his Self-to-part relationship. Simon remained loving toward the wolf so I knew he had plenty of Self-energy. After about 5 minutes the memories, feelings and body sensations ceased and a visible calm settled on Simon.

"Ask the wolf if there is anything more it wants to show," I said.

"He says there's no more," Simon replied.

"How do you feel toward the wolf now?" I asked. Simon still felt loving, so I went on, "Ask if he felt understood."

"He says he hears me talking but he isn't sure he feels understood."

On further questioning we discovered that the wolf could not feel Simon's love because he had been pushed into Simon's right heel by the panther and gorilla, who both wanted the wolf as far away from Simon's heart as possible to protect Simon from his pain. I knew the wolf had to feel understood before he could unburden. To feel understood he needed to feel Simon's love, but even when Simon told the wolf he loved him the wolf did not feel the love.

Wondering how Simon might help the wolf to feel his love, I remembered that touch can increase a feeling of connection. "Ask the wolf if you can touch him," I said. The wolf was amenable and I invited Simon to put his hands around the wolf and imagine love flowing from his hands into the wolf. Still the wolf could not feel Simon's love and said that he lived too far from Simon's heart.

Then it occurred to me that Simon needed to touch the actual spot on his body where the wolf lived. The wolf liked this idea and Simon put one hand on his heart and one on his heel. I said, "Imagine your love traveling from your heart into this hand first, then through your body and into the other hand, and then into the wolf." As Simon did this the wolf instantly felt calmer. After several minutes I said, "Would you like to ask if the wolf wants to come closer to your heart?" The wolf agreed and moved into the left side of Simon's torso, retrieved at last from exile. Then I suggested, "Simon, why don't you move your hand to the spot on your left side where the wolf lives now."

"I'm sending my love from my heart to the wolf over here," he said, holding one hand on his heart and one on his left side. He continued doing this with his eyes closed for several minutes until the wolf said he could feel Simon's love and finally felt understood.

Once this part felt understood, we could begin the unburdening process. I instructed Simon to tell the wolf that he could let go of the painful thoughts, feelings and beliefs he had shown Simon. The wolf told Simon that his burden was in his howl but he could or would not be specific about the burden. This is common in children and, as with adults, it is not necessary to know the exact nature of a burden. We offered the wolf the option of releasing his burden to one of the elements (earth, wind, water, light or air) but he wanted to release the burden into Simon's heart. After several minutes the wolf indicated he had done so and no longer felt empty or alone.

At my instruction, once the burden was released, Simon asked the wolf what he wanted to invite into himself now that there was more space.

The wolf replied, "Love."

Because Simon's hands were still on his heart and torso, I said, "Does the wolf want the love to come from your heart?"

Simon listened and then nodded. We sat quietly for several more minutes as Simon imagined the love flowing from his heart into the wolf in his torso. When we asked the wolf how he was now, he told Simon that he felt loved and lovable.

Before Simon left the office that day we began the integration process, which continued for several weeks. We knew that the gorilla and panther were closely tied to the wolf, so first I had Simon ask if either of them had any concerns about what had happened with the wolf and neither did. In fact, though they were not sure why, both felt relieved. Because we were nearly at the end of the session I had Simon ask if we could check back with them during our next session to see how they were doing. Both agreed.

The next week Simon said, "The wolf feels better. But he's still worried that I might forget him and let the gorilla and the panther send him back to my heel."

"What does the wolf need?" I asked.

Simon asked the wolf, who reminded him that he had the exact same wolf figure at home. The wolf wanted Simon to find that figure and carry it around with him in his book bag. That way the wolf could be with Simon whenever he needed to be. We asked the wolf to designate a signal for when he needed Simon's attention and he offered to show himself as a small stitch in Simon's side.

For the next few weeks Simon took the wolf in his book bag wherever he went. When he felt the stitch in his side, he would remove the wolf and hold him. When it was awkward to take the wolf out Simon would silently let the wolf know he would hold him as soon as he was able. Although Simon could still get angry, the feeling was less extreme and more appropriate to the triggering incident. After unburdening the wolf, Simon never had a destructive episode again.

BLENDED PARTS AND DIRECT ACCESS

Some children have parts who will not unblend either naturally in play or when invited. This tells me that one part is in control and the child's every thought and action is a thought or action of that part. As with adults, when parts are blended and will not unblend, direct access is the modality of choice. In direct access the therapist is the source of Self-energy and to fulfill this role she must be able to unblend her own parts. Here are two clinical examples of direct access.

Jason's parents brought him to therapy because "he has no friends." Jason was easily provoked and hit or pushed other children frequently so no one wanted to play with him. His father also complained that Jason was a "cheater" and said, "No one likes a cheater." Jason was 6 years old.

On his first visit, Jason decided to play the board game Sorry. As we played, I was aware of a series of parts who blended with Jason. While winning Jason was excited and enthusiastic, gloating and telling me that I was a loser. But when the tide turned and I started winning, Jason grew quiet, withdrawn and spoke of feeling hopeless. He said, "I always lose" and "I'll never catch up to you." Finally, when it looked like I was going to win the game, Jason swept all the pieces off the board and declared he was quitting. Then he seemed embarrassed and quickly picked up all the pieces, putting them in the box.

During this time I observed a series of my own parts too. At first, I noticed a part who was sad about losing and did not want to play, especially after Jason called me a loser. Then, I noticed a part who got excited and wanted to gloat when I started to win. Next came a caretaking manager who wanted to reassure Jason's parts and tell him not to feel sad. Finally, I noticed a part who was scared when Jason swept the pieces from the board.

As I observed my parts I asked them to step back so I could stay curious and open while we played the game. That way Jason's parts would not be subjected to my reactions and would continue to feel invited, an unusual if not unique experience for him. Once feeling Self-led, a therapist may choose to be silent and observe the child's parts as they emerge. Early in the direct access process, being silent can help the therapist to gain clarity about the nature of the child's parts and how they have been wounded. In our first session, Jason revealed several parts including a firefighter who gloated; a quiet, withdrawn, hopeless exile; a firefighter who swept the pieces off the board and, finally, a manager who cleaned up.

There is no right way for the therapist to respond when using direct access; the only requirement is for the therapist to unblend her parts and be Self-led. When the therapist is Self-led she can trust her intuition. After observing the child's parts, the therapist could choose to speak for her own parts by saying, "I have a part who feels sad when you call me a loser," or "A part of me doesn't have much fun when you gloat" or "Sometimes a part of me feels bad when I beat you." When speaking for parts there is no judgment about the child's part nor is there any request that the child change his behavior. When a therapist speaks for his/her part it can help the child's part become aware of the unintended impact it has on another person. This simple awareness can help a part begin to alter its behavior.

During this first session I was silent until the end of the game when Jason swept the pieces off the board. Then I reassured him that he could choose to stop the game, and whatever he chose was OK with me. Jason stopped cleaning up and listened but did not respond. After that Jason wanted to play Sorry in every session. Over the next few weeks I began to speak for my own parts by naming not only the ones who felt bad when Jason gloated or called me a loser but also parts who loved to win and got frustrated when I did not. Of course, Jason also had parts who could not tolerate losing. His play revealed two parts who tried to protect him from losing: one cheated and the other quit. In this way I welcomed all his parts and they began to trust me.

Jason's parents both had parts who were polarized with Jason's protectors. They both tried to stop his cheating part, which of course shamed him. However, when it came to Jason's quitting part, his parents had opposite reactions. When Jason tried to quit anything, his father had a part who told him only babies quit and that, to be a grown up, 6-year-old Jason should keep playing.

In contrast, Jason's mother had a part who helped him avoid any activity in which he might not excel. As I helped his parents notice their own parts, they began to understand Jason's parts and were better able to moderate their reactions.

At the same time, I invited Jason's cheating part to join our play. My goal was to welcome rather than shame his parts. Just as I had told the quitter that it could quit whenever it wanted, I told Jason he could cheat whenever he wanted. Jason's cheater loved this and began making different rules to ensure that Jason would win. I continued to speak for my parts by saying things like, "It's hard for me to always lose," or "I wish I could have special rules, too."

Meanwhile Jason's parents were allowing him to play this way at home so his protectors felt welcomed there as well. With some Self-led psychoeducation, Jason's parents had come to understand that it is normal for a 6-year-old to have parts who feel sad, hopeless and out-of-control when they lose. They also learned that trying to manage or prevent Jason's uncomfortable feelings actually intensified them. Over time, as the parents grew less polarized with Jason's parts, they allowed him to feel sad and hopeless without trying to manage or suppress his feeling. Jason's father was less critical and his mother did not always try to protect him. They still had reactive parts but their reactions came less frequently and were less intense.

Once Jason's parts felt more welcomed things began to change. Though he could not articulate the reason, Jason was more comfortable with the cheater, the quitter and the one who cleaned up. It is the norm with younger children for change to occur without the child, the therapist or the parents knowing exactly which parts have unburdened. But the change will be evident, as it was in Jason as he became less volatile. Now when Jason played Sorry his cheater rarely needed to cheat and he rarely quit a game. He was actually able to say that he hated losing while continuing to play. Indicating newfound courage, Jason began picking games that were more challenging and required strategy such as checkers and Battleship. And his parents as well as his teacher reported that he was calmer. Although he still had no close friends, he did begin to have play dates with one boy and these were going well. This is an example of direct access early in the therapeutic process but it was only the beginning of Jason's therapy, which continued off and on for several years.

DIRECT ACCESS WITH ABBY

Abby was a 4-year-old girl whose mother described her as "painfully shy." Abby never spoke at preschool and had few friends. I began the therapy with Abby's parents and her teacher who had parts who were polarized with Abby's "shyness" and encouraged her to participate in things that she was afraid of, which intensified her fear. As I became more familiar with Abby's parents it became clear they both had parts who found anger unacceptable.

They had exiled not only their own angry parts but Abby's as well. While the parents entered into IFS couple therapy (with another therapist) and began to explore their parts, I talked with Abby's teacher. In an attempt to help Abby feel less shy, the teacher had created a rule that Abby must say one thing in school every day. But the more the teacher encouraged and required Abby to speak, the quieter Abby grew. I asked her to suspend the rule while Abby and I were working together and she agreed.

In our first session Abby stared out the window. She did not look at or speak to me. I asked her if it was OK for me to sit on the sofa and she nodded. I quietly told her that she was free to do whatever she wanted when we were together, she could talk or play or not, and that I would not try to get her to do anything. Abby did not respond. She stared out the window for the entire session.

The second session Abby again stared out the window and I sat on the couch after asking if that was OK with her. About halfway through the session she said, "You can't make me look at you."

I replied, "I understand and that's fine because you get to decide what happens, not me."

The third session was a repeat of the second except this time Abby said, "You can't make me talk to you."

Again I reassured her that she was in charge.

Finally in the fourth session Abby went straight to the closet where I kept the toys. Cautiously curious, she began to play. I asked if I should stay on the couch or sit on the floor near her and she indicated the couch. And so it went for many sessions: I sat on the couch watching her play with animal figures but she spoke too softly for me to hear. Eventually she asked me to play with her and we started to build forts with blankets and pillows. In this play, a part of Abby always wanted to tell me what to do and how to build the fort. Her parents started to notice this assertive part at home and (predictable in people with managerial parts who disapprove of anger) described it as "bossy." The part felt like, and indeed was, the polar opposite of Abby's shy part. Noting Abby's polarized shy and assertive parts, I assumed they protected a more vulnerable part.

Polarizations occur naturally in any internal system. In the absence of Self-leadership, protective parts vie for control of the system and cover the options for staying safe with opposite strategies that become more extreme over time. When a child presents with a protective strategy like Abby's shyness, an IFS therapist expects to meet another protector with an opposing view of how to stay safe. And sure enough Abby's assertive part had showed up.

While Abby and I continued getting to know her parts, I also helped her parents adjust to her new assertiveness. Gradually the assertive part felt welcomed at home as well as in therapy. As a result, it began to be aggressive in therapy. It needed to hit something and wanted to hit me. I pondered how to invite this part in and convey that while all feelings (and parts) were welcome, it was not OK to intentionally hurt anyone physically, verbally or emotionally.

I listened to my own parts. Some understood the importance of welcoming Abby's aggressive part, some were afraid of her aggression and wanted to protect me from getting hurt. With this input I discovered how I could be respectful of my parts as well as Abby's. I told her that I could sit on a chair with three large pillows covering my lower body and legs. Her angry part could then hit me where the pillows covered my body. Abby's part agreed to these guidelines and for several sessions she hit me. Occasionally, Abby's hand would stray to my arm and I would remind the part that it was not OK to hit me there. She would immediately return to hitting the pillows.

One day Abby did not want to hit. Instead she asked, "Why do I always have to come to your house to play and you don't ever come to my house?" My office was in an old home.

"Why would you like me to come to your house?" I asked.

Abby replied, "I want to show you how I play at my house."

She could be no clearer than that. In addition, her invitation was confident and enthusiastic, an attitude I had not witnessed before in Abby. We talked with her mother and made arrangements for me to go to her house to play. The day I visited was sunny and warm. We played a board game, built a fort in her playroom, jumped on her trampoline, and played wiffle ball. Throughout, Abby exuded confidence, playfulness, humor and enthusiasm.

The next week Abby told me she did not need to visit me anymore and I agreed. She was no longer controlled by her shy, withdrawn part and neither Abby nor her parents were exiling her angry protector. She was talkative with friends at preschool and she had started taking ballet lessons. I am not certain if our work unburdened any exiles but, as I said, this is often the case with young children. Although we can see the results of the therapy, the child cannot verbalize her internal experience so we rarely know exactly if or what parts have unburdened.

ADOLESCENTS

As with younger children, direct access and insight can be used with adolescents. Some younger teens may require the same externalizing techniques described above. Others can use insight in the traditional way. Still others will benefit from direct access. There is no way to determine in advance who will require which modality. The modality for any age client is based on her needs. Nevertheless, I am including this separate section on adolescents. They can be a challenge for clinicians as well as for parents and having special techniques for working with them can make a significant and positive difference in their therapy.

Adolescents are more challenging in part because of the way they produce firefighters, the protectors who react by numbing or suppressing pain after an exile has surfaced. The reactive behavior of firefighters can seem out-of-control and reckless. Common adolescent firefighter behavior includes: drug and alcohol use, sexual promiscuity, rage, extreme clothing and hairstyles, withdrawal, silence, extreme sports, reckless driving, cutting, bingeing and purging, restricting calories, extreme exercise, excessive TV watching or playing video games and suicidal thinking. And this list is by no means exhaustive. Any part seeking to numb pain would be considered a firefighter.

For the managerial parts of adults, these behaviors can be particularly confusing and frightening. What could make a young person behave so illogically? Focusing on the adolescent's search for identity, Ames, Ilg & Baker (1988) wrote,

> The search for self is, in some ways, what adolescence is all about—finding oneself, learning to identify, count on, and depend on oneself. And to do this one must get free of one's earlier dependence on and veneration of one's parents . . . [a task that requires] much trying on of different personalities. (p. 220)

In the struggle to differentiate and become independent, parts of adolescents frequently adopt new and different behaviors of which parents disapprove. Attempting to protect adolescents, parents, teachers and even therapists try to quell extreme behavior with logic, criticism, anger, punishment, bribery, nagging or worry. Anytime an adult leads from a part rather than from Self, no matter how loving or correct the part may be, a polarization will develop. The blended adult will not have access to curiosity about the teenager's behavior and will automatically be pulled into a polarization with the teenager's firefighter. Once curiosity is lost so is the connection.

With adolescents more than with any other population, therapists must be aware of polarizations. They are common between parts of the adolescent and the parent as well as between parts of the adolescent and the therapist. It also helps if the therapist has a real appreciation for the adolescent's extreme, reactive parts. Every parts-led system needs firefighters because no manager can keep exiles from surfacing 100 percent of the time. Eventually all exiles get triggered and—without firefighters—emotions such as worthlessness, humiliation and terror flood the system. Thus, even if it were possible, it would make no sense to eliminate firefighters. When authorities (including mental health workers) do manage to shut down one firefighter, another steps up to take its place. The only solution is to get to know firefighters and offer them hope that the exile can be healed. Here is a case example of IFS therapy with an adolescent.

Nan, 19-years-old when we met, was referred to me for treatment of bulimia. Her bingeing and purging began during high school but got worse during her first year of college. She took a leave of absence and was home living with her parents. Beginning in high school, Nan had been in a cognitive-behavioral therapy for bulimia and had been hospitalized briefly. When we started to work together, Nan requested that I meet separately with her and her parents until she had a clearer sense of her Self and her parts.

Though 19 years old by the calendar, Nan's developmental age was closer to 13. Nevertheless, from the beginning she was able to focus internally (that is, to use insight) to communicate with her parts. Very early on we discovered some powerful caretaking and pleasing parts and I noticed an absence of anger in her system. Her pleasing parts were so strong that they kept Nan from ever disagreeing with her parents, no matter how large or small the issue. Nan's parents were loving, kind people who also showed no anger. They both had extreme caretaking parts who wanted Nan to be happy and fulfilled at all times and worked hard to keep her from having "bad" feelings.

Nan began her work by getting to know her pleasing part. This protector told Nan that she felt safe and loved with her parents and was afraid that if Nan disagreed or expressed anger they might not love and keep her safe any longer. I helped Nan listen to and appreciate this protector. As Nan did so, the part grew to trust her and agreed to let us help the scared exile it protected. As the pleasing part stepped back, its polarized opposite, an edgy protector, appeared. The edgy part did not experience Nan's parents as loving but believed they were disinterested in Nan's desires and needs and so she was unheard and unloved. This protector did not want Nan to feel unloved. It believed if she could stand up to her parents and be heard, she would feel loved.

This example illustrates Nan's polarized protectors trying to achieve the goal of feeling loved with opposite tactics. One believes that being pleasing will bring Nan love; the other believes Nan will feel loved when she demands that her parents listen to her. As Nan became more Self-led and formed an appreciative relationship with this assertive part, her internal balance of power shifted and the pleasing part was no longer dominant. As a result Nan could now be terse and even irritable with her parents. Initially this shift troubled her parents so I explained that it was normal for her behavior to change as she developed relationships with her parts and that her irritability would not last forever.

They were also concerned because Nan continued to binge and purge. I explained the IFS view of extreme protectors, which is that bingeing and purging are efforts of a protective part to squelch painful emotion. I warned them that this behavior would wax and wane during treatment and might be more frequent if we were actively working with an exile. I assured them it would drop in frequency and eventually disappear as her internal system was healed.

Because her previous therapy had done little to change the eating disordered behavior, Nan's parents made a decision to trust me and the IFS model. Wanting to be sure that Nan stayed healthy, we all (including Nan) agreed that she would visit her physician every 4 to 8 weeks to monitor her health. In addition, her parents did just enough IFS therapy to ensure they would not become polarized with her emerging parts. As they grew more familiar with their parts and emotions, they stopped reacting to Nan with the feelings of hurt and anxiety and subsequent withdrawal or smothering her with attention. Eventually they stopped looking through Nan's room for evidence of her disordered eating and that was enough of a shift for Nan's parts to feel less judged. Once this external judgment abated, Nan's irritated, terse part could step back and began allowing her access to the lonely exile who felt unloved.

Nan's case is a good illustration of IFS therapy with adolescents because the stages in which her exiles unburdened were linked to her level of dependence on her parents—certain exiles were not accessible at all until Nan was financially independent. Our work with one important exile began while she was on leave from college. Over several sessions, Nan discovered that this exile felt unloved, unseen and not good enough. It showed Nan scenes of herself being shy and feeling different, unseen, disconnected and inferior. When it felt Nan understood these distressing experiences, it released some of the burden. But it let Nan know that it could not yet show her everything.

After this unburdening, her bingeing and purging stopped and she was calmer with her parents—neither overly compliant nor irritable in her family—and she decided to take a break from therapy. I supported her, but we both knew the exile still had burdens. Nan returned to college and several months later felt the urge to binge and purge. She called and we began regular sessions of phone therapy. This time the exile showed Nan times when she had felt unloved and unheard by her parents. She saw why neither the pleasing nor the angry part had wanted her to view these scenes when she was still dependent on the people who were central to this exile's burden. When the exile felt understood by Nan, it released more of the loneliness, fear and worthlessness but still not all.

Once again Nan stopped bingeing and purging. And now a part who was angry with her parents emerged. Both the pleasing part and the partially unburdened exile were afraid of this angry part. Nan reassured them that the anger would not take her over and that she could help it feel less angry. The exile agreed, but the pleasing part was afraid the anger would do something to rupture Nan's relationship with her parents permanently and insisted that Nan limit contact with her parents while getting to know the anger. Nan agreed and asked me to explain to them why she would be more distant for a time.

Nan spent many sessions with this angry part who showed scenes in which it had felt unloved and unseen. It also showed Nan the ways in which her parents, teachers and other parts had suppressed its anger. Once the part felt understood and welcomed by Nan, it felt less vulnerable and less in need of protection, and began to relax. In response the angry part gave up being so angry and, referring to itself as Nan's "backbone," decided instead to help her be assertive and say "no" proactively.

Once the anger moderated, Nan resumed regular contact with her parents and enjoyed her growing sense of Self-leadership, which she described as a feeling of calm clarity in which she was able to be with her emotion rather than being the emotion. She decided to take another break from therapy and, as before, I supported her. Nan found a job in her field after graduating and was now financially independent from her parents. Several months later she began to binge and purge again so resumed therapy.

Now that Nan was independent, the pleasing and angry protectors were willing to allow the partially unburdened exile to reveal its deepest burdens. The exile reappeared, this time simply as a sense of abject worthlessness and a burning, empty feeling in Nan's stomach. It took several sessions before the part could even notice love coming from Nan's Self. Once it felt her presence it longed to be held and rocked, which Nan did. The part never showed Nan any images but Nan came to understand through its sensations that it had been burdened early in life. Her parents had been loving but also anxious and eager for Nan to feel good. Longing for a loving heart, this part had gotten loving anxiety instead. Over several weeks as the part felt increasingly connected to Nan and received her love, it released the remaining burden of emptiness and worthlessness.

Nan ended therapy after this and I have not heard from her in several years. There were many parts she did not witness, including the ones who binged and purged. Any time she attempted to help them, a part who felt ashamed of the behaviors would block her access. Because I know that parts will emerge in the best order for their system, I did not push Nan either to witness or avoid these parts. Nevertheless, parts who remain unwitnessed and surrounded by shame are vulnerable to being triggered by life events—at which time I can imagine Nan resuming IFS therapy.

CONCLUSIONS

This chapter illustrates how IFS can be applied to children and adolescents using both insight and direct access. Some young people are able to use insight as adults do; others need their parts externalized into objects. As with most child and family therapies, IFS is most likely to be successful when caretakers also engage in the therapeutic process. Deciding on a case-by-case basis, taking into account the degree to which the parents are Self-led, the therapist may choose to do therapy with the family unit or work with the child separately.

Polarizations between parent and child are particularly important. The therapist will help adults to observe how their parts are polarized with their child's parts, understand their own parts and have compassion for the child's parts. Once parent/child polarizations are relaxed, the child is free to explore her own internal system. And, finally, unburdening can and does happen while children are dependent on their parents but some parts may need the child to be independent before unburdening can be complete.

REFERENCE

Ames, L. B., Ilg, F. L. & Baker, S. M. (1988). *Your Ten-to-Fourteen-Year-Old.* New York, New York: Dell Publishing.

SELF IN RELATIONSHIP: AN INTRODUCTION TO IFS COUPLE THERAPY

Toni Herbine-Blank

INTRODUCTION

Almost immediately after meeting Elizabeth and her husband Mark it was clear to me that they were at an impasse. "We feel terrible," Elizabeth said. "We know we love each other but we fight all the time, we can't talk to each other anymore.

"We disagree about everything," Mark said.

These kinds of statements are common at the beginning of couple therapy. After trying to fix what they believe is wrong with their relationship, many couples enter therapy feeling discouraged, isolated and hopeless. Internal family systems therapy (IFS) invites people first to learn how to be in a loving relationship with themselves and, from that state, to attempt a heartfelt connection with their intimate partner. We offer the concept of parts and Self to help couples reframe their bitter struggles and understand relationships differently. It is my belief that working with parts and accessing Self-energy are the keys to positive change and growth.

This chapter illustrates the theory and concepts of IFS in action in couple therapy, highlighting key interventions with case examples. The reader will learn how the IFS therapist sets the stage immediately for the differentiation of parts from Self, which in turn helps individuals to regulate intense emotion, heal from toxic shame and communicate skillfully.

A FIRST SESSION: LAYING THE GROUNDWORK

As I continued to interview Mark and Elizabeth, I invited them to talk more about what brought them to therapy. To gauge their level of comfort with themselves, I watched their body language closely. I noticed that Mark looked to Elizabeth for affirmation. With a sideways glance at his wife, he seemed to say, "I cannot be OK if you don't think I'm OK. If my experience of me is different from your experience of me, I feel insecure."

What he actually said to me was, "When Elizabeth and I decided to get married we were always on the same page, we didn't disagree about anything. But then we began to fight about the stupidest things. I feel like she's changed. I don't get it."

"And how do you understand all of this disagreeing after you got married?"

"In a disagreement, someone has to be right and someone has to be wrong. Turns out I'm always wrong." Mark said.

"Not true!" Elizabeth responded angrily. "It's you who always has to be right or you stop engaging." She went on to describe a damaging pattern of coping. First each tried to enroll the other to think and feel the same way about things. When this failed, Mark would capitulate and deny his experience to recover the illusion of sameness with Elizabeth. But when his sacrifice failed to help them recover the desired sameness of thinking and feeling, they both grew disappointed and angry. In anger they would retreat into *being right*, discounting each other's perspective.

"What," I asked, "do you hope for in couple therapy?"

"We'd like to get back on track," Mark said.

"What would that look like?" I asked.

"Where we see things the same way and can agree again," Elizabeth said.

"What is the most important thing about agreeing?" I asked.

"Peace! No conflict," Mark said.

"Can I ask what you both learned about conflict in relationships when you were young?"

Rather than getting caught in the content of their arguments, I stepped back internally to notice their patterns of interacting, paying close attention to how they were communicating with me and with each other. Observing for myself at this point rather than out loud, I watched how they turned away from each other and spoke to me as though the other person was not in the room. Mark was quick to defend himself by saying things such as, "If you wouldn't have done this or that, I wouldn't have reacted as I did." In response Elizabeth fell into stony silence.

As with many couples seeking help they could not at this point stay open and curious. They alternated between angry, defensive hyperaroused parts, and withdrawn, collapsed hypo-aroused parts who made them inarticulate. This told me that they could not yet separate, or *unblend*, from reactive protectors.

In most couples protectors vie for power and influence in the relational system. In my experience, the protectors of one person will try to convince me that their partner is the real reason for their relational conflict by making provocative statements like, "He's so out of touch with his feelings. He watches

TV all the time at night and has no interest in communicating." Although I take note of this information, I am very careful not to get lost in a fog of content or be seduced by a critical manager. Rather my first task is to help them understand the behavior and motivation of their protectors in these cycles of reactivity.

"All the concerns and feelings you have make sense to me," I said to Mark and Elizabeth. "I understand that it feels awful between you and has for awhile. It sounds to me as though you haven't been able to stay connected in the way that used to feel so good."

As I continued to validate and normalize their experience, I noticed their bodies relaxing. Mark leaned back; Elizabeth took a deep breath. They looked at each other kindly and nodded at me. I asked them, "What would life be like if you experienced less internal reactivity toward each other and at the same time could listen to each other's perspectives with curiosity and without having to agree?"

"This is what we want!" they agreed.

"We all have parts," I said, explaining how, in the view of IFS, protectors in one person will trip protectors in the other. I went on to illustrate how protectors serve vulnerable parts, and how the self-protective impulses we all share create these very typical cycles of painful interaction.

Then I explained that in IFS therapy we invite couples to embrace what Schwartz (2008) describes as a *U-turn*. This signifies a process that involves asking an individual to discontinue their outward focus on the other person. We invite them to turn back toward themselves, to their own inner experience. The U-turn is a client's first step toward internal differentiation. It is an invitation to form compassionate relationships with wounded parts and end the tidal pull of past trauma on the present. We then invite them to re-"turn" to their partner in a different state of mind; more present, more attuned. It can be a stretch, especially at the beginning of therapy, for people in pain to believe that they can change from the inside out and that doing so will change their experience from the outside in.

"Your most protective parts," I said to Mark and Elizabeth, "may balk at the idea of moving inside to be curious about yourself instead of focusing on changing each other. But my experience—and I have a lot of it—says this will change your relationship and empower you to feel better. Right now, it will probably be a leap of faith."

GOALS OF IFS COUPLE THERAPY

The word *differentiation* can be construed in a number of ways. When I use it, I mean being in relationship with another while maintaining connection with and regulating one's own internal experience. This is a particular challenge in times of stress. The level of differentiation between partners is a reflection of the level of differentiation inside each individual. External reactivity stems from internal reactivity, from conflict between parts in a state of disconnection from Self. To assess internal differentiation I look not only at relationships in the client's internal system, but also at how the client responds in external relationships. Protective adaptations such as avoidance or enmeshment at either level can block healthy differentiation. My goal for couples is attuned and loving relationships inside and out. In this state partners realize they are capable of taking care of their injured parts and they interact from Self-leadership for the sake of the relationship (Schwartz, 2008). Even though the external relational field is our first point of contact with a couple, in IFS couple therapy we prioritize the internal. Our initial aim, which I illustrate in the cases that follow, is to help parts differentiate from the Self to recognize and re-attach to the Self. This internal attachment work paves the relational road of the couple.

We work with the internal system much as we would work with an external system, learning about the roles and protective functions of parts, supporting the development of relationships between parts, and between parts and Self, and then helping our clients to access vulnerable young parts who carry the burdens of relational trauma. As the internal system shifts we can usually observe positive effects on external relationships as well. In brief, we see the external mirroring the internal. We always keep in mind that the painful polarizations, fears, conflict, rage and withdrawal that we see between partners are also occurring internally between the parts of each client.

The art of couple work in IFS lies in balancing in-depth individual IFS work with a focus on the relationship. This entails a variety of strategies: asking one person to go inside while supporting the other one to remain engaged and present; then moving back to external relational work and teaching the couple to speak for parts, listen from Self and try on new ways of behaving that foster differentiation, individuality and connection. This changes old patterns of relating and moves couples forward.

SELF AND AFFECT REGULATION

Although self-defense in the face of interpersonal provocation is hard to resist, in IFS couple therapy we invite both listener and speaker to have curiosity about him- or herself before responding. The ability to be with one's own feelings regardless of intense physiological arousal is key. For example, when a partner gives painful feedback or expresses anger directly from, rather than for, an agitated protector, the therapist might make the following intervention, as I did with my client, Adam, during an interaction with his wife, Erin.

"Adam, I'd like to take a moment and slow you down. May I help you talk to Erin in a way that she just might be able to hear you?"

Adam took a breath and sat back. I waited a moment and then asked, "What's happening in your body right now?"

"I feel tense," Adam replied.

"Where, in or around your body, do you feel the tension?"

"Some in my shoulders but mostly in my gut," he said.

"Would you focus on your gut for a minute?" I asked.

"OK."

"As you focus there," I said, "what do you hear yourself saying to yourself?"

"Let her have it!"

"What's the feeling that goes with those words?" I asked.

"I'm angry," he replied, "and I want to let her have it!"

"Would you be willing to stay focused on that anger and the impulse to let Erin have it?"

"I don't like to focus on my anger," Adam said.

"Tell me more."

"I'm not an angry person. But Erin is so busy not listening to me that I can't help being angry."

"Adam, I'm sure it's true you're not always angry. But just for today, would you consider that this anger is coming from a part of you and is not all of you?"

Adam took a moment. "OK," he finally said.

"Would you consider that for today there is an angry part in your gut?"

"I guess I can be curious," he said.

"Great. And would it be OK to keep focusing on it, just for a little while longer?"

"I can feel it," he said.

"How do you feel toward it?"

"Well, I don't love it if that's what you're asking."

"It's fine not to love it. Given that you don't love it, how do you feel toward it?"

"OK, I guess."

I said, "As strange as this might seem, Adam, let's ask this part of you what it hopes for? What does it want for you right now?" Adam paused for a few seconds, crossing his arms and looking down. Softly, I inquired, "What are you noticing?"

"Maybe I can get her attention and she will know what I'm feeling."

"So the hope of this part is that if you get angry enough, Erin just might pay attention to how you feel?"

"Yes, and maybe she will *feel* what I feel as well."

"Does it make sense that you have a part trying really hard to get Erin's attention?"

Adam took a breath "Yes it does. I never took the time to see it from this perspective before."

"How does it feel to do that now?"

"I can feel myself relaxing."

SELF IN RELATIONSHIP **59**

"Great," I said. "When the time feels right, would you speak for the angry part about whether this strategy for trying to get Erin's attention is working? Is it getting Erin's attention?"

"Not in a good way," Adam said.

"Let's ask it if there was another way to get Erin's attention without having to take you over like this, would it be interested?"

Adam paused and closed his eyes momentarily. Then he said, "Yes, I think it is interested."

"And how is your gut?"

"Relaxed."

This interaction with Adam is an example of how internal differentiation can regulate arousal. Supported by the calm, nonjudgmental presence of the therapist, Adam connected with a distressed inner part and, as that part gradually separated from him, he relaxed. In this way, Adam moved from a dysregulated state to a more optimal state of regulation in which he felt attuned to rather than overwhelmed by his body and emotions. Now he was prepared to talk with Erin.

THE THERAPIST AND SELF-REGULATION

IFS therapy holds that therapists also have exiled parts in pain and protective parts in conflict (Schwartz, this volume). Success in treating couples depends on the therapist knowing her own system. IFS couple therapists will inevitably run into many of their own parts who fear conflict or have strong views on infidelity, caretaking and all the other issues that typically arise for couples. The gift for the therapist in the practice of IFS couple therapy lies in discovering that she is in the same process as her clients with the same rich, exciting inner life.

As the IFS therapist learns to work with her system in the same way as her clients she gains the ability to access Self-energy and regulate her feelings when triggered by the parts of the couple. And, although the locus of healing in IFS is not dependent on the therapist's insight, being insightful, wise and able to speak for one's own parts can create safety and trust in the consultation room.

LEARNING TO COMMUNICATE WELL

Internal differentiation, one of the first goals of IFS couple therapy, begins with attention to parts and their relationship with the Self. However, clinicians should note that learning to unblend from parts and maintain emotional self-regulation can feel disempowering for clients for a number of reasons. First, it often takes couples years to seek treatment once they have identified the need for help, so their patterns are entrenched and protectors can feel that maintaining the status quo is a matter of survival. Second, their protectors are experiencing intense feelings and impulses. And, third, although exploding perpetuates vicious patterns, allowing a reactive part to take over in front of the therapist can be a relief, like taking the top off a pressure cooker. And when one partner is threatening, asking the other (who may already feel critical toward him or herself) to extend compassion is nearly impossible. Even if one partner can do it with my help in my office, the couple will often reengage and reinjure each other on the way to the car. From an IFS perspective we view this type of external reactivity as stemming from internal reactivity, from conflict between parts in a state of disconnection from Self. It takes courage— and encouragement—for couples to agree to try out this perspective and slow down their process.

Alison and Steve had a 3-year-old and 5-year-old twins. The stress of having three young children was enormous and both were angry. More often than not they communicated through protectors who blamed, shamed and countershamed using phrases such as *you always . . . you never . . . if only you would stop . . . if only you would be different. . . .* Highly reactive couples such as this are usually concerned when I ask them to look for answers within because it sounds as if I am asking them to remain isolated with their emotional pain.

"I have to have more help. I'm in this relationship alone, doing all the work! What am I supposed to do?" Alison asked.

"Of course," I replied, "getting your needs met and feeling that your partner is there for you is key." Because helping couples separate from their parts and feel Self-energy is crucial, I repeatedly direct them back to noticing their own experience, as I did now with Alison. "Asking to have your needs met is no problem, but how you ask may be," I went on. "Are you speaking for a part or from a part when you make requests? And if you're speaking from a part, is it working?"

Alison said, "Maybe I'm not doing a very good job of it but I don't think Steve is capable of meeting my needs anyway."

"Alison," I replied, "do you notice what's happening in your body as you speak now?"

"I'm shut down, just shut down!" she exclaimed angrily. "I don't know, maybe I should leave. Just leave!" She glared at her husband.

A couple will accept a therapist as a competent guide once they experience her presence as empathic and nonjudgmental during their most difficult interactions. I became aware of a part of me who was reacting to her as I had to my own mother when I was a child. This part wanted Alison to calm down and see things from Steve's perspective just as I had longed for my mother to do when she was arguing with my father. As the IFS therapist helps clients shift toward inner awareness, she also continually asks her own parts to step aside or soften to allow ongoing access to Self-energy. I recognized my countertransference and gently asked my own young part to move out of the crossfire so I could remain present with Alison's distress.

"Alison," I said, "please look at me for a moment. I believe that you have something important to say to Steve. And I feel pretty sure if the part of you who is so angry continues to speak to him in this way, his protective parts will have no choice but to take care of him and chances are he won't be able to respond in the way you wish he would."

"I know," she began to cry. "I'm so angry! So angry!"

"Your need for help, for connection, and your wish for a partner are all healthy impulses," I said. Alison continued to cry. "What's happening?" I asked.

"I wish I wasn't so screwed up. I'm always the problem."

"You have a part who feels she's always the problem?" I asked.

"Yes, I'm always the emotional one and Steve has me in a box that he won't let me out of."

"I hear you. I hear this part feels like a problem. I would like to know more about that."

Alison closed her eyes. "I feel so much shame."

"Can you stay with that feeling?" I asked. Alison nodded. "Would you be willing to explore the part who feels ashamed?"

"Yes," she said.

"Good. Alison, I want you to be heard and I want Steve to be able to listen to you. And I want to help you know that you can take yourself out of that box. Will you give me some time to help you do this differently?"

"I really want things to be different."

At this moment, I turned to Steve. "I would like to stay with Alison for a little while right now and help her understand what's happening inside. How would it feel if together you and I remained a little bit curious with her?"

"That's fine," he responded.

"If it gets tough to listen or you are uncomfortable, it would be great if you let me know," I said.

"I appreciate that," he replied. "I'll flag you down if this gets too hard."

Before helping Alison communicate differently with Steve, I invited her to understand the source of her anger and alleviate some of her shame response by unburdening an exile who felt worthless. After she understood the relationship between her angry protector and this shamed exile, I began the process of inviting the couple to learn a method of communication that we call *speaking for parts and listening from Self*.

You have probably had the opportunity in your life to notice how difficult it is to communicate clearly when a part of you is enraged or terrified. In IFS we teach couples to help their parts differentiate enough so that the couple can speak *for* their parts and from Self, instead of *from* their parts in a state of intense reactivity. In other words, we help them to speak on behalf of their extreme feelings. But this process, called *unblending*, requires the cooperation of parts. Getting their cooperation requires the therapist to be patient and to cultivate the courage of protective parts: courage to believe that good things will happen when the protector allows the Self to be a resource during difficult communications and courage to relax and wait while listening to a partner during conflict. All this grows experientially, step by step.

With Alison and Steve, I began by making a contract to be their *parts detector*. In service of maintaining safety, I said, "I will not allow you to harm each other and I am asking for an agreement from you both that will permit me to intervene should protectors begin to take over."

Allowing a protector to take over (or, in IFS terms, *blend*) and then attack can feel good, relieving and powerful in the short run. But when protectors repeat this type of behavior expecting to produce change in the other person, they inevitably get back exactly what they hope to avoid. I wanted Steve to experience listening without having to defend. I turned to him, "Are you available to listen while Alison speaks on behalf of what is going on inside of her right now?"

"I'll try," Steve said.

"In my experience listening can be difficult," I said. "Will you check to see if you have parts who might interfere with you listening to Alison?"

Once Steve was able to acknowledge and unblend from parts who might have had trouble listening, I turned to Alison with a similar invitation. "Before you begin speaking to Steve, let me ask you to check inside just as I asked Steve. Can you ask your parts to trust you to speak on their behalf?"

"I can do that," she said. "I have more space inside." At this, Steve reached out and touched Alison's shoulder and they looked each other in the eye. Alison said to him, "I can speak about what's going on in me without attacking you."

When a couple achieves this point of differentiation from protectors and there are moments of Self-led interaction, the therapist can enjoy a moment of quiet, holding Self-energy for the couple who are now guiding their own conversation. It may only last for minutes or seconds but as they achieve untroubled moments they begin to appreciate once again their bond and their friendship. Neuroscience now confirms that repeating newly generated responses changes neuronal pathways in the brain along with old patterns of thinking and behaving (Lind-Kyle, 2009). When we are able to listen with all our senses, hear accurately what is being said, stay in the present and respond with empathy, we are successful in what Siegel (2003) called a contingent, attuned communication, which is self-reinforcing. These moments of heartfelt connection in session are essential to regulating chronic viciousness.

Helping couples learn to communicate well may take a long time and unburdening exiles of their extreme beliefs is key to success. In my experience, effective communication in which partners speak for parts and listen from Self takes the fear out of discussing difficult issues. Also in my experience, protectors balk at practicing communication skills because close, mindful attention to intention and speech takes them out of the driver's seat. Nevertheless, I explain to the couple that if they are willing to practice this as any other skill, their protectors will gain trust and their conversations will become easier. When I work with a couple, I encourage this style of communication, particularly in my office, until controlled practice becomes skilled interaction that is natural and intuitive.

Steve and Alison both noticed that when she *unblended* from her frustrated part and found the need hidden deep below it, Steve's protectors dropped their defenses and he became more available. However, when Alison's protectors took over, yelling and cursing, his autonomic nervous system shifted into fight or flight, a state of hyperarousal in which his heartbeat sped up, his muscles contracted and, though he had not actually done it, he felt the urge to get up and run. With his protectors yelling at him to get away from her, Steve needed help to stay present and listen. In sessions when Steve was asked to listen to Alison *speak for* her frustrated parts, I invited him to stay present to the sensations in his body so that he could understand his inner responses. And I worked with him on accessing Self-energy to soothe his system as he listened. Little by little Alison and Steve started to use the IFS way of communicating, speaking for parts and listening from Self, without coaching. Doing this fundamentally changed their ability to have important and necessary conversations, a key goal of IFS couple therapy. Their successes in my office began to translate to interactions at home. The impulse to withdraw slowly shifted toward an impulse to reach out and stay present.

"I can listen to Alison without interrupting," Steve reported. "My need to defend myself all the time has really shifted. And I'm learning to think about my responses to her without qualifying my answers with a story."

Alison added, "I can listen without interrupting, too. And I don't lead with my angry parts. The thing I like best is asking for my needs to be met clearly and honestly."

This case exemplifies how difficult it can be for couples with impulsive protectors to communicate artfully. Once these parts learn to trust the Self of each individual, they can speak and listen without tumbling into childhood memories that evoke vicious protective responses. Over time, the couple accesses a critical mass of Self-energy so they can trust themselves and each other without having to withdraw or attack.

INTERRUPTING SHAME AND BLAME

"She's so critical of me," John said about his partner, Sharon, with palpable disdain.

"Here it is," I thought, "a classic case of spinning pinwheels." *Spinning pinwheels* is a phrase Schwartz (2008) coined to describe how internal interactions between unacknowledged parts get projected into the relational dynamic of a couple. At the beginning of this therapy my client was able to identify his partner's critical part but not his own.

"What happens inside when you experience her criticism?" I asked to elicit his curiosity.

"I feel hostile," he said, "wouldn't you?"

"Let's stay with the part of you who feels hostile," I said.

"How?" he asked.

"Where do you experience the hostile feelings physically?" I asked.

"In my arms and hands."

"Without wishing it away, would you ask the part in your arms and hands to give you space by separating from you just a little bit?" John nodded. "As you focus on it," I continued, "how do you feel toward it?"

"I'm all right with it. It feels like armor."

"Does that make sense to you?"

"Yes it does. It feels like it has to defend itself . . . to defend me!"

And so I began the journey of helping John turn inward, encouraging him to notice his own experience. John discovered that his angry part was protecting a younger part who had suffered day in and day out at the hands of a critical father. This young boy felt he was a failure in his father's eyes. My goal was to help John understand that his internal critic maintained a vigilant internal watch on this boy to keep him from making mistakes and feeling like a failure in John's current life. His wife's dissatisfactions evoked self-criticism and initiated a miserable internal cycle of blame and shame. Each time we experience shame we go back in time to related experiences and to all the ways in which we attempted to soothe ourselves to feel better. As Nathanson (1992) wrote, human beings will avoid feelings of humiliation at all costs and in a number of ways. John's immediate impulse when he felt criticized was to withdraw, attack himself and then attack his wife. That is, in the blink of an eye his inner critic turned on the young boy inside and then, protecting that injured boy, a rageful part turned on his partner.

"In the hope of what?" I asked.

"I make her feel how she makes me feel."

"And then what?" I asked.

"She stops criticizing me," he said.

"And then what," I asked again gently.

"We aren't fighting anymore," he said. "And I don't have to keep feeling like an asshole who can never get anything right!"

In couple therapy we often see partners whose protectors have become polarized due to shame and humiliation. According to many protectors, the solution to feeling shame is to blame. However the true antidote to shame is self-compassion, which has the additional benefit of helping people take responsibility for their own behaviors and actions (Neff, 2011; Sweezy, this volume). The IFS therapist guides clients to call shamed parts out of the dark and into connection with compassionate inner witnessing while at the same time helping the shaming parts to feel understood so they can retire. This method is an internal correction to the isolation and loneliness that accompany shame (Bradshaw, 1988; Neff, 2011).

We can view the behavior of protective parts like John's as their best guess about how to gain control and be safe, and we know that this guess occurs too quickly for conscious awareness. Neuroscience tells us that it takes much longer for the cortex to process an emotionally dangerous situation than it does for the amygdala, the core circuitry for fear and attachment, to shift into gear. Therefore although "we are under the illusion that we are making conscious, adult decisions based on present day circumstances . . . by the time we are consciously aware of an experience, it's been processed and re-processed in the brain's primitive regions, activating old memory" (Cozolino, 2008, p. 24).

In other words, though we tend to believe we are operating rationally in the present, current emotional responses are actually governed by past experience. Couples in IFS learn that feelings, though valid, are not necessarily accurate barometers of a present interaction, much less of another person's intention. In John's case, childhood experiences of being shamed had motivated protectors to hide his desire for connection. With the hope of getting John's tender needs met, his angry protector demanded that his wife be kind and gentle—and their relationship suffered accordingly. As John developed a relationship with his critic, he came to understand this protective intent. In turn, the critic calmed down and John was able to move closer to the parts who had been chronically shamed by his father. Externally, this shift in John helped Sharon to relax and be curious about her own responses. They both reported feeling more spacious inside and their conversations shifted from bullying and defensiveness to, *let me see if I can really hear what you are saying*, a practice that allowed them to give and receive feedback about their own feelings without wounding each other over and over again.

As we saw with John, exiled parts—the objects of all this protection— are the ones who have taken direct hits in traumatic situations, often early in childhood with caretakers and attachment figures. Children imbibe felt meaning from these events and then go on telling themselves stories about themselves based on that meaning. I call these beliefs *relational burdens.* A relational burden of shame goes something like this, *I am unlovable, I am not good enough, I am bad,* or *I am worthless.* As long as shame rekindles internally and our protectors lead our relationships, love cannot counteract this early injury.

Once John and Sharon began experimenting with saying *yes* and *no* to requests from each other with more clarity, they found courage to speak truths with care and respect and to hear feedback without rigid protection. For example, they reported to me that after a miscommunication in between sessions Sharon caught herself speaking from a critical part. She asked John if he would let her begin again, which he did. While expressing her frustration, she made her request by speaking from Self. John reported, "I felt that young boy inside but it was a blip instead of a nuclear blast. I appreciated Sharon catching herself, so instead of melting down I listened. And it wasn't such a big deal."

Our goal in IFS couple therapy is for individuals to develop the loving and attuned relationships with their own inner children that they have always longed for. As this begins to integrate internally, it becomes easier and easier to interrupt the impulse of a protector and respond differently regardless of what a partner is doing or saying.

THE RISK OF CHANGE

All therapists know clients who hold fast to the comfort of the familiar. Any risk of being different or attempting the unknown can evoke fears of failure, disconnection and rejection. I believe it is important to offer couples hope that change is possible while respecting fear about the risks of letting go. John spoke again, "We've experienced some shifts in our relating but change is a bit risky."

"I'd like to hear more about that," I said.

"Don't know much more," he said, "and I'm not even sure how to know the specifics. I just know it seems scary and risky."

"Is there a part of you who worries about what might happen, John, if you take risks to understand yourself and then you change the way you relate to your wife?" I asked.

"What if she doesn't like the change after all?" he said.

When a therapist asks clients to take a relational risk by doing something different or invites him to ponder the possibility that something wonderful could happen from witnessing the past, resistance from his protectors is predictable and makes sense. For both partners, I suggest small, manageable changes at home and we also do experiments in the office. For example, I may ask a partner to change a behavior and doing it from Self rather than an angry protector or following an impulse to make a move in the other's direction literally or metaphorically. I invite couples to try on new behaviors designed to help them engage in right-brain-to-right-brain interactions, such as sharing vulnerability, maintaining eye contact for mere seconds or staying connected in a virtuous cycle of appreciation followed by loving touch. These experiences rewire patterns of security (Badenoch, 2008; Siegel, 2007) and will eventually lead to more permanent changes in thinking and behaving.

YOU ARE NOT IN THIS ALONE: GETTING NEEDS MET

"I don't want to be responsible for taking care of Karen's needy demands," Joan exclaimed.

When Joan's partner, Karen, approached her with vulnerability, Joan had parts who felt responsible to take care of all Karen's needs. This belief evoked terror and anger in other parts. Because of this internal polarity, Joan withdrew from Karen's bid for connection and was not open to Karen's young parts. Joan's protectors were unable to discern the difference between *care taking* and *being caring*. The former is laden with responsibility while the latter is a natural state of Self-leadership.

"What if," I asked Joan, "your current response to feeling burdened with responsibility was not your only option? Or what if you didn't even have to feel burdened?"

"Interesting but not possible," Joan replied.

Karen, in turn said, "If I can't get my needs met, why am I in this relationship to begin with?"

Karen also had an internal polarity. Hers was between protectors who were in the habit of pursuing external security, pleading and demanding on behalf of exiles who longed to be taken care of exclusively by Joan, and protectors who became critical, demanding and shaming of Joan when she did not meet these needs.

This dynamic speaks to an issue that arises in most relationships: Who takes care of whom? Whose needs take precedence? Schwartz (2008), articulating the pivotal goals of IFS couple therapy, wrote that each person in the couple will retrieve projections, cease blaming, practice self-compassion and generally become the primary caretaker for their own young parts. This U-turn (Schwartz, 2008) brings Self-energy to exiles and allows a partner to achieve success as a secondary source of love and support.

Because vulnerable young parts can flood the internal system with terrifying emotion, IFS couple therapy, just as individual therapy, must attend to the extreme beliefs of exiles. As exiles surface, some couples need individual sessions. However, many can create enough safety to do a U-turn and attend to exiles in the presence of a partner. Because we all have exiles, IFS teaches therapists—and we invite couples—to embrace the U-turn. The goal of a U-turn is not to stay focused inward but to re-turn to the other, empowered by Self-energy. Partners learn to receive the care that is offered while remaining present to themselves and being their own source of constancy when that love is not available. And when partners are no longer called on to meet all needs, they are free to notice the true profound significance of their love and support. These points are well illustrated in the case below.

After acknowledging that Joan and Karen believed their dynamic could never improve, I said, "How might you respond to each other if you were not so angry or terrified?"

"How?" Joan asked.

"The part of you who's terrified of Karen's needs must have a story to tell. Could you be curious enough to listen to what it has to tell you?"

"I guess so," Joan said.

"Think of a time recently when Karen asked you for something and you couldn't help but react negatively," I said.

"That's easy," Joan said.

"Can you feel what happens in your body?" I asked.

"I sure can. It feels like an incredible impulse to push her away."

"Focus on that impulse. How do you feel toward the part who wants to push away?"

"I'm so used to it, so tired of it! It happens so fast, I feel like I don't have control over it."

"Let's ask the part who feels tired of it to back away so you can stay present and focus on it."

"It's like it wants to get me away, out of the room."

"Away from what?" I asked.

After a moment or two of silence Joan responded, "The burden of having to be a parent way too soon, while I was still a child."

As Joan listened to her panicked and repulsed parts, they took her back to early experiences of being used by, and responsible for, her alcoholic mother. Joan's past was dictating her response to Karen in the present. Parts who are activated in the storehouse of past experience have no notion of present time. But even as Joan explored her traumatic childhood experience, I knew I could not for one minute minimize Karen's inquiry about getting her needs met. Why be in a relationship where your emotional needs are never met? "Human beings are hardwired for connection and naturally long for love and security," I said to Karen. "There is nothing wrong with asking to have needs met. And in this work I will encourage you to notice where the request comes from."

This couple's dynamic illustrates how protective parts can get stuck in the belief that bullying, manipulating and pleading will force others to meet the needs of their exiles. When protectors encounter resistance to these tactics they become more extreme, not more thoughtful. The result is a spiral of less understanding, less listening and ever more devastating feelings of disconnection. But when we pay attention to these frustrated protectors and then reach the exiles they protect, we are inevitably taken back in time to witness traumatic relational ruptures. During the witnessing and unburdening phase of IFS, the couple learns about the unmet needs of exiled parts. The frustrations of the present: *clean up after yourself, pay attention to me right now, pay the bills*, actually represent core needs like, *I need to know I'm not alone and I can count on you.*

As Joan and Karen experienced more space inside, they slowly dropped their pattern of pursuit and attack. The quality of their conversation shifted from defensive bullying and punishment to: *let me see if I can really hear what you are saying.* As they listened they recognized that their polarized parts were voicing different concerns but were trying to get the same underlying needs met. This helped them to stop blaming and shaming, which, in turn, opened the door to making requests instead of demands. With a different understanding about the nature of their needs, couples communicate from Self on behalf of exiles rather than from a demanding manager or firefighter.

With eye contact and a calm tone, Joan said, "Karen, you know my history with my mother. Sometimes I feel overwhelmed. There's a part of me that feels like I have no choice but to take care of you. No permission to say no, just like when I was a kid. This part feels trapped and out of control."

Karen replied, "I want you to know it is OK with me if you say no. I would rather have you say no like this than shut me out with no explanation. I may not like it when you say no, but it's much easier for me to deal with a straightforward no."

Joan began to cultivate the ability to say *no* to Karen, realizing that when Karen felt disappointed it was neither the end of the world nor the end of their relationship. She also became aware of her own shame and fear about asking to have her needs met. *No needs here!* was the refrain of her protective parts until she developed a relationship with her exiles. And although I validated Karen's longing for emotional connection, she learned more effective ways of asking for attention from Joan. She also learned to trust that she could care for herself in the moments when Joan was unavailable, a huge triumph for this couple.

CONCLUSIONS

All couples enter adult relationships with burdens from childhood. Relational rupture taps into these burdens, resulting in dysregulated interactions. Some interactions are by protectors who shame and blame internally and externally. These are met with similar protectors in the partner, which causes an escalation of painful cycles of reaction and counterreaction between protective parts. These cycles, circular and repetitive, preclude authenticity, intimacy and forgiveness.

The IFS couple therapy described in this chapter encourages individuals to make a U-turn to be curious internally. Even though the external is the therapist's initial point of contact with a couple, we invite clients to attend first to the internal attachment work with their exiles and protectors, which paves the road for external relational work. When the IFS therapist meets with a couple for the first time, she begins by inviting them into this paradigm shift, asking them to experiment with getting to know how their protective parts try, without success, to get their emotional needs met. We invite partners to explore their difficult interactions and invite them to imagine what it might feel like to have a less reactive response to their partners, to stay connected even during moments of conflict.

This is an experiential therapy that moves between fostering internal attachments and doing relational work between partners. As we help couples understand the nature of protectors and how to move from a wounded position to Self-leadership so they can unburden extreme beliefs and toxic shame, communication becomes less complicated and negotiating emotional needs for safety and connection less painful. Couples discover that a true and lasting source of transformative love inside gives them more than enough love for themselves and each other.

REFERENCES

Badenoch, B. (2008). *Being a brain-wise therapist, a practical guide to interpersonal neurobiology*. New York, NY: Norton.

Bradshaw, J. (1988). *Healing the shame that binds you*. Deerfield, FL: Health Communications.

Cozolino, L. J. (2008, September/October). It's a jungle in there. *Psychotherapy Networker*, 20–27.

Lind-Kyle, P. (2009). *Heal your mind, rewire your brain*. Santa Rosa, CA: Energy Psychology Press.

Nathanson, D. L. (1992). *Shame and pride*. New York, NY: Norton.

Neff, K. D. (2011). Self-compassion, self-esteem, and well-being. *Social and Personality Psychology Compass, 5*, 1–12.

Schwartz, R.C. (2008). *You are the one you've been waiting for: Bringing courageous love to intimate relationships*. Oak Park, IL: Trailhead.

Siegel, D.J. (2003). *Parenting from the inside out: How a deeper understanding can help you raise children who thrive*. New York, NY: Putnam.

Siegel, D.J. (2007). *The mindful brain: Reflection and attunement in the cultivation of well-being*. New York, NY: Norton.

INTEGRATING IFS WITH PHASE-ORIENTED TREATMENT OF CLIENTS WITH DISSOCIATIVE DISORDER

Joanne H. Twombly

INTRODUCTION

Phase-oriented treatment (International Society for the Study of Trauma and Dissociation, [ISSTD], 2011) is standard practice to protect clients with complex posttraumatic stress disorder (PTSD) and dissociative disorders (DDs), including dissociative identity disorder (DID) and dissociative disorder not otherwise specified (DDNOS; see *Diagnostic and Statistical Manual of Mental Disorders*, 4th ed., text rev.; *DSM–IV–TR*; American Psychiatric Association, 2000) from becoming overwhelmed and decompensating or activating protective parts who block and/or minimize progress. This chapter introduces a model for raising and maintaining the client's level of functioning with the tools of phase-oriented treatment in combination with the customary steps of internal family systems (IFS) treatment.

From the perspective of IFS, people with complex PTSD and DDs have exiles who carry burdens of extreme emotion and beliefs, as well as firefighters and managers who are either rigidly controlling or easily overwhelmed. This complicates the inner family of a client with DD in a number of ways. Parts tend to be more dissociated and may seem to have no connection with each other; parts are often phobic of each other and do not want anyone, including the therapist, to know about them and treatment is further complicated by the possibility of the inner family having layers of dissociated parts who reveal themselves only as progress is being made. As a result, the client who begins to function on a higher level can suddenly go into crisis. Although this may truly be a crisis, it may also indicate that progress has resulted in a "new" layer of formerly dissociated parts surfacing who may not know the client, the therapist or much about the present. Or, if they do have awareness of the present, may experience it through the eyes of an abused child.

Because the parts of clients with DD carry extreme burdens and often have difficulty accessing Self-energy, they can easily become destabilized. The first phase of treatment stabilizes and compensates for this by fostering communication and cooperation among parts and introducing coping skills. The second phase focuses on processing traumatic memories, and makes use of the coping skills to pace the process of unburdening by providing the client with more control and protection from potential destabilization. During the second phase, if the client becomes destabilized during or in between sessions, the focus of treatment returns to the first phase until the client is stable enough to continue. The third phase of treatment, in which the client adjusts to a life that is no longer controlled by trauma and neglect, is beyond the scope of this chapter and will be described only briefly.

Like phase-oriented treatment, IFS is organized in steps. The first step involves negotiating with protector parts and gaining access to Self-energy; the second involves witnessing the experiences of an exiled part; the third involves retrieving that exiled part from the past and unburdening its harmful beliefs and extreme feelings; the fourth involves inviting positive qualities to replace burdens and checking back with protectors for questions or concerns. The case of Mary illustrates the integration of a phase-oriented approach with these steps in IFS.

MARY: INITIAL CASE INFORMATION

Mary was a 36-year-old woman, twice divorced, who had three children. Her first husband was an alcoholic who physically abused her; her second husband had a gambling problem. Mary had previously worked as a teacher's assistant but had gone on disability due to "emotional problems." Although Mary could speak knowledgably about parenting, she was unable to say no to her children, who had as a result developed many behavioral problems. The children complained that Mary often contradicted herself and Mary, in turn, complained that they were always trying to get away with things and made her feel crazy.

Mary reported that her father's rage had terrified her during childhood, while her mother had been "a saint" who suffered chronic pain from severe arthritis. She grew up taking care of her mother and younger siblings, and when she was 13-years-old, her father died of alcoholism. As an adult, Mary continued providing most of her mother's care, often putting her mother's needs before the needs of herself or her family.

DIAGNOSIS

When clinicians keep in mind the indications of dissociative disorders during sessions, making a diagnosis can be quite straightforward. These indications include: clients having a history of child abuse, a history of failed prior treatments, three plus diagnoses, amnesia for periods of time during childhood and/or adulthood, somatic symptoms such as headaches, parts who seem to have a separate existence, and uneven functioning (Kluft, 1999). Research also has shown that early neglect, abandonment and/or parents with attachment disorders may be the foundation of DDs and borderline personality disorder (Lyons-Ruth, 2003). Once a diagnosis of DD is suspected, clinicians may want to clarify the diagnosis through easy-to-administer diagnostic interviews such as the Dissociative Experience Scale (Bernstein & Putnam, 1986; or see the ISSTD website, which offers other diagnostic tests and instruments). After clarifying the diagnosis, steps can be taken to integrate phase-oriented treatment with IFS. Teaching the diagnosed client's internal family how to cope and pace unburdenings can prevent complications in treatment and facilitate healing.

MARY: SIGNS OF DISSOCIATION

Although Mary had worked hard in therapy after being diagnosed with attention deficit hyperactivity disorder (ADHD), panic disorder and depression in addition to being treated for migraines and self-cutting, her two previous therapists reported that she never made a lot of progress. This, along with years on disability following a history of work, the report of her children that she contradicted herself frequently, and the indications of child abuse (father's drinking and rage) and neglect (a mother disabled with chronic pain, the role of caretaker for her siblings as well as her mother) all indicated the possibility that Mary had a DD.

Taking note of this cluster of suggestive signs, I began to ask more specific questions about dissociative symptoms, including how much she remembered from childhood. Mary reported that she would hide in her closet and "forget everything" when her father yelled and threw things. She said, "I got so good at forgetting that I once woke up at school not knowing how I got there." I normalized this as something children do to protect themselves when they have no other options, and said that many people continue to forget chunks of time even after childhood. Relieved, Mary went on to report "spacing out" for hours and not remembering what happened when her first husband abused her. She said she still occasionally lost time when the kids were fighting and she felt stressed. She had been afraid this meant she was crazy.

TELLING THE CLIENT—INTRODUCING THE LANGUAGE OF IFS

Clients without dissociative disorders often find the language of parts and Self "quite relieving and empowering" (Schwartz, 1995, p. 90). For clients with DD, it can sometimes be different. If "not knowing" about parts has protected a client from unmanageable experiences and feelings, or made attachment to extremely dysfunctional parents possible, or helped keep secrets necessary for survival, a therapist who suddenly knows about parts may be viewed as dangerous. As one of my clients said, "It terrifies me when you talk about parts. You're not supposed to know about them." These clients need psychoeducation and time to feel safe enough before they can acknowledge the existence of parts.

BEGINNING TREATMENT WITH MARY

Mary exhibited all the signs of having a DD, specifically DID, a DD characterized by more than one part taking over executive functioning and exhibiting areas of amnesia (see *DSM–IV–TR*). Because of this, I approached the subject of parts cautiously, saying, "Some people have a sense of a little kid part or several parts who carry anxiety and sadness from the past. How about you?"

Mary promptly replied, "Can I get rid of her? If I could get rid of her, my life would be so much better!"

I said, "We all have parts and all parts are there to be helpful in one way or another. There's the part of me who's hard working, the part who likes to relax, and the part who plays with the neighbors' kids. If you had an uncomplicated childhood or you have worked through the difficulties of your childhood, there's a flow of communication among your parts and you switch without effort from one to the other depending on what's needed. But when you've had a difficult childhood the walls among parts can become like concrete and you can get stuck in one part or another. For instance, it sounds like one part of you knows quite well about setting limits with your kids but another actually stops you from saying 'No.'"

Mary nodded. "That's exactly what happens. It's like there's a battle going on in my head."

I replied, "As we get to know your parts, we'll understand how they're trying to help. Then we can help them learn to negotiate and work together. That's how change is possible."

THE STEPS OF IFS IN PHASE 1

The IFS concept of Self as a universal, internal presence that is undamaged and compassionate (Schwartz, 1995) is beneficial in the treatment of clients with DD in the long run. Nevertheless, much early work with complex DDs may have to be done through direct access, Self-like parts or what non-IFS clinicians call the "host" or "adult." For clients with parts who carry the burden of worthlessness and whose protectors fear hope because it is linked to the threat of yet more disappointment, the inherent optimism in the concept of Self may feel too threatening at first. Standard practice in the non-IFS, ego state treatment of DDs has long relied on fostering curiosity and compassion within and among parts, and this is a good alternate route to reach the goal of unblending and accessing Self-energy. Along the way, it is important to notice and make use of even small bits of Self-energy. For example, one of my clients could not stop hating all of the parts who were responsible for her seemingly endless array of difficult symptoms. However, she could take a first step, which involved telling them that even though she wanted to get rid of them, she understood that to heal she had to get to know them instead.

The Phase 1 goals are for parts to learn about and feel compassion for each other rather than to process trauma, and for them to become proficient with coping skills. Because parts in the internal systems of clients with DD generally do not listen unless they are addressed directly, it is important to ask all parts to listen when teaching skills. I start by teaching two coping skills, *safe space imagery* (SSI) and *containers*. Both are imagery exercises that help evolve the client's dissociative defenses into coping skills. In addition, I teach the client to retrieve parts from the past and orient them to the present. Until clients have adequate coping skills, I give them permission to continue dissociating traumatic material.

Initially, Mary thought that our treatment, as others before, would focus on "getting the trauma out" by recounting her childhood. I explained that instead we would work first on coping skills to regulate her symptoms and we started with SSI. This exercise teaches clients to block out negative affect and traumatic intrusions, bringing the body to a state of relaxation and calm. For many clients with DD, having all parts develop safe spaces is key to stabilization (Kluft, 1988; Twombly, 2001). I instruct clients to practice SSI every day because, in my experience, this fosters overall calm, helps with daily life management, and eventually becomes a very useful resource during trauma processing.

A SAFE SPACE FOR MARY'S LITTLE GIRL PART

To assure that this exercise would benefit as many parts as possible, I said to Mary, "I'd like everyone who wants a safe space to watch and learn how to do SSI. Then everyone can help each other to do it. What kind of place or space do you and the little girl want to start with? Pick one that is in the present where no one has ever been hurt." The little girl decided she wanted to be inside a mountain.

I continued, "Mary, let the little girl know she can settle there in the mountain, and look around with all her senses and notice everything about it that makes it safe." Because repetition helps to strengthen SSI, after the little girl described her safe space, I repeated her words, "No one else is there and you're surrounded by rock walls that no one can get through. Now notice more and more about how safe it is to be there."

The little girl noticed more about what made the safe space feel safe, but suddenly noticing there was no door, felt trapped. This was a traumatic intrusion. I said, "Tell the little girl to just keep looking around with all her senses and she'll notice something that will help." After a few seconds, I asked: "What is she noticing?"

Mary said, "The little girl sees there's a secret passage out that only she can use."

I asked, "Ask the little girl to focus on the secret passage and notice what happens."

"She notices a sweet smell of flowers," Mary reported. "She realizes there is a secret passage out that only she can use so she feels better."

To provide ego strengthening, I said, "Tell the little girl she's doing great! She's just started learning and she's already figured out how to make her safe space feel safer."

"She's smiling," Mary reported.

We continued this process until the little girl had a full body sense of being safe and relaxed. Then, through Mary, I asked if I could talk to other parts while the little girl relaxed in her safe space for 5 minutes. When she agreed, Mary said she was amazed at how much calmer she felt with the little girl in her safe space. I said, "This was a great start and we will continue to work with all parts who want a safe space, either alone or in the company of other parts."

After the 5 minutes in which I spoke with other parts, I had Mary check in again with the little girl. She was feeling so relaxed and protected that she decided to stay put. I asked Mary to check in with her during the week and suggested that Mary remind her that she could stay in her safe space when Mary was parenting her children. As Mary got to know the little girl through the process of developing her safe space, she understood her better and began to feel Self-energy in relation to her.

Finally, we checked for concerns from other parts.

One alarmed part said, "If the little girl is relaxing, then something bad will happen."

I said to Mary, "Invite this part to look at you. Then let her know how old you are. Tell her about the strengths and resources you have now that you didn't have as a little girl."

The alarmed part replied, "I don't believe you—but the little girl can stay in her safe space for now."

I said to Mary, "Let her know it makes sense she doesn't believe you, and it's OK, she can keep watching you, and checking out the way life is now. She can also ask you and me any questions she has."

Other parts were able to notice the little girl was relaxing, and as is often true, it felt quieter inside.

CONTAINERS

The ability of clients with DD to dissociate can be converted to good use in a coping skill called *imaginary containers* (Kluft, 1988). Containers help the client get control of intensely uncomfortable symptoms and traumatic material. All containers include a commitment to work on everything stored inside when the time is right. For clients with protectors who are already using dissociation to manage strong feelings and block out memory, it is empowering to convert this symptom into a coping skill both for managing daily life and for facilitating the Phase 2 process of unburdening. Some clients will need to create a network of customized containers for their parts; others will prefer to use just one big container.

CONTAINER IMAGERY FOR MARY

I said to Mary, "Let's take your symptom of losing time and make it into a container in which you can purposely store painful feelings and experiences until it is time to work on them."

As the first little girl part continued to rest in her safe space, we identified another little girl part who was burdened with extreme depression and had been around for a long time. At first Mary couldn't get near this second little girl part because a manager, concerned about Mary becoming flooded with depression, blocked her access.

"Ask the little girl to hold on to her depression so you won't be overwhelmed by it," I said. "Now let the blocking part know that our goal is to help this girl manage the depression in a different and easier way. If we can, then the blocking part won't need to use so much energy on the depression. See if it's willing to help us by allowing you a five to ten percent connection with the depressed little girl. And if you do start feeling overwhelmed, this blocking part can always reblock the connection."

By recognizing, respecting and suggesting an upgrade to its skill, Mary made a good connection with the blocking part. As a result, it allowed Mary 10 percent access to the depressed part, enough connection to help the little girl part begin developing a container.

I said, "Ask the little girl what kind of container she wants."

Because the girl did not know, I suggested something like a bank vault or a box, and she decided on a toy box with a big lock.

"But now she's scared and doesn't want to do it!" Mary reported. "She's afraid she'll disappear if all the depression is put away."

I explained, "Tell her that babies aren't born depressed. Depression comes because of what happens after they're born. How about if she starts by putting just five or ten percent in the box to see what it feels like?" The little girl liked that idea so I went on, "Have her focus on the depression and notice that just the right amount of it goes in the toy box and, as soon as it's in, the box locks."

After this, Mary reported that the little girl felt relieved and lighter. "Ask her if she wants to practice being in control by putting a bit more depression in and then taking it out?" I said.

This practice helped her develop a sense of control and mastery over her depression. Once she was secure that she would not disappear and that she had choices, she decided to put 90 percent of her depression in the toy box and she then she went to join the first part who was resting in the mountain. Realizing that this second little girl had helped her throughout life by holding her depression, Mary expressed great respect for her strength.

THE PACE OF DD TREATMENT

Of note, therapy with clients with DD goes slower than standard IFS. If Mary had been a non-DD client with enough Self-energy, her depressed part could have been witnessed directly without using a container and a safe space. However, without enough Self-energy, witnessing at this stage would have resulted in Mary's parts either becoming overwhelmed and destabilized or they would have shut her down. Developing the container helped this part develop a sense of mastery and gave her some relief, and also helped Mary access Self-energy in relation to the part. Later, when we did analyze Mary's "depression" during witnessing in Phase 2, we found it to be a complicated combination of horror, hopelessness, pain, sexual arousal and shame, all resulting from daily sexual abuse by her father, which occurred while her mother lay in the bed beside them "not noticing."

Before ending any session, I check back with parts who have helped. In this session, we started by appreciating the blocking manager and asked for her comments, questions and concerns. The manager said she felt lighter and that her job seemed easier. I asked Mary, "In addition to helping you with feelings in daily life, would she be willing to help manage feelings as we work with other parts?" The manager felt pleased and respected, and became the first of a team of protectors who worked together constructively throughout Mary's treatment.

RETRIEVAL/ORIENTING

While developing coping skills, it is important to be aware that parts tend to live in different time zones or at different points in the past. In Phase 1 we orient parts to the present through *retrieval*. No matter how oriented the client with DD appears to be to the present, questioning will reveal many parts believe they are living in the past with their families of origin and continuing to be abused and neglected. Orienting them to the present can be done by providing them with concrete information about how the present differs from the past.

ORIENTING MARY'S PARTS

We began orienting Mary's parts to the present in several ways, including developing a list of facts about her current life: I am 36, it has been 15 years since I was last abused, I have lived on Main Street in Waltham, Massachusetts for 15 years, my children's names are John and Laurie, my father died 9 years ago, Joanne is my therapist who I have been working with for 3 years. This list was communicated among the parts willing to take in new information and opened her system to the possibility of change. The second and third items, *I am 36, it has been 15 years since I was last abused*, were communicated through fast forward videos that covered the interim years; this tool is effective for helping parts to relocate in the present (Twombly, 2005). For homework, Mary oriented her parts to her current reality by showing them around her house and answering all of their questions and concerns.

FURTHER POINTS ON ORIENTING/RETRIEVING

Parts of clients with DD who are stuck in the past often fear coming into the present. As one very blended client of mine used to say, "The unknown is worse than the known." To give these parts choices, along with the control they have never had, I suggest something different. "Invite them to stay in the past and look from there through your eyes around my office. Or, if they want, they can try being in my office for five minutes and then go back to the past. Or they can go back and forth whenever they want to."

One common problem is that oriented parts can reject distressed, burdened parts and try to keep them from coming into the present. In this case, distressed parts who are stuck in the past can be invited to come closer to the present by placing their safe space in a more recent time. But in either case, until all trauma work is done, parts will invariably slip back into unprocessed trauma and will need to be retrieved more than once.

If clients live with abuse currently, it is important to help their parts differentiate the present from the past. For example, the husband of one of my clients was emotionally abusive. Her exiles, in the all-or-nothing thought process of children, believed his emotional abuse was proof that they were doomed to be as helpless and abused in the present as they had been in the past. We pointed out that although he was emotionally abusive, she never had bruises because he did not beat her. We oriented them to the client's height and age as an adult, to the car she owned, the job she had, and the money she was saving to move out.

DISSOCIATIVE DISORDERS AND MEDICATION

For most clients with DD, medication should be considered. As Kluft (1988) stated, every effort should be made to minimize the pain of this very painful treatment process and medication can help. Checking with parts for concerns about taking medication helps with compliance. And I also instruct my clients to invite all parts to take the medication, which, in my experience, helps it to work (see Anderson, this volume).

USING IFS WITH COUNTERTRANSFERENCE

IFS recommends that therapists prepare for sessions by checking their own Self-energy and this is particularly important with DD clients. Many issues, for example, amnesia, dissociative defenses and preverbal abuse or neglect, will be expressed nonverbally and can be noticed first in the activation of the therapist's parts. Thus, the therapist who is aware of her own parts in session can pick up valuable information about the client's parts while managing the unavoidable dynamics of transference and countertransference (see Schwartz, this volume).

SOME DYNAMICS OF MEMORY

Ethically and clinically it is important to know how to handle requests for validation from the client. Progress can be slowed down or complicated by a therapist "validating" something that is impossible to validate unless you were present when it happened. Courtois (1999) wrote, "The therapist (must) understand that human memory is fluid rather than static and that conditions at the time of encoding, storage/consolidation, and retrieval may affect memory retention and accessibility" (p. 275).

Courtois (1999) had three recommendations: first, the therapist strives to practice from a neutral perspective regarding memory; second, the therapist understands the malleability of human memory and the differences between historical and narrative truth and third, in attending to traumatic memories the therapist maintains the goal of facilitating mastery and resolution.

MARY'S QUESTIONS FOR ME ABOUT MEMORY

When Mary asked me if I believed her story, I explained that I believed in her and that we would help her parts to feel witnessed in their experiences, and that as the parts were witnessed and their burdens lifted, Mary would figure out what was important to know about her childhood.

HOW I KNEW MARY WAS READY TO MOVE TO PHASE 2

Once a client comes to sessions reporting that she has used coping skills for symptom and affect management, the process of unburdening can begin. As Mary and her internal system practiced coping skills, understanding and problem solving, she began to present examples of progress. When a part experienced anxiety, panic or guilt, Mary and other parts were increasingly able to access enough Self-energy to be curious, ask about the part's concerns, and use various coping skills. She taught her system to orient to the present: "Our dad is dead, he can't beat us anymore, he died in 1990." She taught them cognitive strategies: "What's the evidence that you're going to be killed?" And to use their safe spaces, "Remember you can go to your safe space and let me handle the kids." When Mary got caller ID on her telephone, she used it to decide when to answer her mother's frequent calls. Initially, a part felt guilty and feared abandonment if she waited. Reminders that she could rely on the adult Mary to handle phone calls allowed her to go to her safe space. Eventually, the part had the confidence to just stay there and watch (via an imagined web cam) as Mary handled her mother's phone calls. This, in turn, reinforced the part's feeling of security. Mary reported that it became easier and easier to manage the calls and she no longer felt a surge of anxiety every time the phone rang.

Mary also made progress in parenting. Using safe spaces for the young parts who got scared when her kids yelled and having help from a manager who could block the sound of the yelling, Mary was able to set appropriate limits and notice how well the children responded. We acknowledged progress regularly and noted that some burdens, including anxiety, hopelessness and helplessness, began to grow lighter. Mary was quietly becoming proud of her accomplishments. All of this indicated that she was ready to begin Phase 2 of treatment.

TITRATING UNBURDENING IN PHASE 2

Phases of trauma treatment are not linear and destabilization can occur at any point, necessitating return to Phase 1. It might be due to external events (e.g., when Mary's mother had a minor heart attack), internal ones (as she made progress, a formerly unknown layer of parts surfaced who had no coping skills or orientation to the present), or it might be inadvertent and therapy induced (e.g., when we worked on too much traumatic material at once).

I pace work with traumatic material and unburdening so the client can maintain her highest level of functioning. Organizing the unburdening into manageable steps is key to pacing. During trauma processing, I follow the *Rule of Thirds* (Kluft & Fine, 1993). In the first third of a session, I discuss the plan for processing trauma; in the second third, I follow the plan and in the last third, I make sure the client is stable and we plan the next session.

The goal for the client in choosing an initial target is to have a successful unburdening. Fine (1991) recommended starting with "an isolated or relatively recent event of concern to the client" (p. 672). After choosing this event, I build in further protection by storing all other traumatic material in containers to reduce the possibility of flooding. In addition, Figure 5.1 offers a model for reducing the risk of destabilization by organizing the client's internal family. In this model, all parts who are not either directly involved or being witnessed are asked to go to their safe spaces and put up sound and feeling proofing (Twombly, 2005). Parts who handle daily life activities such as work and parenting also are asked to go to their safe spaces to be protected from the impact of witnessing. The witnessing itself is done with the assistance of a part (or parts) who have enough Self-energy and who were not involved with this particular event. Once the event is fully witnessed and the exiles are unburdened, information about the event will automatically become available to the adult/Self-like parts (Fine, 1991).

Once the internal family can be organized in this way, the next step is to decide—with the client's parts—which segment of the traumatic material to witness first. Witnessing a percentage of a large, complicated burden supports the client's stability and sense of control. I often start with two seconds of traumatic material and increase the time as the client's confidence grows (see Figure 5.2).

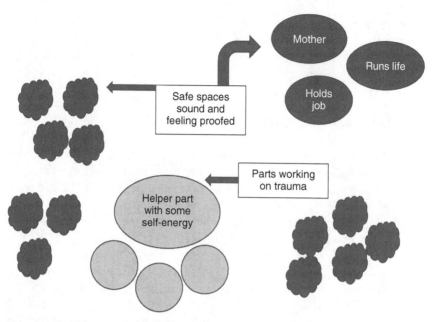

Figure 5.1 Set Up for Protected Witnessing and Unburdening Parts

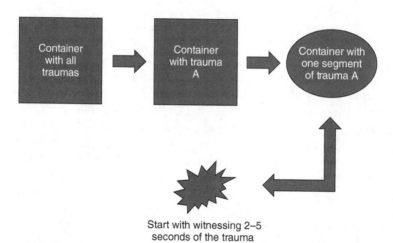

Start with witnessing 2–5
seconds of the trauma

Figure 5.2 Protected Witnessing and Unburdening using Safe Spaces and Containers

MARY'S PHASE 2: WITNESSING AND UNBURDENING BY PERCENTAGES

Mary decided to begin work in Phase 2 with the memory of a teacher yelling at her for failing a test in high school. All parts who did not hold burdens from this event took the precautions described. Checking for Self-energy, we discovered Mary was blended with a critical part who said, "Mary is to blame because she's so stupid." Once this part felt assured that she did not have to give up believing that Mary was stupid (a burden based on old messages from her father) unless she wanted to, she was willing to relax back and watch.

This left three parts who all carried burdens from the incident. We decided to place 70 percent of their burdens in a container and to ask for one volunteer to be the spokesperson for all three. Because Mary was still concerned about becoming overwhelmed, we invited the blocking manager to stand by and block out feelings either when Mary asked her to or whenever she noticed Mary feeling overwhelmed. With this arrangement, Mary felt the confidence to begin witnessing.

The parts began to tell their story. The night before flunking the test, Mary had been awakened by sounds of her father in a drunken rage beating her mother. Mary, thinking her mother might be killed, ran out of her bedroom and tried to stop him and he turned to beating her while her mother ran out of the room. The next day Mary failed the test and her teacher threatened to drop her from the honors program. When the three affected parts felt Mary understood this portion of the incident, they were ready and able to unburden it. The realization that they could attend to and unburden such an incident without feeling overwhelmed brought them relief, pride and calm.

Her parts then decided to work on the next 30 percent, the physical pain from being beaten. When we checked for concerns, we discovered that one of the three parts believed she needed to hold on to the burden of numbing in response to pain for use in future beatings. Mary oriented this part to the present and assured her that only old feelings would be unburdened so she did not have to lose the ability to be numb. Then all the parts were able to continue with witnessing and unburdening this 30 percent. The unburdening brought such great physical relief that the numbing part decided to store her burden in a container and take a rest. Mary, who felt relief and a new sense of inner strength, realized why the smell of alcohol was always triggering.

During the last third of this session, we shifted focus from unburdening to stabilization. The container with the remaining 30 percent of the incident was reinforced and the three parts who had been witnessed and felt tired went to rest in their safe spaces until the next session. Finally, we checked for concerns, comments and questions from the rest of Mary's system. During the following session, the remainder of this incident was witnessed and the parts were fully unburdened, which caused them to reconfigure spontaneously into one teenager. She declared, "This is so different! None of us are lost. Even though we're one, we're all here. And we feel strong!" As other parts were updated, Mary answered their concerns and questions, heard their comments and left the session feeling calmer and stronger.

PROGRESS AND THE EMERGENCE OF DISSOCIATED EXILES

Over the next several weeks, as Mary and her system spent sessions witnessing and unburdening several other incidents, her functioning became more stable than ever. Parenting was going well, she accomplished things she had been putting off, and she began socializing. Although Mary knew there was more traumatic material to work on, she wanted a break so we spent several sessions consolidating gains and talking about her progress. Then one day Mary came in reporting that she had experienced horrible flashbacks, which she had stopped with the old habit of banging her head against a wall. She felt devastated and feared that she had lost all progress.

I said, "Let's ask inside. Who can help us to understand why this is happening now?"

We discovered a part (referred to as Z) who had been deeply dissociated and had now surfaced, probably due to Mary's progress. Other parts had serious concerns about Mary having any connection with Z. But once the blocking and numbing parts agreed to act as safeguards, Mary was allowed to recognize Z's presence and offer her Self-energy. We retrieved her from the past, oriented her to the present and made her a safe space.

Next session, we prepared to unburden Z. Because many parts were extremely concerned that Z could destabilize Mary, we decided to leave Z in her safe space. The participating parts agreed to a plan in which the teenager would take on 5 percent of Z's burden and be witnessed by Mary. As always, all other parts went to their safe spaces, and all other traumatic material was left in the container.

As Mary began witnessing, the teenager described a scene in which Mary's mother watched passively while Mary's father molested her. Even with all the preparation, some protectors blended repeatedly, using avoidance and denial to protect Mary's attachment to her "good" parent. By checking and rechecking for Self-energy, and pointing out that the blocking and numbing parts were doing what they had promised to do, we were able to continue the witnessing.

In this session with Z, the teenager unburdened a total of 10 percent. Afterward the teenager went to rest in her safe space, and we noticed that Z was also resting more comfortably in hers. Mary commented, "I knew about Z but some part believed I would die if I connected with her. I wonder why she came up now?"

I suggested, "When you make progress, parts who've been deeply dissociated can start surfacing. Your stability seems to signal to these parts that you're now in a place where you can help."

As Mary's internal family managed these initial unburdenings, her daily life functioning continued to improve and she felt confident enough to get a job during school hours with a nonprofit organization. Many parts still needed help and crises still arose, but at this phase of treatment Mary had enough Self-energy to cope with them more effectively.

POSSIBLE CHANGES AFTER PROCESSING AND UNBURDENING TRAUMATIC MATERIAL

Clinicians and clients will notice that dissociative barriers change as traumatic material is resolved and the client's system of parts reconfigures. This might involve parts who were once very active taking a back seat as others become prominent, or it might involve groups of parts integrating into one part (like Mary's teenager).

PHASE 3: INTEGRATION AND REHABILITATION

Once parts have become unburdened, clients transition to a life that is not controlled by dissociation and burdens from the past. Groups of parts may integrate into one and the client has access to Self-leadership. Most clients with DD have at least underperformed at work and have been in dysfunctional relationships, including ineffective, counterproductive psychotherapy relationships. This transition involves grieving all that was missed and lost. Relationship patterns usually become a focus. Many clients find that couple or group therapy is helpful while they negotiate interpersonal changes. Eventually, the client and therapist can look back on the whole treatment and terminate.

CONCLUSIONS

This chapter introduces a model for integrating IFS with the benefits of phase-oriented treatment of trauma disorders. The goal of this integration is to enable clients who would otherwise become destabilized to maintain their highest level of functioning during the treatment process, which makes IFS treatment safer and more productive for clients who have dissociative symptoms, complex PTSD and dissociative disorders. Clients who are dissociative and whose managers cope with the feelings of parts by blocking, numbing, avoiding and dissociating, often stop making progress in standard IFS treatment. Phase-oriented treatment teaches those managers more effective ways of coping and enables progress.

Although IFS clinicians are trained to assess the client's Self-energy throughout a session, those without specific training in dissociation are usually less familiar with the diagnostic indicators of dissociative disorders and less practiced at assessing a client with DD's ability to witness extreme traumatic material. The initial IFS step, which involves negotiating with parts and gaining access to Self-energy, can be accomplished in Phase 1 with the addition of several tools: the assessment and diagnosis of a DD along with cautious use of the language of parts; getting to know parts through direct access; developing Self-energy in the form of cooperative, caring relationships among parts and with the therapist; teaching parts to convert dissociative symptoms into coping skills including safe space imagery and containers and retrieving parts from the past and orienting them to the present.

In Phase 2, the second and third IFS steps, which involve witnessing the experiences of parts, retrieving them from the past and unburdening harmful beliefs and extreme feelings, can be safely accomplished with attention to several particulars. Witnessing and unburdening only commence when the client demonstrates stability and self-assertion. When the client becomes destabilized during Phase 2, the therapy returns to the stabilization focus of Phase 1. And, finally, the intensity of witnessing and unburdening is titrated with safe space imagery and containers, while the content of containers is processed incrementally, by percentages.

Integrating IFS with phase-oriented treatment for dissociative disorders, as suggested here, may at first appear to be slower. Nevertheless, this approach can help avoid hospitalizations and excessive periods of under functioning as well as therapeutic impasses. In this way, applying a few additional tools consistently and with patience can save time and money while improving the chance of therapeutic success.

APPENDIX

International Society for the Treatment of Trauma and Dissociation: www. ISST-D.org

Recommended reading: Adult Treatment Guidelines: www.isst-d.org/jtd/ 2011AdultTreatmentGuidelinesSummary.pdf

Also recommended: *Coping with Trauma-Related Dissociation: Skills Training for Patients and Therapists* by Boon, Steele, and van der Hart

DIAGNOSTIC TESTS

The Dissociative Disorders Interview Schedule and the Dissociative Experience Scale are located at www.rossinst.com.

Somatoform Dissociation Questionnaire (SDQ) 20 and 5 (Nijenhuis) are available at: www.enijenhuis.nl

REFERENCES

American Psychiatric Association. (2000). *Diagnostic and statistical manual of mental disorders* (4th ed., text rev.). Washington, DC: Author.

Bernstein, E. M., & Putnam, F. W. (1986). Development, reliability, and validity of a dissociation scale. *Journal of Nervous and Mental Disease, 174*, 727–735.

Courtois, C. A. (1999). *Recollections of sexual abuse: Treatment principles and guidelines.* New York, NY: Norton.

Fine, C. G. (1991). Treatment stabilization and crisis prevention: Pacing the therapy of the multiple personality disorder patient. *Psychiatric Clinics of North America, 14*, 661–676.

International Society for the Study of Trauma and Dissociation. (2011). Guidelines for treating dissociative identity disorder in adults, third revision: Summary version. *Journal of Trauma and Dissociation, 12*(2), 188–212. Available at www.ISST-D.org

Kluft, R. P. (1988). Playing for time: Temporizing techniques in the treatment of multiple personality disorder. *American Journal of Clinical Hypnosis, 32*, 90–98.

Kluft, R. P. (January, 1999). Current issues in dissociative identity disorder. *Journal of Practical Psychiatry and Behavioral Health, 5*(1): 3–19.

Kluft, R.P., & Fine, C.G. (1993). *Clinical perspectives on multiple personality disorder.* Washington, DC: American Psychiatric Press.

Lyons-Ruth, K.L. (2003). Dissociation and the parent–infant dialogue: A longitudinal perspective from attachment research. *Journal of the American Psychoanalytic Association, 51*(3), 883–891.

Schwartz, R. C. (1995). *Internal family systems therapy.* New York, NY: Guilford Press.

Twombly, J. H. (2001). Safe place imagery: Handling intrusive thoughts and feelings. *EMDRIA Newsletter, 6*(Special Edition), 35–38.

Twombly, J. H. (2005). EMDR for clients with dissociative identity disorder, DDNOS, and ego states. In R. Shapiro (Ed.), *EMDR solutions.* New York, NY: Norton.

EMBODYING THE INTERNAL FAMILY

Susan McConnell

INTRODUCTION

Somatic IFS (internal family systems) is based on my understanding of how parts, their burdens and the Self are embodied. It is compatible with the findings of trauma research that our thoughts, emotions and beliefs all have somatic components (Levine, 1997; Van der Kolk, McFarlane, & Weisaeth, 1996). Combining the standard IFS protocol with the methods of body psychotherapy, bodywork and movement therapies (Johnson & Grand, 1997; Macnaughton, 2004), Somatic IFS can be used with the full range of issues typically seen in psychotherapy.

This chapter presents the concept of embodied Self, describes the five tools of Somatic IFS and then illustrates their application to cases involving addiction, complex trauma and chronic illness, as well as body image and sexual orientation.

EMBODIED SELF

Prior to IFS, my involvement with martial arts, yoga and bodywork trainings helped me to cultivate an experience of what I now call "embodied Self." I learned that physical tension and postural misalignment could both reduce my sensitivity and be transmitted to my clients. But if I let go of muscular effort, I could connect with a calm center. On learning the IFS model, I began to identify effort, striving, tension and resistance as *parts* and the feeling of being calm, aligned, centered and harmonious with *Self*. I found that both parts and Self were continually revealed through my own physical experience and the experience of my clients, and I noticed that when parts differentiated from Self, the body became a physical field for the flow of Self-energy. Over the years, many clients have reported experiencing Self-energy as an internal spaciousness; others have seen bright light or a ball of energy; still others have reported warmth, tingling or a sense of fluidity. This is the fluid, fluctuating state I call embodied Self.

Using the five interdependent tools of Somatic IFS, the therapist can help the client embody Self and bring Self-energy to the healing process. These tools are: *somatic awareness, conscious breathing, somatic resonance, mindful movement* and *attuned touch*. Each one is designed to address the impact of attachment injuries on the body and each can be applied at any point in the IFS model: accessing parts, facilitating the relationship with parts, witnessing, unburdening and integration.

SOMATIC AWARENESS

The human body is a living web, an extensive network of intricately interwoven bone, tissue, viscera and fluid, which constitutes a vast sensory field susceptible to environmental injury from prebirth onward. In response to injury, protective parts can block body awareness and dissociate from sensation, which, in turn, can affect the full range of sensual experience. Developing awareness *of* the body, and restoring awareness *in* the body, is therefore fundamental to Somatic IFS. Awareness of the body can bring laser-like focus to one sensation or it can be global. When parts regard the body as an object, their agenda tends to involve judging, changing, containing or controlling. Exploring the body subjectively facilitates a very different relationship in which sensations and movement are met with nonjudgmental curiosity.

In Somatic IFS, the therapist should attune first to her own internal state. To establish vertical alignment in the body, she can sit on a chair so the spine and rib cage are supported from a base and the breath can come freely. In this way, the therapist's entire body can be present with the client's parts. When her parts become blended, she can notice the resulting physical tension and ask the muscles to let go. Working from this state of embodied Self, the therapist can attune to the client's physical as well as emotional experience.

CONSCIOUS BREATHING

Noticing the breath, which usually occurs out of awareness, is a simple yet radically effective tool for accessing parts and evoking Self-energy. Many techniques for breathing influence the sympathetic nervous system and help regulate body processes that can be mediated by parts, such as blood pressure, heart rate, circulation and digestion. Inhaling mindfully helps to awaken, nourish and energize the body while also inviting spaciousness and calm. Even without specific breathing techniques, guiding a client to send his breath to a part or a place in his body can be useful during unblending and unburdening.

Conscious breathing is especially important in working with clients who have experienced trauma. These clients often cycle between dissociative protectors who inhibit the breath and agitated exiles who make the breath rapid and shallow. In addition, fight, flight and freeze responses can continue to influence the breath far into the future. Clients who dissociate in response to traumatic memories can learn to stay present by taking full, deep breaths with awareness. Because breathing patterns are clues to internal experience, breathing can be synchronized between therapist and client, or between partners in couple therapy, to attune to and foster connection. Conscious breathing creates the conditions for use of the next tool, somatic resonance.

SOMATIC RESONANCE

With somatic resonance we enter more fully into the relational realm, the arena of empathy and countertransference. As the client communicates an unspoken story through posture, gesture, muscular contractions, breathing patterns, dissociation and sexual energy, the therapist becomes somatically attuned to these physical shifts and is able to convey an unspoken empathic joining. These instances of nonverbal, somatic resonance are an invaluable source of information for the therapist—especially with trauma and abuse—because her body is "sharing" the client's exiled, dissociated experiences. This form of witnessing can help the client to move historical, nonverbal experience into narrative.

MINDFUL MOVEMENT

Mindful movement can be used therapeutically in many ways. It can help re-embody early movement patterns associated with trauma and disordered attachment, externalize blended parts, witness the stories of exiles and facilitate unburdening. It can also foster and stabilize Self-energy and, toward the end, integrate and anchor the shifts that have occurred in the client's system due to witnessing and unburdening. Attending mindfully to movements a client makes—even barely perceptible ones that normally go unnoticed—is a way to locate both protectors and exiles and is a very useful source of information that might otherwise be lost.

As with all somatic tools in this chapter, the therapist focuses first on her own movement. For example, as I sit with a client and notice my head reaching forward slightly in her direction, I associate this familiar movement with a part striving to hear, see and help my client. I ask the muscles at the base of my head to lengthen so that my head can rest back on my cervical vertebrae before focusing on the client.

ATTUNED TOUCH

Attuned touch rests at the top of the pyramid created by the other Somatic IFS tools. In actual practice with my clients, it occupies the least space. Although therapists rely the most on seeing and hearing, the "distance senses" (Montagu, 1971) in contrast to the "proximity senses" of taste, smell and touch, attuned touch is powerful and can be appropriate. Touch from embodied Self can let a part know that we are literally "in touch," which can facilitate the part's willingness to share a story that needs to be heard but may not yet have words.

Nevertheless, particular caution is in order with touch because therapist's parts can easily communicate their burdens to the client through it. Parts who diagnose, judge, push for change, feel needy or parental, fear the client's attachment or are erotically aroused can all inflict subtle—or not so subtle— injury on the client through touch. When it is used, touch should come from embodied Self and only with the permission of all the client's parts.

SOMATIC IFS WITH ADDICTIONS

So far Charlie had benefitted from the somatic approach to his internal family. Although he had been ambivalent about living at the beginning of our work, over the course of a year he had unburdened those parts and had felt more and more able to "choose life." His addictive behaviors with food and computer games had decreased, and he had focused on diet, exercise and healthy sleep habits. After losing forty pounds, he felt more energetic and motivated.

Then, abruptly, he was unable to continue. This session with Charlie illustrates all five Somatic IFS tools.

"I can't stay on this health program," he announced.

My first goal, looking at Charlie's slumped posture and the misery on his face, was to stay embodied. I noticed my thought, "Now he'll gain all that weight back, *again!*" This part of me was worried about both of us feeling like failures. Charlie had experienced many failed attempts at losing weight. I knew how much courage it took for him to try one more time. My part did not want to fail him. I experienced this part pulling my stomach muscles inward, restricting my chest as I inhaled and leaned my head forward. I breathed compassion for this part deep into my stomach and the muscles in between my ribs until they relaxed. Then I resumed an aligned posture. My energy now felt centered in my lower abdomen, and I was more present.

Charlie agreed to focus on this part, which had not signed on for choosing life and was now overwhelming him. I said, "How do you experience this part in your body?"

Charlie closed his eyes. "It's just paralyzing," he said.

"Stay with that feeling and notice the emotions, voice, thoughts or images of the paralyzing part as well," I said.

"It says it wants me to be stuck in all my old behaviors and literally stuck on my sofa. I feel like my whole body is glued to the sofa."

Although Charlie was clearly attuned to the paralyzing part, I wanted to be sure it was not blended with him. So I said, "How do you feel toward the paralyzing part?"

Charlie said, "I'm frustrated with it."

"Stay with the frustration for a moment and notice it in your body."

This frustrated part showed up as tension in his forehead and jaw. He touched his face and head spontaneously and then held it with both hands. I asked, "How is the frustrated part responding to your touch?"

"It has relaxed," he reported.

"How do you feel now toward the part that doesn't want you to get off the sofa?" I asked.

"I'm open to getting to know it," Charlie said.

As he lay on my sofa, he felt truly unable to move. The next step was to discover the concerns of this paralyzing protector. Charlie asked what it feared would happen if he were to move. In response, the protector showed Charlie a young, scared boy who was alone and felt powerless. The protector let Charlie know that moving would be dangerous for the boy.

I said to Charlie, "Can you still feel that energy of choosing life in your body?"

After some internal reflection, he said, "I hear a small voice saying it would be good to stand up and move around."

As Charlie took a deeper breath, I noticed a slight lengthening of his spine and forward movement of his chest. "Stay with that voice and notice if any sensation or impulse to move is connected," I said. He nodded, touching his chest. "See if the paralyzing part would trust you to move if it knew you wanted to help the boy." Charlie nodded, shrugged his shoulders and then sat up. As the paralysis continued to let go, he stood up. "Look around," I said, "and find something in this room to represent that energy for choosing life."

Charlie looked around slowly. He glanced at my bookshelf on the far side of the room and focused on a figure of a bear carved out of stone. He began to move slowly across the room toward that figure, his body still stiff with fear. So that the protector would allow the boy to sequence his story through movement and feel Charlie's supportive presence, I said, "Go very slowly. Can you feel the paralyzing part in your body still?"

"Yes. It's got a grip on my muscles, like I'm moving through water in slow motion."

"Can you feel the one it protects?"

"Yes. He's deep inside my body. He's really buried in there. He's scared of being noticed."

"What happens if he's noticed?" I asked.

"His father hits him. His mother tells them all to be good but it doesn't help. He hits everyone. My stomach is cold," Charlie reported, his face grim and pale.

"Stop there for a moment," I said. He had reached the middle of the room and he stopped, closing his eyes. "How do you feel toward the boy who's so scared?"

"I wish I could care about him," Charlie said. "But voices are telling me that he's weak. He let his mother and sister and brother get hurt. He's far away."

"Will the voices who are criticizing him trust you?" I asked. "Let them know you can take care of him."

"They don't believe me," he said.

"Ask these voices to notice the strength of your legs as you are standing."

After stopping to notice, these protectors realized Charlie was not the boy and agreed to see what Charlie could do for him.

"Now I feel compassion for him," Charlie said. "I feel a softening in my chest."

"Put one hand on your chest and the other on your belly and breathe that compassion down to the cold," I said. "Let the boy feel your compassion through your hand. What happens to the cold sensation as you do that?"

"It's getting warmer. I feel some energy moving through my body, like an internal shower."

"Are there any words you want to say?"

"I want him to know he is safe with me and it's not his fault. It's OK for him to be powerful."

"Let him hear those words and feel your touch and see if he is ready to let go of all he's been holding in his stomach."

Using the tool of somatic resonance to facilitate Charlie's process, I brought more awareness to my own embodied Self-energy, especially the warmth in my heart and stomach and the strength in my legs. Charlie's face relaxed. He moved his shoulders and tipped his head from side to side as if coming back to life. Opening his eyes, he nodded, and I nodded back. Continuing to the bookshelf on the far side of the room, his movement was fluid with the energy of a young boy. He picked up the stone bear and held it to his cheek. "I feel calmer," he said. "The paralysis is gone. And this part knows I am strong and can care for the little boy."

The little boy who had been stuck with his terrifying family and frozen in Charlie's stomach was used to being soothed with food. Once food became unavailable, the paralyzing protector had gone to work on Charlie when the boy got scared. By embodying his compassionate Self and moving purposefully toward something of his own choosing, Charlie was demonstrating his strength and reliability to this protector, a crucial first step toward getting permission to witness and unburden the boy.

Charlie returned to the sofa, holding the stone bear tenderly in his hands. "How do you feel?" I asked.

"Amazingly good," he said. "Alive, I guess."

"Let's take time now to invite that energy to travel around in you and get comfortable."

We sat together in a state of somatic resonance as we noticed our embodied Self-energy. After a few minutes of silence, Charlie reported, "I can imagine my brain is being rewired, like there is a switch inside my brain that turned on and now it won't be so hard to choose the right foods to eat."

"Let's check back next session and see how it goes choosing foods this week," I said.

In this session it became clear that the paralyzing protector had first been trying to override the boy's fear of his father, lodged in the pit of Charlie's stomach, by filling him with food. Although this protector had appeared to accept the health campaign of Charlie's managers, it had actually believed that getting healthy would stir the father's wrath. Therefore as soon as Charlie achieved a dangerous level of success, it took over. Charlie used awareness, breath, movement and touch to embody Self and facilitate a relationship with the protector so it could step aside. My awareness of my body allowed me to resonate with his parts as well as to foster his Self-energy. Charlie then brought awareness to the boy's burdens, buried deep within his stomach. He demonstrated compassion for the boy through touch and breath. As he did so, all his parts experienced the confidence of Charlie's Self claiming an object that represented health and life. In this way Charlie ended a cycle of dysfunctional protection and rescued his exile. Although some of Charlie's parts still had occasional urges to collapse and overeat, Charlie could now acknowledge their concerns and choose alternatives, such as going to hear music with friends or taking a walk.

SOMATIC IFS WITH TRAUMA

The following session with Anne illustrates Somatic IFS with trauma. Using awareness, breath and movement we navigate the territory of a traumatized exile and her protectors—an overachieving manager and a dissociating firefighter. Bringing embodied Self-energy to the exile allows it to unburden the trauma physiologically and be restored to its original qualities.

Anne was a successful corporate executive, wife and mother of three who had a complex history of childhood trauma. "I am unraveling," she said in our first session. Anne's early trauma included sexual abuse by neighboring boys when she was 12-years-old, and physical and emotional abuse by her father throughout her life. Her mother abandoned her at the age of 14. Now that exiles were taking over her body and awareness, she was living in a state of nearly continual panic.

In a session about six months into treatment, Anne described a sensation of pulling downward from her solar plexus along with a strong urge to collapse. Meanwhile, the manager, who had long resisted the impulse of this exile, was pushing energy up through her trunk and out into her limbs. The manager admitted it was very tired and, despite its best efforts, collapse was imminent.

"Would it be OK to give the impulse to collapse permission to go as far as it wants?" I asked.

Anne nodded and then crumpled slowly to the floor, curling into a fetal position. She lay quietly for several minutes. Finally, speaking from the exile, she said, "I hate myself. I should have been able to stop those boys. I am weak. I must have wanted it. What was wrong with me? Even my own parents hated me."

I noticed a slight feeling of disconnection with my body. I checked to see if this was related to my parts or if my body was resonating with a dissociative process in Anne. I did not find any parts within, so I asked, "What is happening in your body right now?"

"Now I'm getting that numb feeling, like I can't feel my body and I can hardly think."

Accessing the self-loathing of the collapsed exile in this way caused the dissociating part to come in and protect Anne from feeling overwhelmed. Because body sensations help keep experience in the present moment and sometimes counteract dissociation, I decided to focus solely on the sensations of the exile to see if this might happen.

"Let's set feelings and words aside for now and focus on your solar plexus. What do you notice?"

"I feel a pull, like a dark rope going through the middle of my body and pulling me down. Like it wants to pull me into a tight little knot until I disappear."

"Is it OK to stay with this pull? Notice the sensations in your solar plexus, where the pull starts. Notice if it pulls on your sternum or your head, and how tightly it is pulling."

With my help, Anne was able to explore the impulse to collapse more specifically without dissociating. Although she wanted to interpret her physical experience, I knew it would calm her emotions and regulate her system to stay with sensation alone.

As Anne was able to be more present in her body, she said, "This part is a little girl who knows she wasn't wanted as a baby and thinks there was something wrong with her. All those bad things happened to her were because she is bad."

"Where is this little girl now?"

"Here," Anne touched her stomach. "She's the one who wants to curl up and die."

"How do you feel toward her?"

"I want to get away from her."

"The part who wants to get away from this little girl might be the one who has run your life up till now. Let's invite it to show itself in your body."

Anne sat up, her body straightening with the upright posture of the manager who had long opposed this exile's state of collapse. "Yeah, this is familiar." she said. "This is how I usually live in my body. This part makes me work till I'm ready to drop. My body feels like it's straining to stay up out of something. This part is tired of having to do this! It doesn't know how much longer it can keep this up. It's afraid I'll just collapse and not do anything. I'll be a failure, a nothing!"

I mirrored the posture of both of these parts in my own body to get a better sense of the polarization between the little girl who showed up in the urge to collapse and the manager with the desperate strain to stay up out of the strong earlier emotions of the little girl. Resonating with her somatic experience helped me to hold them both with compassion.

Exiles experiencing strong negative feelings create physiological hyperarousal, which can override Self-energy and evoke parts who dissociate (Anderson, this volume). The therapist has the challenge of using a steady flow of Self-energy to stabilize a system that is oscillating in this way between extremes of hyper- and hypo-arousal.

"Anne, try moving between the collapse and the strained, upright posture," I suggested. As Anne did this, I mirrored her movements. She noticed I was joining in with her and that seemed to encourage her to stay with her experience. We breathed in and extended our spines, and breathed out and curled up. Her movements gradually became less extreme until we both were sitting upright but relaxed.

"My solar plexus feels open now. I don't feel that pull. I feel easy and calm."

"Let both parts feel that ease and calm. Let the one who pulls you up know that you will be taking care of the little girl and it will be OK," I said. As the session ended, I added, "Let the little girl know we want to go on spending time with her next week."

As Anne's superfunctioning manager felt more trusting and relaxed, the exile who wanted to collapse and die emerged. This, in turn, threatened Anne's dissociating firefighter. So that Anne would stay grounded, I directed her to focus on her body and its movements. Mirroring her movements, I helped witness her protectors. Once they relaxed and Anne had more access to her embodied Self, we could work with the traumatized little girl.

In the next session we invited the little girl to show herself in Anne's body. Her spine became rigid and felt compressed. Her neck, trunk, arms and legs were immobilized, and her gaze was locked straight ahead. She was frozen, an automatic survival response when there is no hope of escaping a threat.

I asked Anne, "How are you feeling toward her?"

"I feel so sorry for her," Anne said, demonstrating that she could remain unblended even as the part embodied. "She was so alone and terrified. Just paralyzed with fear."

"Does she get that you understand what she's been through, and why she had to freeze?" I asked. Anne nodded again. "Is it OK if you let that go out of your body now so that all your care for her can come back in?" Anne nodded. "OK. Here's something that has worked for you in the past. Gently and slowly twist from side to side while you breath, feel your spine unlocking. How is that?"

"When I look right, I feel her there, frozen. Then when I move left there's like a wave of space that flows in. And then I move back toward her, bringing the space to her. And she breathes it in and looks more alive. And I move left again to get more. I'm conveying this space full of light and energy to her and she's taking it in. Her body is changing from a frozen to a living thing. I'm picking her up now and I can feel how soft she is, how little. She feels my love for her." Anne wept and she said her body felt grounded, soft and strong.

At the end of this session, Anne said, "That was like cryotherapy—you freeze the person and then thaw her out when you have a cure."

Anne invited the exile who wanted to die to blend with her so Anne could witness the effect of the trauma fully. She then asked it to unblend enough so it could feel her presence. Her movement and breath allowed the exile, frozen in time as well as in her body, to experience Anne's embodied Self. Her touch conveyed this presence to the little girl, who felt loved. Even though Anne had more exiles to unburden, in that moment she experienced a new sense of connection and joy.

SOMATIC IFS WITH ILLNESS

Danielle's childhood was dominated by chronic kidney disease from the ages of 3 to 13 years. She was now a single, working professional in her forties, and at the outset of therapy she was obese and diabetic. When she started therapy with me, she was aware that although her kidney disease had been cured in childhood, she was not healed. Her parts carried burdens of shame and loneliness both from the illness and from medical treatment. She had been taunted by schoolmates as well as poked and prodded by physicians. Some parts carried disappointment from the years of hoping for a cure; some were discouraged about having been behind in her classes due to illness; some believed that she needed to be sick to get attention and love; others believed her body was bad and defective. These exiles had many extreme protectors who worked tirelessly. They sought to master her environment and numb her body while blaming her for the childhood illnesses and urging her to cut herself, watch TV, overeat or stay on the couch. They believed she would get sick again and die if she got up. As we worked with these protectors and exiles she opened up to new friendships and began to envision having a body that could allow her to join with them as they went biking and dancing. However, these changes were a threat to yet other protectors.

"I want to work with the Girl on the Couch today," Danielle said.

"Are your parts OK with that?"

"Yes, I think they trust us to talk with her as long as she stays on the couch. She hurts, aches all over. Her body is bloated. She thinks she *is* the aching and bloating."

"Does she know you are with her?" I asked.

"Yes. She's glad. She's feeling alone. Momma is too busy with my baby brother. She knows I care about her."

"Good. Ask if she wants anything from you."

Danielle said, "She wants to get off the couch but feels she has to stay there because she's sick."

"Let her know that your body has healed now. Maybe you can show her somehow that your kidneys are fine."

Danielle began to touch herself all over her body. She took several deep breaths. She told the Girl on the Couch that she was now healthy. She saw the girl get up off the couch and begin to move. The Girl on the Couch informed Danielle that she wanted to be called Margaret from now on. Once they had let go of a burden, Danielle's parts wanted a real name rather than a description.

"Tell Margaret to check and see if she still carries any belief that she is sick, or that she has to stay on the couch."

"No, she has let that go. Margaret knows she is healthy and she is free to move without worry. I feel energy surging throughout my body."

With the help of the tools of awareness, touch and breath, Danielle had her first experience of retrieving and unburdening, and it gave her hope. In the next session, Danielle reported, "I've been off the couch more. I'm keeping the house cleaner. I've gotten back into painting and I've written some poetry. But I'm sensing a part who is afraid the disease might come back and believes my body is still not healed."

"Do you sense this part in your body?" I asked.

"Yes," she said. "There's a place in my stomach that feels empty and lonely."

"Tune into the sensation of emptiness. Notice the size, shape and quality of it. Ask if there is anything the emptiness is wanting you to know."

"I am remembering a house we moved into when I was 3. All of my sick years were in that house. My bedroom was right next to Mom and Dad's. The doctors had just told them my kidney disease was back. I could hear Mother cry. I told myself I was making her cry. Now I'm hearing that I must never make Mother cry again. Just my existence made Mother cry. It wasn't something I could stop. I feel guilty. Why am I here if I am just making Mother cry?"

"Not just guilt but a belief that it's not OK for you to be alive?" I said.

"Yes," Danielle agreed. "I've often wished I was dead. That is the dangerous edge."

"Where in your body do you sense this dangerous edge?"

"Heaviness in my chest, a sense of gloom, darkness, no way out, no solution. She said, 'I'm bad, my body is bad, I should not be alive.'"

As I took in her words and her emotions, I tuned into my chest to allow my body to resonate with her part. I asked her, "How are you feeling toward this part?"

"I understand. I feel sad for her and want to help her."

"Let her know that you understand. Let your breath touch the heaviness in your chest. See if there are words you can say that will help her."

"I am telling her with my breath that she doesn't have to stay in that darkness; she can come with me and be with me where it is lighter."

Staying in touch with the sensations in my chest, I knew what to say next. "Ask if there is something she can leave behind in the dark."

"I'm wondering if she would like to leave behind that sense of being bad because she made Mother cry."

"What does she say?"

"She'd like to not feel that way anymore but it's such a part of her. It's like a gloom that surrounds her."

"Even so, if she's ready she can leave that sense of being bad behind the same way she leaves the darkness behind."

"She likes the idea. She is sort of easing out from under the gloom. She is in my presence. She has left behind the sense that she is bad now," Danielle reported.

"What are you feeling in your body now that she is here with you?"

"My chest is lighter, more open. I'm taking full breaths." Her hand went to her chest.

"Let her know through your touch that you are glad to be with her. Can you continue to spend some time with her today? Perhaps through your breath and touch?"

Again, the tools of awareness, breath and touch helped Danielle to access the part of her who believed she was bad for being sick and making her mother cry. They were helpful in developing a relationship with this part, witnessing its story, unburdening the sense of being bad and leaving the gloom. My body's ability to resonate with the heaviness in her chest helped to guide my interventions. More parts of Danielle's system arose over the next several weeks. One part felt all its hard work of protection had been wasted. Another worried that the girl would not be safe from taunting peers. One part longed to be able to love her body, but another part was threatened. We focused on the latter, a part who thought therapy was opening doors that should stay closed, creating false hope for a better life, and risking deep, dangerous despair.

"What is this one saying to you?" I asked Danielle.

"It wants me to accept that I got a bad body from the beginning and it's not my fault if I get sick." She was quiet for a moment, attending inside and then added, "The cutter agrees therapy is dangerous and says anyway the whole process is going too slow."

"Cutting brings immediate relief?"

"Yes. It looks like a red cross. It's young and it makes a hurt and then takes care of the hurt so it will heal. It wanted me to have that kind of healing success when I was sick. It wanted me to feel soothed."

"How do you feel toward it?"

"I appreciate it. I know it means well. It knows I am not mad at her. I'm not blaming it. She wants us to call her Priscilla. I'm telling her that I know how to take care of those deeper hurts. Priscilla says she is considering this and she agrees to let us know if she feels the urge to cut."

Although her deep Christian faith had been a major resource for Danielle, some parts believed they were unacceptable, even to God.

"I want to bring those parts to the light," Danielle said. "I want them to feel claimed as God's creation. This is all like prayer to me."

Several months later, Danielle was diagnosed with breast cancer. Luckily she found it early. We worked first with the parts who reacted to this diagnosis—parts who were shocked, angry, afraid of the surgery and radiation and afraid of dying. They wanted her to get back on the couch, daydream, and watch TV, so we revisited these parts from her childhood illness. Then we found a part who believed Danielle herself had caused the cancer. It did not like all this body awareness we had been cultivating. This part ranted that Danielle was fat, weak and had a rotten body.

"Where in your body do you find the part who blames you for having cancer?" I asked.

"It's hard to find this one in my body. I just feel sort of numb."

"How do you feel toward it?"

"I wish it was not here. I'm afraid it caused the cancer."

"Ask the fearful one to trust you to be with the one who numbs your body."

Danielle was quiet for a couple of minutes. While she was silent I took the opportunity to attend more fully to my body. I opened to the fear of my body's vulnerability, and my despair about her healing. I noticed heaviness in the pit of my stomach. I brought my breath to it, and felt a tingling. I had the intention of sending this embodied Self-energy to Danielle.

Then Danielle said, "Yes. I am with the blaming part. It insists I have to be sick to be loved."

"How are you feeling toward it now?"

"I want to help it. I want it to feel that I'm here."

"Tune in to the numbness. How deep does it go?"

"It's all the way to the bone."

"Are there places that are less numb?"

"Yes, in my middle."

"Try bringing your breath and touch or some small movement to the numbness." She touched her upper left arm with her right hand. "What happens?"

"I can feel more where I'm touching," Danielle reported. "I'm telling this part that I don't blame it for numbing and that it doesn't have to make me sick anymore." Tears began to trickle down her cheeks. "It's showing me how lonely it's been."

Working with illness involves working with parts who have reactions to the illness as well as parts whose behaviors may have contributed to the illness without suggesting blame. Somatic resonance, breath, movement and touch all helped Danielle to have Self-energy with the part who blamed her for the cancer.

Cut off from her peers as a child because of the illness, Danielle found comfort in what was available: fantasies, food, numbing and the care she got when sick. We talked about how these needs are based in physiology. Oxytocin, a hormone and a neurotransmitter that is stimulated by touch and social connection, helps in recovery from illness, injury and stress (Uvnas-Moberg 2003). Oxytocin is also stimulated by alcohol, nicotine and high fat foods, so when this hormone is not being stimulated through social connections, the body turns to substances for comfort. This helped her to have compassion for parts who were both driven and affected by her physiology.

Danielle's cancer diagnosis provided an opportunity for deeper healing of her body, mind and spirit. During the weeks of painful radiation treatments she was open to receive the help, connection and comfort that flowed from her community of friends. Once the cancer treatment was behind her, Danielle began a practice of walking mindfully. As she practiced daily, she reported feeling astonished at the developing awareness and effortlessness of moving her feet and legs. This movement was bringing her joy and eventually gave her the confidence to begin an exercise program. After we worked with parts who hesitated to have her identify herself as a cancer survivor, Danielle went on a walk for breast cancer. After this, Danielle realized that a part of her was still exempting her breasts from her newfound physical awareness. She explored this part's fears and helped it allow more awareness into her breasts. I suggested anointing them with oil and she later sent me a poem about blessing her breasts.

At this point Danielle was ready to focus on losing weight. During the cancer treatment she had comforted herself with food and had added pounds. Her doctor warned that she was morbidly obese. The history of cancer provided a strong incentive to lose weight and improve her self-care. "I need to lose a lot of weight but one of my parts is really freaked out about this plan. She tells me her name is Betsy," Danielle reported.

"How does Betsy show up in your body?"

"I feel tension in my jaw. She just wants to eat and eat."

"Good. Stay with that tension to let her know you're there."

Danielle's arms began to move in a frantic, grasping gesture of her hands pulling toward her mouth.

"Try slowing this movement down to find out what Betsy wants to show you."

"Betsy is trying to fill me with goodness."

"Let's thank her for that. Ask if she's willing for you to help. We can show her other ways to do that."

"She says she is willing to work with me on this."

Awareness of the sensation of tension led to movement. Attending to Betsy's frantic movement with mindfulness helped Betsy know that Danielle understood her more than words could say.

Danielle had a habit of eating alone while watching TV. She experimented with eating a wholesome breakfast, mindfully, without TV. She invited Betsy to sit at the table with her. In this way, Danielle lost ninety-five pounds over the course of a year, and was able to halve her diabetes medication. Danielle's weight loss was an opportunity to discover how her fears were connected with eating. Danielle had enough embodied Self-energy to engage in an extended dialogue with Betsy.

"She says she's scared of losing weight," Danielle reported. "I'm telling her it's OK, I'm here with you. Do you want to tell me why you're scared?"

Betsy replied, "I'm scared about who will be attracted to us."

"Tell me more," Danielle said.

"In 7th grade we were getting skinny and our body was getting shapely and we were attracted to our friend, Angela. Then we got sick. We were being punished for being attracted to Angela."

"Oh?" Danielle said to Betsy, "How did you feel about being attracted to Angela?"

"I was scared. I knew we were doing something wrong. So what if we get skinny now and we're attracted to a woman and she's attracted to us? That would be disastrous."

"Why would that be a disaster?" Danielle asked.

"Because those feelings aren't allowed. That kind of relationship is bad."

"Betsy," Danielle said, "I feel your panic right now. Let me be with you. I want you to know that I appreciate how hard it was for you to tell me. You've kept this fear secret for a long time. But it's OK now. You can trust me to handle it. A relationship between two women is not bad."

"You really mean that?" Betsy asked. "I thought God punished us for this by making us sick."

"Yes, I really mean that. We are the way God created us, and that can't be bad. Would you like to drop this belief that we were punished for being attracted to a girl and the fear that if we lose weight we will be attractive to women?"

"Can I really do that?" Betsy asked.

"Yes, we can get rid of it when you're ready."

"That sounds nice!" Betsy replied. "I'm ready."

At this point, Danielle needed help from me with the unburdening. I asked her to find where Betsy held the belief in her body.

"I feel embarrassed to say this, but I feel it in my genital area, kind of like a tension in my pelvic floor."

"What would Betsy like to do with the belief?"

"She wants to soar up and incinerate it in the sun."

Betsy gave the tension and the belief over to the sun and felt the relaxation spread throughout her body.

In the next session, Betsy said she was also afraid of men being attracted to Danielle.

"When they are attracted to us, they touch us in ways we don't like," Betsy said. Betsy showed Danielle scenes from a date rape in college and reminded her that she had started cutting shortly after the rape.

Looking up at me, Danielle said, "Some really young part is connected to that rape but it's not ready to be contacted yet."

"What does Betsy need to hear from you in the meantime?" I asked.

"That I can handle anyone who is attracted to our body," Danielle replied.

Although this session is an example of working with several chronic illnesses, it illustrates the interconnection of illness with addiction, trauma and, in this case, sexual orientation. We utilized all the tools of Somatic IFS to heal Danielle's burdens from childhood illness—the shame, guilt and fear, the belief about needing to be sick to be loved, and the belief that her body was bad. These burdens had all led to behaviors—overeating and being sedentary— that contributed to her obesity and diabetes. Attending to these by coming to therapy, in turn, gave her the opportunity to heal her childhood injuries.

Throughout our work, Danielle's embodied Self emerged more and more. She reclaimed her body as healthy and good, sacred and deserving of love. She embraced her lesbian identity and launched her first relationship with a woman while maintaining her relationship with God and her community of faith. Danielle began to engage in a variety of creative activities for the first time. Although she struggles with old habits of eating, especially when she is with her family, she has a committed intention to exercise and eat mindfully.

CONCLUSIONS

As parts absorb burdens over the course of a lifetime, the body's awareness; breathing patterns; ability to resonate with others; ability to move with ease, grace and freedom and to give and receive touch are all adversely affected. The first tool, awareness of the body, is the basis for the other four tools, conscious breathing, mindful movement, somatic resonance and attuned touch. As these sessions illustrate, all five tools of Somatic IFS can be integrated with the IFS model at each step as long as the therapist also embodies Self. Every case presented demonstrates that psychic as well as physical injury occurs in the body and can be healed in the body directly. Together, these five tools are geared to help the client heal old injuries by embodying the internal system—the parts, their burdens and the Self.

REFERENCES

Johnson, D., & Grand, I. (Eds.). (1997). *The body in psychotherapy: Inquiries in somatic psychology* (Vol. 3). Berkeley, CA: North Atlantic Books.

Levine, P. (1997). *Waking the tiger: Healing trauma.* Berkeley, CA: North Atlantic Books.

Macnaughton, I. (2004). *Body, breath, and consciousness: A somatics anthology.* New York, NY: Random House.

Montagu, A. (1971). *Touching: The human significance of the skin.* New York, NY: Harper & Row.

Uvnas-Moberg, K. (2003). *The oxytocin factor: Tapping the hormone of calm, love and healing.* Cambridge, MA: Da Capo Press.

Van der Kolk, B., McFarlane, A. C., & Weisaeth, L. (Eds.). (1996). *Traumatic stress. The effects of overwhelming experience on mind, body and society.* New York, NY: Guilford Press.

"WHO'S TAKING WHAT?" CONNECTING NEUROSCIENCE, PSYCHOPHARMACOLOGY AND INTERNAL FAMILY SYSTEMS FOR TRAUMA

Frank Guastella Anderson

INTRODUCTION

This chapter is focused on integrating psychopharmacology for acute or chronic complex trauma with psychic multiplicity and Self-energy, the central themes of internal family systems (IFS) therapy. In the service of this goal I developed five main strategies for working with clients. First I identify a list of symptoms, keeping in mind that *medications treat symptoms not feelings*. Second, I open a dialogue with the client's parts, to help differentiate a part response from a biological condition. This dialogue with parts helps me to be clear about what I am treating and helps me track symptoms so that I am sure the medications are actually working. Third, I validate the experience parts have had with medication and address any future concerns. Here my policy is *no medications are prescribed unless all parts are in agreement*. Obstacles to reaching consensus are common and will be discussed later. Fourth, I educate parts about what to expect from medications and maintain open communication with them throughout the prescribing process. My fifth and last strategy is to be aware of my own parts as they arise while prescribing. I developed a policy of *I educate, you decide*, which helps my parts to step back and make space for Self-energy. In sum, I *identify* symptoms, *differentiate* emotional from biological, *validate* concerns, *educate*, *collaborate* and *monitor my parts*. These strategies are illustrated with case examples later but first, because the neurobiology of trauma must guide medication choices, here is a review of the relevant basics of neuroscience and neurobiology.

NEUROSCIENCE

Neurons in the brain strengthen and grow new synapses when activated by experience. *Neuroplasticity* refers to connections changing in response to experience (Doidge, 2007). When these neurons fire, new nerve cells can grow. This is called *neurogenesis* (Doidge, 2007). Experience thus creates structural change in the brain. *Neural integration* is a process of coordination and balance between different brain regions that are functionally linked (Siegel, 2011). For neural integration to occur, the brain needs to function optimally, with all parts working together in harmony so that new neural networks can form and behavioral change can take place. Because trauma affects several key areas of the brain, recovery involves reestablishing balance. The first area affected by trauma is the brainstem, the most primitive part of the brain, which receives input from the body and regulates heart rate, breathing, alertness, sleep and the fight-flight-freeze response (Siegel, 2007). The second area that is affected, the limbic system, is composed of the amygdala, hippocampus and hypothalamus. This area controls affect, attachment, memory and meaning making (Siegel, 2007). The third area affected by trauma is the cortex, which includes the right and left hemispheres and the prefrontal cortex. The right hemisphere deals with perception, holistic, nonverbal and autobiographical memory whereas the left hemisphere is factual, linear, logical and deals with language (Siegel, 2007). The right hemisphere takes information from the body and brainstem and integrates it with the left hemisphere (Schore, 2003). The prefrontal cortex, a key structure involved in mindfulness, is vital in coordinating all the areas of the brain mentioned above to function as a whole (Siegel, 2007). The anterior cingulate within the prefrontal cortex is involved in emotional processing and working memory (Siegel, 2007). *Mirror neurons*, crucial to empathy and connection, also reside in the cortex (Siegel, 2010). The therapeutic protocol of IFS, with its mindful focus on parts, helps protectors relax so that Self-energy can emerge. This can create the optimal environment for the brainstem, limbic system, cortex and especially the prefrontal cortex to work together, promoting neural integration and creating new pathways in the brain.

TRAUMA AND MEMORY

Memory is either implicit or explicit. Implicit memory occurs within the first 18 months of life and is primarily focused on perception, emotion and bodily sensation (Siegel, 2011). It functions to generalize experience and primes the brain for future action (Siegel, 2011). It does not involve focal, conscious attention and it lacks the awareness that comes from the past (Siegel, 2011). Many memories and reenactments of trauma come from implicit memory and are often expressed by firefighters or exiles. For example, Jane came into a session after being stuck in a hotel room on a business trip, unable to return home because of a tornado. She was describing the storm when a train went by, a common occurrence at my office, where Jane had been many times. But this time she threw her coat over her head and screamed, "Make it stop, help me, please help me!"

Not sure what was going on, I said, "Jane try to look at me. Can you hear my voice? See if you can open your eyes to see me and see where we are. Look me in the eye. You are safe here."

Jane looked at me and then around the office for a few minutes and gradually calmed down. "The sound of the train was like the tornado," she finally explained.

For those moments Jane had been re-experiencing the roaring of the tornado bearing down on her. She was flooded with feelings and sensations identical to that time and was totally unaware of her present surroundings. When a client is blended with a traumatized part in this way, perspective and context disappear and she is engulfed in the past. Jane had no words, no narrative to attach to the experience—implicit memory was taking over her brain.

Explicit memory starts to develop at age 2 years. Requiring focused attention, this form of memory is factual and episodic (Siegel, 2011). Because explicit memory includes the hippocampus, it involves a sense of time and narrative (Siegel, 2011). A major goal of trauma therapy and of the process of unburdening in IFS is to turn implicit into explicit memory, bringing a cohesive narrative to traumatic experience. Some protectors have qualities of implicit memory. Firefighters, often extremely intense, reflexive and all-or-nothing in their responses, are unable to see the present reality. For example, when I asked a client why she had confronted a colleague at work, she responded, "See you are just like everyone else in my life, you don't understand me and you don't like me, no one does and no one ever will." This was the response of a blended firefighter, who, by my interpretation, lived in her brainstem or limbic system, where it embodied implicit memory. Clinicians and clients alike can learn to notice the ways in which these protectors and some exiles seem to come from the fight-flight-or-freeze brainstem region, or the highly emotional amygdala in the limbic system. Over time, I suspect we will learn where all parts are located in the brain.

Softening these implicit memory parts is particularly helpful for the goal of evoking Self-energy, the optimal environment for neural integration. I believe research will demonstrate that the method of IFS, which allows traumatized protectors and exiled parts to unburden toxic beliefs and feelings in the presence of the Self, is a way to deconstruct old pathways in the brain and is an effective strategy for converting implicit into explicit memory, paving the way for the formation of new neural networks. Once an unburdening has occurred, the brainstem, limbic system and cortical structures can work together in a newly integrated way.

NEUROBIOLOGY AND MEDICATIONS

The neurobiological effects of trauma on the body are widespread, affecting anatomical structures in the brain and neurotransmitter concentrations along with alterations in the endocrine and immune systems. High levels of stress have been shown to decrease hippocampal volume (Sherin & Nemeroff, 2011), an area of the brain that is essential for explicit memory, and to increase firing in the amygdala, where implicit memory is encoded. It also reduces the volume of the prefrontal cortex, specifically the anterior cingulate (Sherin & Nemeroff, 2011), which normally calms down amygdala firing. Several neurotransmitters are altered by high stress conditions. There is a significant increase in norepinephrine levels and activity, thought to be a key factor in the development of posttraumatic stress disorder (PTSD), along with increases in dopamine and glutamate (Sherin & Nemeroff, 2011). Serotonin and GABA (gamma-aminobutyric acid) levels are decreased (Sherin & Nemeroff, 2011), both of which have calming effects on the brain. Malfunction in cortisol levels (high in acute trauma and low in chronic trauma) is common, as is a dysregulated hypothalamic-pituitary-adrenal axis (Sherin & Nemeroff, 2011). We also are aware of thyroid and endocrine abnormalities. Alterations in endogenous opioids may be associated with numbing, analgesia and dissociation (Sherin & Nemeroff, 2011). Thus, the body's response to stress is widespread and, under these conditions, it makes sense that the therapeutic process of IFS becomes difficult and neural integration and new pathway formations are hard to achieve.

To understand how medications play a role in restoring balance in the traumatized brain, we must take a brief look at individual nerve cells. Nerves in the brain mainly communicate by electrical impulse traveling down the cell to the synapse (the end) where vesicles contain neurotransmitters. These are released into the synaptic cleft and the neurotransmitters attach to a postsynaptic receptor, stimulating the electrical impulse by means of voltage dependent sodium or calcium ion channels along the next nerve cell (Schatzberg, Cole & DeBattista, 2010). Medications work by increasing or decreasing the concentration of neurotransmitters in the synapse, or stabilizing the electrical signal by affecting the voltage-dependent channels, promoting the proper communication between nerve cells. New technology allows us to measure neurotransmitter levels, which gives us a clearer picture of which levels need to be corrected (NeuroScience, 2009). Two types of neurotransmitters that medications affect are relevant to trauma: excitatory (glutamate and norepinephrine) and inhibitory (serotonin and GABA) (NeuroScience, 2009). In the excitatory category, glutamate is the primary neurotransmitter involved with learning and memory (NeuroScience, 2009). Too much glutamate is toxic for the hippocampus and can cause dissociation (Sherin & Nemeroff, 2011). Norepinephrine, which decreases in relation to depression, is primarily involved in arousal, alertness and emotional memory and in excess can contribute to the development of PTSD (Krystal & Neumeister, 2009). And, finally, dopamine (for the most part excitatory but can also be inhibitory) is involved in the reward (pleasure) circuitry connected to addiction as well as explicit memory and motor control (LeDoux, 2002). In the inhibitory category, GABA prevents overstimulation throughout the brain while the other inhibitory neurotransmitter, serotonin, modulates pain and libido. Serotonin also produces a sense of calm and contentment as it regulates norepinephrine and dopamine and can help reverse the atrophy in the hippocampus and prefrontal cortex (Krystal & Neumeister, 2009). In acute trauma where there is an excess of excitatory neurotransmitters, psychopharmacology can help to calm the brain by decreasing excitatory neurotransmitters and increasing inhibitory neurotransmitters. PTSD can also be associated with periods of numbness and disconnection. Here we would be interested in increasing excitatory neurotransmitters to reverse the heightened inhibition of the brain. Research demonstrates that medications can stimulate neurogenesis (Schatzberg, Cole & DeBattista, 2010), and I believe that restoring the normal concentrations for neurotransmitters helps the brain reach the optimal state for neurogenesis and neural integration, which enables a client to unblend more easily from protectors and exiles and to access Self-energy.

Now let us match medications with neurotransmitters. Some antidepressants increase the inhibitory neurotransmitter serotonin, others increase the excitatory neurotransmitters norepinephrine and dopamine and some do both. Often the goal with clients who have experienced trauma is to calm the brain and antidepressants that increase the inhibitory neurotransmitter serotonin are generally more helpful for this. Mood stabilizers, which decrease the excitatory neurotransmitter glutamate and increase the inhibitory neurotransmitter GABA, can also be useful for trauma. And they serve to calm the nervous system by affecting voltage channels and stabilizing nerve membranes. Anti-anxiety medications also increase GABA and can be helpful on an as-needed basis. Atypical neuroleptics, which decrease dopamine and affect serotonin (see Table 7.1), tend to be useful with trauma because they bind to the NMDA (N-methyl-D-aspartate) receptor, believed to be central to memory processing and inhibiting dissociation (Alderman, McCarthy & Marwood, 2009).

Several studies have shown the effects of high levels of norepinephrine on the pathogenesis of PTSD (Sherin & Nemeroff, 2011). On the one hand, anti-adrenergic drugs, which decrease the excitatory neurotransmitter norepinephrine, are useful for treating acute trauma as well as intrusive memories and flashbacks (Alderman, McCarthy & Marwood, 2009). On the other hand, stimulants, which increase low levels of norepinephrine and/or dopamine, are useful to "activate" the prefrontal cortex in cases of numbing and disconnection that develop over time. Stimulants are not, however, advisable

Table 7.1 Common Medications and the Neurotransmitters They Affect

- Serotonin & GABA (Gamma–aminobutyric acid)= Inhibitory Neurotransmitters
- Norepinephrine, Dopamine & Glutamate= Excitatory Neurotransmitters

ANTIDEPRESSANTS

- SSRI (Selective Serotonin Reuptake Inhibitor)
  - o Prozac, Zoloft, Paxil, Celexa, Lexapro, Luvox (↑ Serotonin)
- Dual Agents
  - o Effexor, Cymbalta, Remeron (↑ Serotonin, ↑ Norepinephrine)
  - o Welbutrin (↑ Norepinephrine, ↑ Dopamine)

MOOD STABILIZERS

- Tegretol, Neurontin, Lyrica (Stabilize nerve membranes)
- Lithium (Stabilize nerve membranes, Balance neurotransmitters)
- Lamictal (Stabilize nerve membranes, ↓ Glutamate, ↑ Serotonin)
- Depakote, Topamax, Gabitril (Stabilize nerve membranes, ↑ GABA)

ATYPICAL NEUROLEPTICS

- Risperdal, Zyprexa, Seroquel, Geodon
  - o (↓ Serotonin 2a (side effects), ↑ Serotonin 1a (calming), ↓ Dopamine)
- Abilify
  - o (↓ Serotonin 2a (side effects), ↑ Serotonin 1a (calming), ↑ or ↓ Dopamine)

BENZODIAZEPINES

- Ativan, Klonipen, Xanax, Valium, Serax, Librium (↑ GABA-A)

ANTIADRENERGICS

- Clonidine, Inderal, Minipress, Tenex, Intuniv (↓ Norepinephrine)

STIMULANTS

- Ritalin, Concerta, Adderall, Vyvance, Metadate, Focalin
  - o (↑ Norepinephrine, ↑ Dopamine)
- Strattera (↑ Norepinephrine)

NONBENZODIAZEPINE SLEEP AIDS

- Ambien, Sonata, Lunesta (↑ GABA-A alpha 1 receptor)

Source: Physicians' desk reference, 2012; Schatzberg, Cole & DeBattista, 2010.

for acute trauma. Medication for trauma clients can be chosen according to its effect on inhibitory and excitatory neurotransmitters. Optimizing neural integration by balancing neurotransmitters opens the door, in IFS language, to unblending extreme parts and bringing Self-energy to the fore.

WORKING WITH MEDICATIONS AND PARTS IN TREATMENT

Richard Schwartz (personal communication, August 2011) said, "Parts can push the biological button." I agree and I also have seen the reverse, that biology can affect parts. If a client is not on medication and feels stuck with parts who cannot unblend, then consider a medication consult because it is a good unblending agent. If, on the other hand, a client has tried several medications and none have worked or she complains of multiple side effects, direct communication with parts about medication decisions is a good policy. The clinician can query the client's internal system of parts about any responses to medication, or ask a specific part how it feels about taking medication in general or wonder how the part may be reacting to a specific medication. I believe that parts need to be included in the decision-making process for a medication to work properly. Ideally, the prescribing clinician should do this work but many prescribers are not familiar with parts work. In this case, the therapist can help the client understand the feelings of her parts about medications and how to *speak for them* when seeking medication support. Here is an outline of my method for working on medication with parts.

First, I open a dialogue with parts around medication decisions and help the client to *identify* a list of symptoms for treatment. Remember medications *treat symptoms not feelings* and medications work by correcting the neurotransmitters, imbalances (which cause symptoms) thus bringing a client's system back into equilibrium. It is important for the clinician and the client to be clear which symptoms they want to treat and to be able to track progress over time. Low energy, reactivity, panic and numbness, for example, are symptoms while sadness, anger, loneliness and despair are feelings. Parts can help differentiate a psychological (part response) from a biological condition. Biological conditions that can be associated with trauma are PTSD, dissociation, depression, substance abuse, eating disorders, attention deficit disorder and obsessive–compulsive disorder, to name a few. When symptoms related to these diagnoses occur it is important to determine if they are purely biological in origin or if they come from, for example, a depressed part who is protecting an exile by withdrawing, isolating and disconnecting; or a frightened, overwhelmed part who pushes the biological button and causes a panic attack. When asked, parts are often helpful in determining the relationship between a part and biology. In my experience, they are often clear about whether a part is causing a symptom or the system of parts is experiencing the symptom as something happening to them through a biological process—when in doubt, ask the part.

Once you have determined the origin of the symptoms, it is important to *validate* the experiences of the client's parts as well as addressing any concerns they have about taking medications. When parts feel validated they are much more likely to be cooperative with a medication trial. I will not prescribe medications unless all parts are in agreement. However, some obstacles to reaching consensus are common. Hypervigilant parts can interfere. As well, differing responses among parts to medication can be a problem. When this happens, I make sure the client has heard the feelings of all parts and that the parts feel the client understands. For example, there may be a part who feels exhausted and desperately wants relief along with a part who is afraid to take anything into the body and a third part who needs more information to feel comfortable. It is important for all parts to feel the client really hears them and will proceed only after taking their view into account. And polarizations, which can motivate parts to affect or block medication, often surface when we explore parts' fears. When I notice a polarization between parts, I explore the feelings, opinions and agendas of both sides. In my experience, this often leads to an exile, and the polarization around medication decisions must be addressed before the exile can be unburdened.

Finally, I *educate* parts about what they can expect from a medication. I invite all parts to communicate their experience and concerns, and I promise that the client and I will maintain an open dialogue and *collaborate* with them throughout the process. In addition, I am mindful of my own parts whenever they interfere with me prescribing from a place of Self-energy. I find that my helper and helpless parts come up frequently. My frame of *I educate, you decide* helps my parts let me stay in Self-energy. Here are several case examples illustrating various ways in which biology can affect parts and vice versa.

BIOLOGY AFFECTING PARTS

Nina, whom I saw for both therapy and medication management, was going through the break-up of a long-term relationship. Feeling consistently over-whelmed and blended with a little girl part, she did not believe she had the resources to endure her pain.

"Let's check in with your parts," I suggested.

"The little girl feels like there is a thick layer of Plexiglas between us and it's keeping her from feeling connected to me," Nina reported. "She's frozen and sad."

"Is the Plexiglas a part?" I asked.

"No. I'm getting 'no' on that," she said.

"Are all of your parts feeling the same thing?" I asked.

"Yes," she said. "And they are missing the connection with me."

"Ask them if they all want some help with this," I said.

"Yes, they all want help."

"Ask if they are willing to take a medication to help make the Plexiglas go away," I said.

"Yes they all are willing," Nina reported.

"I think an SSRI will give your body the best help with the Plexiglas feeling," I said.

After educating her about what to expect from the medication, including potential side effects, I gave her clear instructions on how to increase the dose slowly. Then I asked her to check in with her parts again to see if they had any questions and if they still wanted to proceed. All her parts said yes. "If they have any concerns at any point in the process, ask them please to let you know. And promise them that we will address their concerns," I said.

After agreeing to a brief weekly check in to see if she noticed any changes or heard any concerns from her parts, Nina left with a prescription. After the third week of using the medication she reported that she could feel it starting to work. She felt lighter and was able to hear from her parts more easily. I asked her to check with her parts to see how they were feeling. Tears came to her eyes as she heard them chiming in about how pleased they were to feel better and how grateful they were that someone actually cared enough to ask them how they were feeling, which they were not used to. They described being able to see and feel her presence more clearly.

In this example, a medication was given with all parts participating in the decision, the medication helped and therapy could proceed. Generally speaking, medications work better when all parts instead of only one part are affected by the symptoms and when all parts agree to take a medication. In this case, a biological condition was affecting a client's parts and interfering with the process of therapy.

PARTS AFFECTING BIOLOGY

Sue had been in therapy for several years and had done remarkably well over all. She had a significant trauma history including sadistic sexual abuse by her cousin. Over the spring she had been feeling much better. She had been coming twice a week for approximately 6 years and was thinking of cutting down on the frequency of her visits. This seemed reasonable to me. We agreed to finish a piece of work with her 12-year-old girl and then she would change to weekly visits by summer.

As work with the 12-year-old progressed, Sue's behavior changed. She cancelled appointments for the first time and stopped paying her bills consistently, developing a running balance. She seemed increasingly depressed although she remained on antidepressants. She gained 10 pounds and lost motivation to connect with friends. It was even difficult to discuss these changes in her behavior due to her inconsistent attendance. I knew something was up but did not know what it was. This pattern of atypical behavior went on for weeks before I was able to bring it up.

"Sue," I said, "are you sure there isn't something going on with any of your parts? We both know that missing appointments and not paying your bills is not typical for you. Really, take time to ask inside if any parts have anything to tell you about this?"

Sue sat in silence, checking inside, and then began to cry. "I am so afraid you are going to hate me," she said.

"What are you talking about?" I asked.

"It is my twelve-year-old. She has been so afraid to deal with this last piece of work. She doesn't want to come to therapy." Sue continued to weep. "She feels so ashamed. She likes you so much but she's afraid to go on. This is the only way she knows to make things slow down."

"I understand completely," I said. "That makes perfect sense. Tell her that we can slow things down and I'm sorry I didn't hear her sooner." I added, "Ask if she has anything to do with you feeling depressed and withdrawn?"

"Yes definitely!" Sue said. "She's been feeling so bad and not knowing what to do to fix it."

"Ask her if she wants help with that," I said.

"She wants help and she wants to make sure you're not mad at her," Sue reported.

"Tell her that I'm not mad. I'm grateful that she is now able to let us know what she feels. Ask her if the medication is still working and, if so, does she want to increase it?"

"She says the medicine is not working and she would be willing to try another one," Sue reported.

"Check and see if all parts are OK with a change in medication," I said.

"Yes," Sue said. "They all want to feel better."

In this example, a 12-year-old part who was terrified of paying attention to her experience tried to slow the therapy down in the only ways she knew, including pushing the biological button to increase Sue's depression even though she was already on an antidepressant. Once Sue connected with this part in a Self-led fashion the part responded, Sue listened to the part and changed the medication. The depression lifted within a couple weeks and the atypical behavior around appointments and payment resolved immediately.

This example illustrates an exile pushing the biological button because it was feeling totally overwhelmed. The part slowed the therapy down by missing appointments, not paying bills and increasing Sue's depression. She was afraid this behavior had made me angry but after validation and reassurance, she was able to request a medication change that helped her deal with overwhelming feelings and the therapy could proceed.

VALIDATING AND ADDRESSING CONCERNS

As mentioned, I will not prescribe medication unless all parts agree. In this way, though the client may be unaware of them, I am able to address concerns that parts may be carrying. Protective parts often feel suspicious about the client's motive for taking medication and fear being eliminated. Once these feelings have been expressed and validated, the client's Self can explain the actual goals of taking medication, which includes helping—not eliminating—hard-working protectors.

Tom, a client who was in IFS therapy with another therapist, came to me to discuss medication. He had been on a selective serotonin re-uptake inhibitor (SSRI) for social anxiety for several months with no significant improvement.

I said, "Let's check with your parts about the Paxil you are taking to see if there are any parts who may feel resistant to taking it."

"Hmmm," Tom said with a puzzled look. "I asked my little boy about the anxiety and medication and he doesn't even know what anxiety is."

"Check to see if any other parts do know about the anxiety and medication," I said.

"There seems to be a part that is older, like a teenager that wants to keep me anxious!" Tom said in surprise.

"Are you open to hearing more from this part?" I said.

"It says the anxiety is helping. If I am feeling better I will start going out with friends, meeting new people, and they will see how inadequate I really am."

"Does this make sense to you?" I said.

"Well, yes it does but I had no idea a part was feeling this way," he said.

"Do you understand it now?" I asked.

"Yes," he said.

"Ask the part if it has had anything to do with the medication not working," I said.

"Yes it has been blocking the medication," he said.

"Does the part feel like you understand where it's coming from and why it's doing this?" I said.

"I think so," he said.

"Ask if we can help find other ways of protecting you from getting hurt so it doesn't have to work so hard," I said.

"It likes the idea of not working so hard," he said.

"Good. Let it know that the medication can also help it not work so hard," I said.

"It's open to that," he said.

"Tom," I said, "I need you to be committed to listening to this part and its fears as we move forward with medication. Are you willing to do that?"

"Yes I am," he said. "The part really likes that idea."

So Tom got permission from the part to increase the Paxil by 12.5 milligrams, and he assured the part that he was open to hearing any of its concerns. At the follow-up appointment he was significantly less anxious.

In this example, a manager was blocking the positive effects of medication to protect an exile who was burdened from being hurt and humiliated in social situations. Validating the manager and addressing its fear helped it feel willing to relax and cooperate with Self in allowing the medication to decrease his anxiety.

POLARIZATIONS

Parts often become polarized around medications. One part wants relief while other parts fear, dislike or disapprove of medication. A history of failed medication trials is a red flag for polarized parts, who can override medication responses when they do not feel heard. Carol came in to consult about medications for trauma and dissociation. She was in an IFS therapy but no one had ever asked her parts how they felt about the various medications she had been taking over many years. When she checked with her parts on their feelings about medication, she was surprised to hear, "Can't get better; can't get better!"

She asked why and the part replied, "If we get better we will get beat."

"Beat by who?" I asked.

"My mother," Carol sighed. "Mom has always been threatened by us doing well."

"Does this make sense to you? If so let this part know," I said. After she had done so, I went on, "I suspect that this part has something to do with the medications not working well for you. Let's also check to see if any other parts have feelings about medication."

Now I am hearing, "*We always do what the people in charge say. I am a good little girl.* Wow!" Carol said. "Now I understand why I've always taken anything anyone has ever wanted to give me even though nothing ever helps!"

"Let her know that you get how important it is for her to be a good girl," I said.

After Carol understood the root of her complicated medication history she was able to begin working with her parts more directly around medication decisions. When she got consensus to try a low dose of Abilify for dissociation, we proceeded.

"Make sure that both the scared girl and the good girl understand that the goal of this medication is to help them so they don't have to work so hard against each other. Let them know you're not trying to get rid of either one of them," I said.

"I think they get it now," she said.

This example illustrates how polarizations can complicate medication responses and choices. Not listening to parts had resulted in a long history of failed medication trials. A polarization was revealed. One part was afraid of medications working while the other part would take any medication given. This dilemma was resolved by the client's Self validating the parts and offering them the option of not having to work so hard.

MANAGER VERSUS FIREFIGHTER RESPONSES

Specific categories of parts tend to respond differently to medication. Managers are proactive protectors whose mission is to avoid emotional pain while firefighters are reactive protectors whose mission is to douse emotional pain. Firefighters tend to be absolute and severe (an example of living in implicit memory). They often override medication responses out of fear of being made to disappear or lose their job. They develop trust slowly and may only be willing to take medication as needed (known in the medical world as PRNs). Atypical neuroleptics and benzodiazepines, which decrease severe reactivity and anxiety, can be taken as needed. These medications are good choices when negotiating with a firefighter, however with addictions atypical neuroleptics are preferred. At times it may be necessary to use direct access to learn about the feelings and beliefs of a particular part, but enough Self-energy must be available to facilitate working with and hearing from all the client's parts so they can reach consensus. As the next example illustrates, in cases of severe trauma it may take time for protective parts to unblend so that Self-energy is available.

Phoebe, who had dissociative identity disorder (DID), originally came for a medication consult. She had been to several psychiatrists over the years and in our first session she stated, "Medications do not work for me, I have tried everything and I can't tolerate anything."

"Do you know how your parts feel about taking medications?" I asked.

She said, "I have no idea. No one has ever asked them before."

I said, "Is it OK to ask them now?"

Phoebe went inside and pretty quickly heard from a part who said, "You know you can't trust doctors. They are all the same."

The part went on to remind her that the therapist who had sexually abused her in graduate school kept pushing her to go to a psychiatrist and take more pills. She believed he wanted her to be in an altered state so that she would be more compliant with the abuse.

"Boy, that makes a lot of sense doesn't it?" I said.

"Yes I guess it does," she said.

"Let this part know that you get its fear about taking medications," I said. "Also let it know that you will not take any medication until it trusts us and we have its total permission."

Over the next 4 months Phoebe and I met weekly and she decided to transfer her therapy to me. Her skeptical part also began to trust me and eventually it was willing to try a very small dose of Seroquel 6 milligrams (compounded by a pharmacy). Hypervigilant parts are often associated with physiologic hypersensitivity and so tend to respond well to "microdoses" of medications. Standard doses of medications are often associated with intolerable side effects that can frustrate a prescriber who is unaware of this and leave a client feeling misunderstood. Some parts are resistant to traditional medications and should be educated about alternative treatments such as herbal remedies, natural products or acupuncture. Products that naturally support neurotransmitter production are also available. Two such examples are: 5-Hydroxytryptophan (5-HTP), a serotonin precursor, and phosphatidylserine, which can restore cortisol receptor sensitivity and help HPA axis communication.

The part was willing to try the medication but wanted permission for Phoebe to e-mail me with any questions. It also wanted to try the medication on the weekend when not much was going on. Phoebe said, "That is all fine with me."

"Check in to see if all parts are OK with this plan," I said.

"I don't hear any complaints," she reported.

Managers, in contrast to firefighters, are often willing to admit exhaustion and seek relief. They will usually take medication and they like the sense of distance and perspective that can be created by selective serotonin re-uptake inhibitors (SSRIs). Therefore, at least for these parts, SSRIs seem like good unblending agents. In addition, exploring medication options serves the helpful function of revealing polarizations between managers, firefighters and/or exiles. In this example, both client and prescriber worked with a vigilant protector to alleviate its fears, address its concerns and develop a trusting relationship.

KEEPING COMMUNICATION OPEN

Parts appreciate knowing what to expect from a medication and can be helpful in assessing dosage. They can also help by tracking and classifying physical sensations that could be caused by the medication or could, instead, be the communication of a part. Here is an example of the importance of keeping communication open and paying attention to sensations that arise in relation to medication.

Sean came in for a psychopharmacology appointment saying he felt good and wanted to find out if he could maintain this improved mood on a lower dose of medication.

"Ask your parts how they feel about tapering the Lamictal," I said.

"I am noticing some tension and tightness in my shoulders right now," he observed.

"Would it be OK to focus on that sensation and ask what's up?" I said.

"Well, there is a part that's worried about tapering," he said. "It says there is a lot going on right now. My wife is particularly stressed and I am getting a new boss at work. This part thinks it's not the best time to make changes."

"How do you feel toward the part?" I asked.

"It makes sense," he said. "I'm glad the part spoke up but I still want to taper."

"Let this part know you really get what it is telling you and ask what would help to make it feel comfortable with you tapering," I said.

He closed his eyes for a moment and then said, "If I promise to listen and pay attention then it will feel OK about trying. It says I need to listen to the tension in my shoulders." So they agreed to stay in close communication.

"Check to see if any other parts have concerns," I said.

"No I don't think so. I never knew my muscle tension was a part," he said. "That surprises me. I feel good that my parts can help me make this decision. I am more confident moving forward with the taper."

This example illustrates the importance of listening to and working with a manager who communicates through the body. Here a part expressed fear about tapering medications due to stressors in the client's life. After listening to the body, his parts agreed to taper more slowly if the client would agree to listen to them along the way.

STAYING IN SELF, ADDRESSING THERAPIST'S PARTS

Just like any IFS therapist, the prescribing clinician must work with his or her parts. Both my helper parts and my helpless parts can be activated when I prescribe medications. When I experience a dilemma about whether to witness a client's pain or prescribe a medication to reduce or remove a symptom, my helper parts tend to get activated. A therapist who is considering whether to send someone for a psychopharmacology consultation could have a similar dilemma. My helpless parts tend to get activated when parts of the client feel frustrated because medications are not working.

Paul had been feeling disconnected lately and believed he was depressed. He had a history of bipolar disorder, which was well controlled with a mood stabilizer. He came into a session saying he wanted to try an antidepressant as well.

"Check in with your parts to see how they feel about this," I said.

"No response—all quiet inside," he said quickly.

He really wanted an SSRI so I agreed and he started on a low dose, but over the next several weeks he became numb and felt worse. At this point I realized that a part had been activated in me. This part had agreed too easily with Paul's wish to take an SSRI. When I turned my attention inside, I heard a young part say, "If I give him what he wants he will like me," and I realized I was blended with my helper. I knew if this part had stepped back I would have been more curious about Paul's statement, "No response—all quiet inside," and I would have asked about his urgency to try a new medication.

I asked my helper to relax now and let me be curious. As it agreed, I said to Paul, "Check in with your parts again and see if we can learn anything about what is going on here."

On going inside, much to his surprise, he discovered a new part. He said, "I think it's a numbing part."

"See if this part can tell you more about its job," I suggested.

"It says it is protecting me from having any feelings. It has been around for a while and does not want me to have any feelings about my sister's new diagnosis of leukemia. It says to me that I will never be able to handle it if anything happens to her."

"Does this make sense to you," I said.

"Yes totally," he said.

"Let this part know you understand and ask it if it would like some help or relief with a medication," I said.

"It says no, it feels glad that I finally know that it exists."

"Check in with other parts now to see if it's OK to taper off the medication," I said.

"Yes totally."

We planned a taper schedule and he began to work more directly with the part. Taking this new tack, his numbing protector softened and he was able to get to know an exile who had taken care of his younger sister when they were kids. This exile felt that his sister only had him, and conversely, he only had his sister so she was essential to his survival.

Here we see that a symptom that initially looks biological can turn out to be a protector. In this case a numbing protector was trying to keep Paul from feeling deep pain about the neglect and losses that he and his sister suffered in childhood as well as the coming loss of his vital connection to her. My helper part had gone along with his protector and had gotten in the way of my curiosity about his silence and the urgency he felt to take a medication. I discovered all of this only after he started the medication (which was biologically unnecessary) and noticed that he felt overmedicated. This example illustrates how a part in the prescriber can interfere, allowing a medication to be prescribed which was unnecessary and proved unhelpful.

MY PART FEELS PUSHED

John and Michael come in for their usual appointment, however this particular week John seemed more agitated than usual. "I can't take it anymore," he said. "Michael is so depressed and unable to get anything done at home. I feel like I am doing everything! I work all day and then have to come home at night, cook dinner and clean the house. He does nothing all day long but sit on the couch playing games on the computer. We have been coming here for a while now," John looked at me fiercely. "You are a psychiatrist. Why don't you give him a pill or something to stop the drinking?"

I looked at Michael. "How do you feel about what John just said?" I asked.

"I am tired of being criticized by him," Michael said. "I can't do anything right. I think I would drink a lot less if he would back off. I'm not that bad."

"John," I said, "I think Michael might be able to take a look at his drinking if he felt less criticized."

"I knew it!" he said. "His drinking is my fault. Once again the responsibility lies on my shoulders. It always turns out that way, my whole life. I want out!"

Aware at this point that a part of mine had incensed a part of John, I took a moment to check inside. I quickly found a part who felt pushed by John into trying to fix Michael. And this part did not like being told what to do.

Taking a deep breath, I said, "John, I hear how upset and frustrated you are about Michael's drinking. And I hear that a part of you would like me to prescribe a medication to help him stop and function better at home. That makes a lot of sense to me. And Michael you seem upset and shut down by what you describe as John being critical and attacking. And you don't really feel that your drinking is a problem. I cannot tell if a part of you is drinking in reaction to John's criticism or there is a biological addiction we are working with. But before we discuss that, let me educate you both about some of the options available for alcohol treatment, including medications. Revia is a medication that reduces cravings, Antabuse treats binge drinking and Clonidine helps with withdrawal symptoms. I am here to answer your questions every step of the way." They looked at me and then at each other, their faces softening, and I proceeded to explain their options.

In this example, once I was able to connect with my reactive part who felt pushed into doing something, it was able to relax and I could proceed to the job of assessing and possibly prescribing with Self-energy. I generally find that the stance *I educate, you decide* elicits Self-energy in the client and allows my parts to step back.

CONCLUSIONS

In summary, I have developed five strategies to integrate psychopharmacology for trauma with the basic principles of IFS therapy. First, I identify a list of symptoms; second I differentiate a part response from a biological condition; third, I validate the experience of parts and address their concerns, with a policy of only prescribing when there is internal consensus about trying medication; fourth, I educate parts about what to expect from medications and collaborate with them throughout the prescribing process and, fifth, as I guide and educate the client (who makes the decisions), I am mindful of my own parts.

Neuroscience shows that the brain is capable of changing (neuroplasticity) and developing new nerve cells (neurogenesis), which ultimately result in the formation of new pathways and behavioral change. For the formation of new networks, certain parts of the brain need to be working together (neural integration). In trauma, the physiological effects of stress cause activation in the brainstem, increased amygdala firing and hippocampal atrophy in the limbic system and hypothalamic-pituitary-adrenal dysfunction. Stress also affects the cortex, resulting in decreased volume in the prefrontal cortex and atrophy of the anterior cingulate. One of the ways to correct abnormalities in brain function is to restore neurotransmitter concentrations with medications. I believe these abnormalities cause symptoms, which can block treatment, and that correcting them allows IFS therapy to progress more efficiently.

To work at the interface of biology and psychology, I open a dialogue with parts that is geared to differentiate the physical from the emotional and cognitive. Medications treat symptoms not feelings and when asked, parts will describe a biological process that "happens to them," or will describe themselves feeling overwhelmed and fearful and "pushing the biological button." Validating the concerns of parts about medication helps them to feel understood and be willing to cooperate with a medication regimen. When not included in the decision-making process, parts can block the beneficial effects of medication. It is also common for polarizations to develop, with different parts having different feelings about a particular medication. When the client can hear both sides with Self-energy, a consensus will often emerge. On the whole, medications help to support and relieve hard-working protectors.

Typically, different medications are helpful for different symptoms following trauma. Knowing which neurotransmitters are affected by which medication can help prescribers to determine which symptoms can be treated. Generally SSRIs, which work by increasing the calming neurotransmitter serotonin, are helpful for symptoms related to PTSD. Mood stabilizers help by stabilizing nerve membranes and increasing the calming neurotransmitter GABA and decreasing the excitatory neurotransmitter glutamate. The atypical neuroleptics tend to be helpful for dissociation because they affect serotonin, block dopamine and affect the NMDA receptor. Antiadrenergic medications, which decrease the excitatory neurotransmitter norepinephrine, are helpful for intrusions, flashbacks and acute trauma. Benzodiazepines work by increasing the calming neurotransmitter GABA and should be only used as needed due to their addictive potential. They are, however, helpful for treating acute anxiety. Last, stimulants can be used for trauma when an increase of dopamine and norepinephrine is needed to activate the prefrontal cortex while treating numbness or desiring an increase in focus and attention.

Just as different medications treat different symptoms, different parts tend to respond to different medications. Firefighters with their reactive all-or-nothing responses come from implicit memory and, most likely, originate from more primitive brain structures such as the brainstem and limbic regions. Firefighters typically take a long time to develop trust with Self and will often only take medications on an as-needed basis. They tend to respond to atypical neuroleptics and benzodiazepines. Managers, on the other hand, are often more willing to take medications because they want relief. They tend to benefit from SSRIs and mood stabilizers. Hypervigilant parts tend to respond well to microdoses of medications. They also like natural remedies that are less potent and tend to reject sleep medications, which thwart their goal. Educating parts and keeping communication open throughout the medication process is vital for developing trust between Self and parts.

The connection between neuroscience, psychopharmacology and IFS is an exciting frontier. In my opinion, correcting chemical imbalances in the brain by eliciting the help of parts in the process of prescribing medications paves the way for protectors to step back and Self-energy to emerge so that exiles can unburden (old pathways are deconstructed) and new neural networks can form in the brain.

REFERENCES

Alderman, C.P., McCarthy, L.C., & Marwood, A.C. (2009). Pharmacotherapy for post-traumatic stress disorder. *Expert Reviews Clinical Pharmacology*, 2(1), 77–86.

Doidge, N. (2007). *The brain that changes itself.* New York, NY: Penguin Books.

Krystal, J.H., & Neumeister, A. (2009). Noradrenergic and serotonergic mechanisms in the neurobiology of posttraumatic stress disorder and resilience. *Brain Research, 1293*, 13–23.

LeDoux, J. (2002). *Synaptic self, how our brains become who we are.* New York, NY: Penguin Books.

NeuroScience. (2009). *Institute of education, hormone bios.* Available at www.Neurorelief.com.

Physicians' desk reference. (2012). Montvale NJ: PDR Network.

Schatzberg, A.F., Cole, J. O., & DeBattista, C. (2010). *Manual of clinical psychopharmacology.* Arlington, VA: American Psychiatric.

Schore, A. N. (2003). *Affect regulation and disorders of the self*. New York, NY: Norton.

Sherin, J. E., & Nemeroff, C. B. (2011). Post-traumatic stress disorder: The neurobiological impact of psychological trauma. *Dialogues in Clinical Neuroscience, 13*, 263–278.

Siegel, D.J. (2007). *The mindful brain*. New York, NY: Norton.

Siegel, D.J. (2010). *The mindful therapist*. New York, NY: Norton.

Siegel, D.J. (2011). *Mindsight*. New York, NY: Bantam Books.

THE INTERNAL FAMILY SYSTEM AND ADULT HEALTH: CHANGING THE COURSE OF CHRONIC ILLNESS

Nancy Sowell

I began to use the internal family systems (IFS) model with symptoms of disease out of desperation. My knees and feet were so swollen and inflamed that walking had become extremely painful. At the time, there was no specific training in the application of IFS to medical illness and pain, so I had not used it with my clients. The autoimmune disease from which I had been in remission for some years was flaring. The behavioral medicine approach, which I used professionally and had found useful in controlling my symptoms as well as my comorbid anxiety, was not getting to the heart of my stress. So I tried going *inside*, in the language of IFS, to see if I could get some helpful information from my internal system. There, I discovered that my parts were in serious disagreement over what to do for me.

Some parts of me stoically ignored and minimized my pain. They kept me working, business as usual. Other parts felt scared or angry. They advocated for major changes in both my professional and personal life, saying I should stand up for myself more and set clearer limits on my time, energy and availability. Meanwhile, a part of me was afraid of conflict and upheaval. As inner tension mounted, I would sometimes escape into movies, fiction and the computer. But more often than not, when I was not working, I was so exhausted that I would collapse on the couch or skip dinner and go straight to bed. I knew from years of using biofeedback that this inner turmoil took a physiological toll. Nevertheless, it was happening outside of my moment-to-moment awareness. In turn, my primary modes of coping with the stress and pain, such as overworking, were exacerbating both.

As I listened inside to my parts, I understood that I needed to take action to reduce the stress. First, I made more time to be in touch with my Self and to tune in to the parts I had been ignoring. Rather than avoiding the physical pain in my joints, I focused on those symptoms with compassion and curiosity. I became aware of sadness and fear, for instance, as I focused on the pain in my knee. I also became aware of deep physical fatigue. I heard from parts who were speaking through my symptoms and parts who were reacting to my disease and the pain. I found both vulnerable and protective parts who were trying to get my attention. The panicky part balanced out the minimizer. The angry part was trying to keep the overcommitted accommodator in check. As I listened in this way, I could no longer ignore what I was hearing. Even the parts of me who had taken on the role of ignoring the pain and inflammation needed to be understood and appreciated. Ignoring the pain had helped me to get up and start moving each morning, but acknowledging each part's inherent value contributed to a growing understanding and cooperation in my system. The most vulnerable parts, such as the young girl whose needs had gone unmet for too long, finally had my attention.

And I started advocating for myself and setting clear limits with others in the external environment. At work, I added more administrative support and reduced my hours. I stopped working evenings and accepted fewer clients. I made time for self-care: more rest, exercise, good food, play and relaxation. Parts of me who had become polarized in dealing with the illness, such as the hard-working stoic and the one who collapsed on the couch, became less extreme. They felt heard and cared for with my Self in charge. While making these changes, I went to see my health care providers. For a short time, I started taking anti-inflammatory medication again. Within a few months, I was back in remission and off medication.

This experience convinced me to start using IFS with others, and today IFS is my primary intervention with clients who seek help for medical problems. As I gained more experience in the medical application of IFS, my curiosity about the interplay of genetics, parts and environment in relation to health and illness grew. In the example of Marty, described in depth later, as for myself, there is a family history of the disease in question. However, the vast majority of people in my family—as in Marty's—have never developed symptoms. Why and when some family members become symptomatic is unclear. A literature search informed me that although life experience—as carried in memories, beliefs, emotions and behaviors—influences health, we still do not know how or to what degree personal history manifests in genetic or epigenetic vulnerabilities and strengths, or how it impacts our susceptibility to infection and our ability to heal. Nevertheless, there is a growing body of research linking stress (Archie, Altmann, & Alberts, 2012; Sapolsky, 2005), personality traits (Haukkala, Konttinen, Laatikainen, Kawachi, & Uutela, 2010; Kiecolt-Glaser et al., 2005), attachment (Kotler, Buzwell, Romeo, & Bowland, 2011; McWilliams & Bailey, 2010), coping style (Deimling et al., 2006) and a history of adverse childhood experiences with adult health problems (Romans, Belaise, Martin, Morris, & Raffi, 2002). My personal and clinical experience led me to believe that therapy can affect physical health profoundly.

IFS is designed to help clinicians and clients identify, understand and relate with compassion, courage and clarity to all our parts. In my experience, when Self-energy is aimed at the intersection of nature and nurture, physical as well as emotional healing can occur. This chapter offers a framework for understanding and exploring the relationship between parts and medical problems, underlines the connection between past and current environmental stressors and, in a case example, illustrates the healing effects of one man's growing self-awareness and self-compassion.

Marty's initial message on my office answering machine gave me the impression that he was an opinionated, strong-minded man. When we spoke for the first time, he said matter-of-factly that he was 59 years old and had coronary heart disease and chronic obstructive pulmonary disease (COPD). He then moved quickly on to the business at hand. Was I taking new clients? He had gotten my name from his primary care physician who told him about my work at Brigham and Women's Hospital using IFS in a randomized controlled trial with rheumatoid arthritis patients (Shadick, Sowell, & Schwartz, 2010). "I need help dealing with stress and some family issues," he said.

In our first session, Marty said that he had had "bypass surgery" (a coronary artery bypass graft, or CABG) several years before. After many years of doing much better, he recently had been feeling a little worse. When I inquired about his medical prognosis, he replied, "I haven't asked. I know I need to reduce my stress. My doctor wants me to stop smoking and maybe lose some weight. Let's just work on the stress and see how it goes."

I was struck by the contrast between Marty's avoidance of important facts about his health and his otherwise direct style of communicating. He was quick to tell me his views on politics, social issues and my waiting room design, but omitted the fact that he had had more than one heart attack. He showed disparate characteristics in other ways, too. He sometimes displayed an edge of anger but was generally relaxed and personable. Although he enjoyed occasional blunt, almost shocking statements, and seemed pleased to break the rules of social decorum, Marty was averse to asking for help and appeared almost repelled by his own emotional needs.

"I smoke like a chimney. I'm fat. My arteries are filled with sludge. I have trouble breathing. And, now I do the Florida shuffle walking up the stairs! What's all the hubbub?" Marty quipped and waited to see my reaction.

"Does this mean you're not planning on running the marathon this year?" I joked back. After sharing a laugh, I began, "Seriously, Marty, you've talked about your wife's fears and your doctors' concerns, but does your health worry *you*?"

"I don't think about it much. My wife does enough of that for both of us. I have a lot of other stuff on my mind," he replied.

"I know you do. If you think about it now, though, would you say that you, or a part of you, will avoid thinking about your heart problems or your COPD?"

Marty paused as he thought over my question. "Probably. I get tired of hearing about it. I know what I gotta do. Honestly, I *don't* like talking about it. I guess I don't like thinkin' about it either. And, like I said, I have a lot of other stuff on my mind."

After the initial sessions, I knew that his protectors—the parts who keep vulnerability and pain out of awareness—were in charge most of the time. Marty's physicians and his family, of course, all wanted him to stop smoking and take better care of himself. And Marty was clearly dedicated to his family. His wife sometimes accompanied him to his appointments and read in the waiting room during our sessions. They had two adult daughters, but his son, Gary, had been killed in a boating accident a year earlier at the age of 32 years. Marty softened tremendously when he spoke about his grandson, Gary's four-year-old boy. "The little guy," as Marty called him, had grown very attached to Marty after Gary's death. Outings with his grandson and the projects they did together were some of the brightest spots in Marty's life, and with some encouragement, he described the boating accident that had taken Gary's life. He confided in me his feelings of responsibility for helping his son's family, now that Gary was gone.

One tenet of IFS is "All parts are welcome." I do not argue with parts or try to talk them out of how they feel or what they do. And, as an IFS therapist, it is my job to notice my own internal system as well. In this case I noticed my patient's increased anxiety both in response to pressure from the external system and his internal system. Externally, Marty's family and his other health care providers were all quietly watching and hoping that his work with me would help him process his grief and stop smoking. Internally, his protective parts were clearly exacerbating his symptoms and his life was in danger. I knew that it was crucial for him to reduce his risky behaviors, such as smoking and overeating, along with his stress.

If I am feeling anxious about my client's medical condition and self-destructive behaviors, my effectiveness as a clinician is diminished (Schwartz, this volume). As I begin working with a medical patient, I help my protectors know that I am here with them and with my patient. I often find myself subtly communicating with my own parts during a session, telling them, "I'm right here. I hear you. Let me be with this person now." Marty's behaviors and risk level did make my parts anxious and I checked in with them periodically throughout our work.

After spending a few sessions in which we got to know each other, Marty began to open up and even started looking forward to coming. When I judged it was time for us to agree on which parts he wanted to get to know better and help, I described our treatment dilemma by directly engaging the part of Marty who felt pressured by his family and medical team. "Marty, everybody wants you to quit smoking! Have you noticed that? I'm feeling a little pressure! What about you?"

Marty chuckled, "Now you know how I feel!" After we laughed together, he added, "What? We can't just keep yucking it up? You wanna get down to business?"

We talked about the anxious concern coming from his family and doctors. He acknowledged that he was making himself more symptomatic with smoking, overeating and not "doing feelings." His symptoms had increased in the months since Gary's death. We talked about his stress and his dedication to helping Gary's family on top of all his other responsibilities, including his daughters and their families. We decided to start the IFS work by looking at these stressors and identifying the parts involved. Marty was interested to know how I was thinking about his illness and our work together. I offered a simple framework, illustrated later, for identifying and getting to know how his parts were related, directly and indirectly, to his illness. But I described the framework gradually, whenever it seemed relevant and helpful. I do not routinely go over the theory or protocol of IFS with clients who have medical problems. Because some are not interested and some do not find it particularly helpful, this is a judgment call. In Marty's case it did prove helpful. Information, along with a structured way to think about the relevance of IFS to his physical problems, helped Marty's strong, hypervigilant managers to relax and participate.

My framework for applying IFS with medical symptoms includes identifying and checking for: (1) parts who trigger or exacerbate symptoms, (2) parts who maintain symptoms, (3) parts who know something about improving or healing symptoms, (4) parts who are fearful of improving symptoms and being well and (5) parts who want to die. I never assume that all are present, nor do I impose my views on clients. But because I often find that these parts, alone or in combination, are present in clients with a medical illness, I keep this range of possibility in mind.

I also look for current stressors and behaviors, as well as burdens rooted in the past that are carried by parts and impact the client's health now. Polarities among the parts dealing with these burdens and stressors are common and can precipitate disease and provoke and maintain symptoms. Marty's system illustrates this well. In this example you will see that his protectors are polarized with a sad, exiled part. Some protectors promote escaping or numbing the sadness, and others promote management and control.

Our job was to help his polarized parts become less extreme, then to identify the parts who maintained or exacerbated his symptoms, who feared getting better or who wanted to die. Once we could do this, I felt certain that his anxious, grief-stricken, sad and angry parts would feel relief, which would, in turn, affect his illness. I knew that my patience, kindness and hope would be crucial in guiding him. But I also knew that the actual healing would occur in the relationship between Marty's Self and his parts.

Clients who have serious medical conditions like Marty often have very active protectors who focus on functioning and want to "leave well enough alone" when it comes to emotional suffering in the internal system. That is their job and Marty was no exception. So we started with these parts: "I need to keep this business afloat. Not just for my wife and me but for Gary's family, too. They're counting on the income. I need to work and keep the money coming in for everybody. I don't have Gary's help now. I'm trying to figure out whether to hire somebody, or what to do! There aren't enough hours in the day."

In their desire to help Marty keep his fear and sadness under control, manage his business and support his family, these parts kept Marty working long hours with very little down time to attend to his physical needs and exacerbated his symptoms. Other protectors, such as the smoker who numbed feelings, were precipitating Marty's symptoms more directly. The smoker did not want him to be sick; rather it did not want him to be vulnerable and overwhelmed. When Marty went inside and found the protector who smokes, he reported the following, "It's not a part I can see. It's in the dark. It's trying to keep me away from sadness—some big bubble of sadness. Smoking pushes it away. He also tries to distract me away from it. When this part smokes it stops whatever I'm doing or thinking and it takes me away."

"Away from the sadness?" I asked.

"Yeah. The sadness doesn't get a chance to come up, and then it passes. Sort of like a door closes shut," he said.

"Hearing this, how do you feel toward the part who wants to smoke to keep the sadness away?" I asked.

"I totally get it. I know what it's thinkin'. It's not a bad guy who's out to get me. It's trying to help me. It doesn't want me to get overwhelmed!" he said.

"Is this part aware of you right now, Marty?"

"Sort of. He can feel me paying attention to him."

"Invite him to really notice that you are there and you understand him," I said. There was a long pause. I could see a change in Marty's face reflecting a connection with this part. I added, "Invite him to feel your positive feelings toward him and your interest in him."

Marty nodded to let me know that the part saw him more clearly. "He's very aware of me now. Not that he sees me, but more like he just knows I'm here. Like he feels me. It's like we're sharing something. We're sharing an understanding." Marty went back to listening and occasionally reporting what was happening between him and the part.

After a while I said, "Marty, find out if he knows the physical consequences of smoking to keep sadness away?"

"No, he doesn't think about the smoking making me sick," Marty reported.

"Is there something you'd like to communicate to him about that?" I asked. Marty was quiet for sometime as he concentrated inward.

"I showed him what's happening to me—kind of had a look inside at my heart and lungs. He's sorry it's hurting me, but he can't stop, he says."

"Find out what would need to happen for him to seriously consider not smoking in the future," I said.

"The sadness would have to stop," Marty reported.

"Check to see if he would want to stop smoking if you could help the sad parts."

"He's interested but not so sure about this idea. A bunch of thoughts just jumped up. He doesn't know what he would do if he stopped smoking. He's feeling a little suspicious and wonders if I'm trying to get rid of him, or if you are?" Marty said, looking up at me.

"Let him know that I respect him for protecting you all these years. I'm glad he kept you from getting overwhelmed." There was a pause before Marty nodded to signal that he had done so. "Also tell him that he'll always be part of you. This is about helping him with options, not trying to get rid of him."

"He's listening but he doesn't understand what you mean about options," Marty said.

"I mean when you, in your Self, connect with the sad parts and help them, then he won't be locked into smoking and he can figure out what he'd rather do. I will help guide you through the process if he's willing." After a pause, I added, "What would he rather be doing if he didn't feel smoking was so necessary?"

There was a long pause as Marty listened inside. "'Ticket to Ride'—that Beatles' song—just popped into my head. He's thinkin' about music! He hasn't listened to music in a long, long time," Marty chuckled. In hope that he actually could be free to relax and do things like listen to music again, the smoking protector eventually agreed to allow Marty to find, know and help the sad parts.

Like the smoker, the parts who snacked and watched late-night television wanted to keep the pain and suffering of Marty's exiles at bay and they were not aware of the toll this took on his health, nor would they stop until Marty had helped his exiles. When Marty and I talked about the stress of being sick and having other responsibilities and he started to feel emotional, these protectors would spring into action. In one such conversation Marty said, "I can't afford to be sick. I have too much to do. People are counting on me!" This belief, a burden acquired by an adolescent part when his father died, had reignited with the death of his son Gary. It showed up in thoughts like, "I must do whatever is necessary for my family's survival!" Or, "I can't afford to play and relax." And it showed up in behaviors such as overwork, self-sacrifice and the tendency to ignore fatigue or emotional needs. Burdens like this, carried forward in time by parts, may help to explain how adverse experiences of childhood (Felitti et al., 1998), personality traits (Eaker, Sullivan, Kelly-Hayes, D'Agostino & Benjamin, 2004; Everson et al., 1996), coping (Moos & Holahan, 2003) and attachment style (Feeney, 2000) continue to effect physical health in adult life.

Self-monitoring is a standard behavioral medicine tool, which I have modified for use with IFS to identify and track parts associated with target behaviors, beliefs, emotions and body sensations. To find the parts whose burdens were affecting Marty's health, we began tracking his internal and external experience. For a couple of weeks Marty kept a log that had a series of checklists. First he noted the circumstance, such as interacting with others, working or being at home; then his emotions such as anger, sadness, anxiety or joy; then his behaviors such as smoking, eating, working, drinking and TV watching and finally his medical symptoms such as shortness of breath, wheezing, coughing, dizziness, fatigue and heart palpitations. In this way, Marty became more and more aware of the relationship between external circumstance and his internal experience of emotions, thoughts, behaviors and physical sensations as well as his medical condition.

In a session about four months into treatment, Marty and I talked about work and family stress related to Gary's death. He had made Gary a partner in the construction company where they both worked, and from which he had been planning to phase out his active involvement just before Gary was killed. In a year or two, Marty would have become a silent partner, allowing him to retire and take a long-planned cross-country trip in an RV with his wife.

"That was the plan before . . ." his voice trailed off and he looked upset, his face flushed. Now he looked directly at me and sounded angry. "What's the point in talking about this? I don't think whining about my problems does me any good!" He put his hand to his chest.

"What's happening, Marty?" I asked.

"It's harder to breathe," he said.

"Would it be OK to check inside and ask what just happened?"

Marty closed his eyes and was silent for a moment. Then he said, "I don't want to talk about Gary today."

"Marty," I said, using direct access with this protector, "what are you concerned will happen if you talk about what it's been like since Gary died?

"Look, I can't afford to go there!" he exclaimed. "Not the physical stuff, but more this," he gestured to his chest and heart area, "and all this 'feelings' business. I'm like a fucking piano wire about to let go!"

"Like you'll explode, feeling it all?"

"Right! Exactly! What's the point?" he said angrily, shifting in his chair with discomfort, his breathing still labored. "Let's just say I'd rather leave well enough alone. There's nothing I can do about what happened." He paused, suddenly looking more approachable. "I know what you're saying about stress. I *should* talk about it, but I don't know . . ." he trailed off.

"I understand why you wouldn't want to go there if it would just overwhelm and make you feel worse. I wouldn't want that either."

Marty relaxed a little. Then he said, "I need a cigarette." He stared into the distance, beyond the walls of my office. "There's nothing I can do! See?" He looked back at me directly now. "If you make me start emoting or something I don't know what'll happen! Do you understand?"

"I think so," I said. "You don't want me to pressure you into anything or stir things up." He nodded. "This feels too big, too risky. Right?" Marty nodded again. We settled into a comfortable moment of quiet in which Marty's shoulders slowly relaxed and he leaned into his chair, the coloring in his face returning to normal and his breathing coming easier. "You've got some very strong protectors there!" I said finally.

"The tip of the iceberg, believe me!" he replied. "I hope I didn't scare you."

"You didn't scare me, but I *did* notice the strength of your part's conviction. Would it be OK for us to get to know this part better? The one who thinks talking about feelings is a bad idea."

"I don't know how the hell you're planning to do that," Marty said, "but let's give it a try. That's why I'm here, right? You can bet I'll let you know if it's not workin' for me!" He cocked his head and gave me an exaggerated, semimock look of warning coupled with a slight smile. "And, listen, I get the point, too. In a way, I'm sick and tired of being all bottled up."

With the self-monitoring and increasing awareness, Marty came to know the parts who were determined to keep his sadness and grief at bay. In *unblending*, he was able to observe each part with curiosity and interest, getting distance from their beliefs, body sensations and worldview without denying it or turning away. When he found the stoic, young protector while accessing Self-energy, his appreciation grew.

In turn, this protector reminded Marty that his father, who ran the family cranberry farm, had experienced heart problems when Marty was a young boy. As a result, Marty had begun to take on adult responsibilities early in life. When he was 14, his father died of a heart attack, leaving Marty to work and take care of others and this manager took over, saying, "It's all up to me now." These young ones longed to leave adult responsibilities to his parents; they felt terrible sadness and grief over his father's death, and now they were activated over the loss of Gary. The manager, along with a few other protectors whom Marty identified later in therapy, worked hard to keep them out of his awareness, causing them to feel ever more silenced and hopeless. In response, another protector felt trapped and furious. In short, Marty's early losses converged with Gary's death, leaving him in a state of tremendous inner turmoil.

When these proactive manager strategies failed and Marty's sadness, hopelessness and fear emerged, then his reactive firefighter protectors would step in, pushing smoking and overeating to numb his pain.

Although these short-term comforts helped him soothe the pain of his exiles, they also exacerbated and maintained his cardiac and lung disease. As he became more familiar with these protectors, he learned to appreciate how each one had a job and helped him function. Some of these parts had helped him keep the family farm afloat when he was a boy coping with his father's illness and death. An example of this is the 14-year-old who had decided to fill his father's shoes to avoid feeling overwhelmed with grief and fear. As Marty's appreciation and understanding grew for this young "manager," he earned enough trust to get access to the exiled boy, the sad one who was so frightened after his father's death. Here is an excerpt of that session.

Marty's eyes were closed with his attention focused inward. He had been talking about running his business without Gary and from there he had become aware of the boy inside him who felt so scared and sad living on the family farm after his father's death. His self-monitoring and our tracking had taught him that these feelings could trigger difficulty breathing. He also had recently become aware that his sad, scared parts activated his firefighters who smoked, ate and otherwise numbed his feelings.

"I feel fear around my stomach, like a knot in my gut," he said, his face pale and grim and his breathing harsh. "I can feel sadness coming up." There was a long pause. "Now, I feel this tightness in my chest and around my throat," he said as he placed his hand on his chest around his heart.

"Is it OK emotionally and physically to feel this right now or is it too much?" I asked. Marty did not answer. He looked like he was holding his breath. "Marty," I said, "Are you feeling overwhelmed?"

He nodded and spoke quietly, his breathing still labored, "Yeah, a little."

"Check inside to see if this part would be willing to turn the volume down a little on these feelings. We don't want him to go away. Just check and see if he's willing to not overwhelm you." Marty quietly focused inward for several minutes, his breathing slowly easing. "Better?" I asked.

"Yeah. I can still feel him around my chest. He's really sad. He doesn't know what's gonna happen to him or the farm. He's worried about his mother and his brothers and sisters. He's scared. He has no one to talk to."

"I can see that you care for him." Marty nods to affirm my statement. I continue, "Invite him to feel your care and concern—your hand on your heart as you listen to him inside."

Marty continued to focus inward through a long silence. Holding his hand to his heart, then he began to choke up. "I *really feel* for him!" As tears streamed down his face, he signaled to me that he was OK by patting the air with his hand.

After a few moments of quiet in which Marty wept, I asked, "Is he aware that you're here really feeling for him?"

"Sort of. I feel him there." As he pressed his hand to his chest, he said, "I have a kind of image of him. It's dark. It seems like his back is to me. He's still sad, *really* sad, and he doesn't know what he's gonna to do without his father. He misses his dad."

"I can see how much you care about him." Marty nodded. "It's possible to communicate your compassion, even without words," I said. "You can beam it to him like warmth or light, or communicate through your hand on your chest, or any other way that works for you and for him."

With eyes closed and his focus inward, Marty remained quiet for a while. Then tears began to stream down his face again. "He knows I'm here. He's turned around to see me. It's OK. He's relieved. He's crying." Marty trailed off into a long, tearful pause. A minute passed before he spoke. "He needs somebody. He just *needs* somebody!"

"That's right. Take your time. Be there exactly the way he needs you to be," I said.

"He wants his dad. He misses him. He doesn't know what he's gonna do without him." There was a long pause as Marty continued to connect with this part.

"That's right. Stay with him. Invite him to bring it all to you. Be there exactly the way he needs you to be," I said as tears continued to stream down Marty's face.

"I've got him," Marty whispered.

I could see from his face, breathing and body language that what was transpiring between Marty and this 14-year-old boy inside was very tender. I was careful not to disrupt the experience. Sensing no distress, I was attentive but I waited.

"He's so relieved that I'm here with him. He's showing me something in the pumping station at the cranberry bog." There was a long pause. Marty looked alert but calm. His eyes remained closed as he described what was happening in his inner world. "There's a problem with the machinery but he's not sure what to do. He's so overwhelmed. He doesn't know where to begin. He misses his dad! He feels lost. It's too much for him. He's just a kid. He needs his dad!" Marty broke into sobs.

"Marty . . ." I started to speak to make sure it was OK for Marty to feel such strong emotion. But before I could get the words out, he held a hand up to signal that he was OK and I could let him continue without interruption. I waited, trusting Marty's Self.

"He feels ashamed crying in front of me. He feels like a big baby. He doesn't think anyone wants to know how he feels. He's *so* alone. He doesn't feel like he deserves . . ." the words trailed off. "He doesn't feel like he deserves my love," Marty whispered. "He's afraid I'm going to leave him, too."

"What do you want to tell him about that?" I ask.

"I understand how he feels. He's right! Nobody there knows how to talk to him about anything that matters. I'm letting him know that I'm not going anywhere." Marty paused. "He's right here with me now. I've got him," he said.

THE INTERNAL FAMILY SYSTEM AND ADULT HEALTH **137**

"Invite him to feel your energy and to take it in," I said encouragingly. After several minutes passed, I saw Marty's face and body relax. "How's he responding to that?" I asked.

"He's calmer—relieved. He's beginning to trust that I really want to hear whatever he needs to tell me."

"That's great," I said. "As you tune in to him like this, see if there's more that he needs right now."

"He needs me to stay with him, to *be* with him," Marty said definitively. "I'm getting flashes of different moments—lots of scenes. I'm there with him." Several minutes passed. Marty was concentrating. His eyes remained closed. He was sitting in relaxed stillness in a green chair across from mine, tears quietly sliding down his cheeks again. I waited without interrupting.

Once Marty began to stir, I quietly asked, "How's it going?"

"It has all sort of slowed down. There was a lot happening for a while—things that I had forgotten about. He showed me some of the funeral and what happened after—what it was like for him. I could feel his pain and confusion."

"Find out if there's more that he needs you to know or to see," I said. I waited while Marty went back to the boy again.

"He doesn't have more to *show* me. He just wants to stay with me."

"What do you tell him about that?" I asked.

"I'm staying right here with him."

"See if he would like to leave that time and place, if he's ready, and go with you?" I asked.

"He's shocked to hear you ask that. He didn't know he could ever leave! He'd love to get out of there but he's worried about leaving his brothers and sisters—and his mom," Marty said as he opened his eyes.

"Is there anything you want to tell him about that?" I asked.

"There is. Give me a minute," Marty closed his eyes and focused inward again. "OK."

"OK?" I asked, surprised.

Hearing my surprise, Marty smiled and opened his eyes to look at me as he said, "I told him that they'd be OK. I reassured him that everyone was going to be fine. I told him that I could show him."

"So, he's ready to leave now?" I asked knowing that I could trust Marty's judgment.

"He's ready."

"Bring him someplace where he can release all the burdens that he's been carrying. Someplace that would feel just right for him—wherever he'd like. He could release them into water, wind, light, earth, fire or anything else that works for him," I said guiding Marty and the 14-year-old boy through the unburdening process.

"He wants to release them into Vineyard Sound from my skiff," Marty informed me. "We've dropped the anchor and he's standing on the bow in front of me. There's a southwest breeze. He's got his back to the wind and he's letting them go into the wind and water."

"Invite him to name the burdens as he releases them. Like his loneliness . . ." I trailed off as Marty picked up on this and continued.

"The overwhelmed, feeling like a baby, the pain and sadness, shame—lots of shame."

"Make sure he gets it all. Encourage him to check his body for more," I said.

"He's letting the fear of being left alone go now and the feeling that it was his fault, the weight of it all on his chest and shoulders! "

"Anything else?" I asked.

"The metallic taste in his mouth when they told him that his dad had passed and the emptiness in his gut."

"Invite him to notice how it feels as the wind and water take it all away," I said, watching expressions of relief cross Marty's face. "Anything more?" Marty shook his head.

"He's standing on the bow still. He's taking in the light on the water. It's like he's been carrying around a boulder that just got lifted off his chest. He can stand up straight. He feels freer than he ever has. And, I feel like *I* can breathe easier now that he's doing better."

In our next session, Marty said, "I feel less clogged up in my chest and not so tense anymore." Over the next few sessions Marty connected with the parts who had either been protecting the adolescent boy from further injury, or protecting the rest of Marty's internal system from his emotional pain. Their roles were designed to keep his grief, fear and shame exiled. These protectors needed to know that this sad adolescent was no longer stuck in the past. Knowing that he had released the burdens that he had been carrying all the years since his father's death, and that he had Marty to guide him going forward would help to free them from their rigid protective roles. These protectors could potentially become more flexible and less extreme in their mode of operating now. They needed to develop a trusting relationship with Marty, as well and to know that his Self was there for them, too.

Marty invited one of these, the 14-year-old protector who had felt driven to fill his father's shoes, to see how the sad boy was doing now.

"Ah!" Marty chuckled. "He says he never thought he'd see the day."

"What day?" I asked.

"The day someone would find that boy and help him," Marty said, more serious now.

"How does that affect him?" I asked.

"Well, now that you mention it, he's wondering what he should be doing."

"So he doesn't feel he has to go on keeping all of your emotional and physical needs at bay?" Marty nodded. "Well, what would he like to do?"

"He'd like a vacation."

"OK with you?"

"Yeah! He deserves one."

Once this protector's rejection of help from others softened, Marty's symptoms were affected in a number of ways. Perhaps most important, he felt less depressed and more hopeful. "I used to say, 'Life stinks and then you die.' And part of me really felt that way. It used to say to me, 'What's the point? Take me out now and save me the trouble, why don't ya?' It doesn't talk like that anymore. I want to stick around and have a good life."

To have that good life, Marty began to notice and take care of his own needs. He tuned into fatigue; rested when he got tired; worked less and accepted the help, support and love from his wife, family and friends that he would previously have rejected. His wife noticed that he was less angry and was sharing more with her and the rest of the family. He had started talking about the future again and was discussing the business with her, one of his sons-in-law, and his daughter-in-law, Karen, Gary's widow. Marty had begun to involve Karen in the administrative aspects of the construction business, which Gary had been covering before he died. Marty said he was "testing the waters" with his son-in-law and considering offering him a significant role in the company. One evening after a session, Marty's wife confided in me that he seemed much more relaxed—playing with the grandchildren and enjoying the family. She reported feeling closer to him than she had in a long time.

Soon after this Marty was ready to quit smoking and did so quickly. Unburdening an exile like his grief-stricken boy is usually essential to changing a habit like smoking. In Marty's case, the unburdening released his polarized protectors, the stoic manager who tried to fill his father's shoes by working endless hours and the angry, resentful firefighter who wanted less work. Then the part who believed Marty could only truly be free when he died began to see other possibilities. As the promise of living a life beyond work, self-sacrifice and loss seemed possible, attending to self-care and quitting smoking made more sense to Marty's system.

Marty developed a different take on the emotional life of his parts, too, which he explained like this, "Once I knew that boy and realized it was a part of me that I *cared* about, something changed. Don't get me wrong, I'm never gonna be Rod McKuen. I just don't have to smoke or work myself to death, or get mad so that I won't have to admit I'm tired or having trouble keeping up at work. I'm not running around anymore, knocking myself out doing everything for everybody, trying to keep things under control inside and out."

This instinct to "keep things under control" is characteristic of patients whose parts are desperately trying to manage historically based feelings of responsibility, abandonment, grief and fear. These are patients for whom IFS therapy holds much promise—of healing their destructive (but well-intentioned) habits and often their physical ailments. IFS is not about dominating or getting rid of our parts, but rather accepting them while becoming

Self-led. We would no more condemn that vulnerable and desperate teenage Marty than we should the adult behaviors resulting from that young part's wounds.

Even when a disease or injury cannot be cured, it's still possible through therapy work with parts to develop a healing relationship between the Self, the body, the internal family and the external world. A desire to heal rather than control or manage symptoms motivated me to use IFS with my own illness. And because stress, adverse childhood experience, personality traits, negative beliefs and thoughts, lack of exercise, poor nutrition and smoking have all been linked to physical illness, it made sense to me that IFS could be effective in conjunction with medical treatment.

IFS is concerned with knowing and befriending all of who we are. The enormous energy used by protective parts to keep physical and emotional suffering from awareness can be liberated, and the psychic roller coaster attendant to pain and disease can slow down. When it does, we are more able to experience the present moment. Inner conflicts, such as stoicism repressing fear and sadness, can be resolved. As internal conflict softens and vulnerability is transformed, self-care naturally improves. In meeting the challenge of acknowledging and welcoming all of ourselves, we realize that we have the power to soothe and heal our own bodies and hearts and enter more fully into life.

REFERENCES

Archie, E.A., Altmann, J., & Alberts, S.C. (2012). Social status predicts wound healing in wild baboons. *Proceedings of the National Academy of Science, 109,* 9017–9022. doi: 10.1073/pnas.1206391109

Deimling, G.T., Wagner, L.J., Wagner, L.J., Bowman, K.F., Sterns, S., Kercher, K., & Kahana, B. (2006). Coping among older adult, long-term cancer survivors. *Psycho-Oncology, 15*(2), 143–159. doi: 10.1002/pon.931

Eaker, E.D., Sullivan, L.M., Kelly-Hayes, M., D'Agostino, R.B., & Benjamin, E.J. (2004). Anger and hostility predict the development of atrial fibrillation in men in the Framingham Offspring Study. *Circulation, 109,* 1267–1271.

Everson, S.A., Goldberg, D.E., Kaplan, G.A., Cohen, R.D., Pukkala, E., Tuomilehto, J., & Salonen, J. (1996). Hopelessness and risk of mortality and incidence of myocardial infarction and cancer. *Psychosomatic Medicine, 58,* 113–121.

Feeney, J.A. (2000). Implications of attachment style for patterns of health and illness. *Child: Care, Health, and Development, 26,* 277–288.

Felitti, V.J., Anda, R.F., Nordenberg, D., Williamson, D.F., Spitz, A., Edwards, V., Koss, M. P., & Marks, J.S. (1998). Relationship of childhood abuse and household dysfunction to many of the leading causes of death in adults: The Adverse Childhood Experiences Study. *American Journal of Preventative Medicine, 14*, 245–258.

Haukkala, A., Konttinen, H., Laatikainen, T., Kawachi, I., & Uutela, A. (2010). Hostility, anger control, and anger expression as predictors of cardiovascular disease. *Psychosomatic Medicine, 72*, 556–562.

Kiecolt-Glaser, J. K., Loving, T. J., Stowell, J. R., Malarkey, W. B., Lemeshow, S., Dickenson, S. L., & Glaser, R. (2005). Hostile marital interactions, proinflammatory cytokine production, and wound healing. *Archives of General Psychiatry, 62*, 1377–1384.

Kotler, T., Buzwell, S., Romeo, Y., & Bowland, J. (2011). Avoidant attachment as a risk factor for health. *British Journal of Medical Psychology, 67*, 237–245. doi: 10.1111/j.2044–8341.1994.tb01793.x

McWilliams, L. A., & Bailey, S. J. (2010). Associations between adult attachment ratings and health conditions: Evidence from the National Comorbidity Survey replication. *Health Psychology, 29*, 446–453. doi: 10.1037/a0020061

Moos, R. H., & Holahan, C. J. (2003). Dispositional and contextual perspectives on coping: Toward and integrative framework. *Journal of Clinical Psychology, 59*, 1387–1403. doi: 10.1002/jcip.10229

Romans, S., Belaise, C., Martin, J., Morris, E., & Raffi, A. (2002). Childhood abuse and later medical disorders in women. *Psychotherapy and Psychosomatics, 71*, 141–150. doi: 10.1159/000056281

Sapolsky, R. M. (2005). The influence of social hierarchy on primate health. *Science, 8*(5722), 648–652. doi: 10.1126/science.1106477

Shadick, N. A., Sowell, N. F., & Schwartz, R. C. (2010, April). *The living well with rheumatoid arthritis program: A randomized controlled trial of a psychotherapeutic intervention to reduce rheumatoid arthritis disease activity.* Paper and poster abstract presented at the 31st annual meeting of the Society of Behavioral Medicine, Seattle, WA.

IFS AND HEALTH COACHING: A NEW MODEL OF BEHAVIOR CHANGE AND MEDICAL DECISION MAKING

John B. Livingstone and Joanne Gaffney

INTRODUCTION

Illness often calls for the assimilation of complicated medical information and requires making tough medical decisions and difficult changes in habits of self-care. This, in turn, can activate fear, anxiety and confusion in patients and equally strong reactions in family members and health care professionals, putting patients on an emotional roller coaster ride. If we consider the patient, her supports and her medical professionals as one system, we can see that this system can fall under significant stress at just the time when calm, clarity and collaboration would best serve the patient's interests.

Medical and public health professionals agree that behavior change is crucial to prevent and manage chronic conditions (e.g., obesity, diabetes, arthritis) and improve the quality of treatment decisions for complex medical conditions (e.g., cancer, coronary arterial disease). But despite 50 years of academic research on behavior change and more than 15 years of academic research on medical decision making, sound evidence about how to accomplish these goals is sparse. To date, the cognitive paradigm in psychology has dominated the agenda of this research, omitting the pivotal roles of emotion and interpersonal dynamics in both patient behavior and treatment outcome (Livingstone & Gaffney, 2011).

Despite the dominance of the cognitive paradigm, the importance of emotion and relationships in patient care is well established. We know that emotional reactivity compromises intake of new information (Sanbonmatsu, Uchino, & Birmingham, 2011) and affects decision making (Lowenstein & Lerner, 2003). We also know that relational dynamics can trump intellect and information (LeBlanc, Keeny, O'Connor, & Legare, 2009). The presence of an emotional connection with the health care provider is the gateway for patients, including the parents of young patients, to assimilate new medical information (Livingstone, Portnoi, Sherry, Rosenheim, & Onesti, 1969).

Yet the current medical system continues to separate the physical from the emotional and cognitive, focusing on physical symptoms with little time and attention given to how thoughts, beliefs and feelings impact bodily states and health behavior. The two national initiatives in patient-centered care, which were designed to lower costs, and remedy gaps in patient care (Institute of Medicine [IOM], 2001) and shared decision making (Braddock, 2010; Ottawa Decision Support Framework, 2006; Zikmund-Fisher et al., 2010), have not been widely implemented because they do not include ways for clinicians to effectively navigate the internal and interpersonal forces that impact their daily work. Medical care and the modality of health coaching would, in our view, improve with a paradigm shift, for which we offer one option.

This chapter illustrates a model of health and wellness coaching called self-aware informational nonjudgmental health coaching (SINHC™), an IFS-based coaching model that integrates the IFS approach of *direct access* with our new process *Information Interweave*™. We view health coaching as a modality rather than as a profession and consider SINHC an essential component skill. The concepts and clinical methods of the internal family systems model (IFS) have arrived at a fortuitous moment in the evolution of patient care. Many nurses have already learned components of SINHC, and we believe that a wide variety of health professionals could usefully add these skills to their education and training, for example, primary care physicians, physician assistants, physical therapists and medical social workers. Although the use of SINHC to provide "medical decision support" requires some knowledge about diseases and treatments, we believe that creative training programs, good informational databases and partnering with physician specialists will fulfill this requirement. Successful pilot studies indicate that additional research on health coaching is warranted (Appel et al., 2011; Wennberg, Marr, Lang, O'Malley, & Bennett, 2010; Wolever et al., 2010), and the specificity and clarity of SINHC methods should enable well-designed comparative studies to be conducted on its effectiveness.

Although direct access, one of the approaches sometimes used in IFS treatment, can sound like ordinary conversation to the outside observer, the SINHC-trained coach who is using it is actually listening for the feelings and beliefs of the patient's personality part(s) (hereafter referred to simply as *part*). Throughout the SINHC process, while remaining within the patient's comfort zone, the coach will engage the patient's parts with interest and concern but will not offer alternative beliefs, feelings or advice. Her goal is to honor and validate the part(s) who then tends to soften and becomes willing to differentiate from the patient's Self. This process, called *unblending*, helps other parts to relax and can often be observed in shifts of the patient's tone and vocal intensity. The coach notes these shifts as well as the level of connection between her and the patient and then assesses the readiness of the patient for new information. As the patient appears ready, the coach communicates evidence-based information in a manner that connects to activated parts and matches the patient's pace, literacy and cognitive style.

Our goal in creating SINHC was to offer health care professionals, including nurses and doctors, effective tools for meeting the needs of patients who must make behavioral changes to regain their health, or who face the emotional challenges inherent in making choices about their medical care. Health professionals also have reactive parts and often feel frustrated when the treatment option viewed by the patient as most desirable yesterday is rejected today, or when an accepted surgical procedure evokes postoperative dissatisfaction and remorse. The daily stress of delivering care and interfacing with vulnerable patients can stir up feelings of helplessness and the urge to manage both the patient's choices and his feelings about illness. Yet contradictory behaviors in patients are not solved by additional information because they are not based on logic or rationality. They come from the feelings and beliefs of parts who are activated within the patient. In our experience, health professionals are often unaware of the emotions and behavioral tendencies aroused within them by patients. This is a blind spot that increases stress, compromises the professional's ability to empathize with the patient and blocks discernment of the patient's true needs. SINHC is specifically designed to provide health professionals with pathways to work with their own parts as well as with those of patients.

This chapter illustrates how the interviewing protocol of SINHC helps the coach as well as the patient discover and work with feelings, beliefs and action tendencies that affect health behavior change and decision making. To be clear, we use the terms *health coach*, *coach*, and *interviewer* interchangeably to refer to any health professional who learns and practices SINHC. The range of issues presented to health coaches is broad and includes any problem that appears to be associated with the patient's health issues. Here are some examples: a nursing home resident has been reported for resisting rehabilitation; the mother of a child has terminal cancer and is experiencing marital tension; a woman has had several miscarriages and is confused about whether to have amniocentesis; a man has quit taking his beta blockers because they make him feel depressed; a patient cannot decide which treatment (for breast cancer, prostate cancer, angina, etc.) is best for him or her. The SINHC protocol is not linear. It guides the interviewer to start by connecting with the patient's affect and exploring the concerns of the activated parts rather than focusing right away on medical facts, such as the importance of continuing on beta blockers. SINHC creates a road map between coach and patient, which helps them stay connected as the patient's needs are revealed. The interview may move well beyond medical concerns and parts to other relevant factors, including difficult economic and environmental circumstances and the insensitive behaviors of relatives or care providers.

SUMMARY OF THE SINHC PROCESS

Before starting an interview the coach becomes grounded in her body and notices her own parts (McConnell, this volume). Holding the intention to keep these parts relaxed and unintrusive, she maintains a double awareness of the patient's internal system and her own. Using this self-awareness during the interview, she checks frequently but briefly on any of her own parts who could interfere with her coaching goals, promising to listen to their concerns later. Her initial goal, in addition to feeling open and grounded, is to establish a connection with the patient's parts(s). Although protector parts often show up first, the patient may lead with vulnerable parts. The coach accepts all vulnerability with compassion but, in the initial contact, will refrain from stimulating any more emotion to keep vulnerable parts from blending, or overwhelming the patient.

The coach tracks the patient's internally generated conflicts as well as those activated by family or medical providers. To increase the patient's self-awareness, she expresses curiosity about the meaning of his emotional tone, sighs, pauses and any storyline contradictions. When opportunity arises, the coach encourages him to identify his feelings but may not call them "parts." Rather than providing him with answers, she stays affectively connected, follows clues and explores his parts' concerns. Emotional readiness for more information tends to emerge after parts have been acknowledged and met with understanding and compassion. Guided by the patient's readiness, the coach does the Information Interweave by offering small chunks of pertinent medical information.

Although training in SINHC includes learning some core concepts of IFS and some terminology, the coach refrains from teaching the IFS language to patients. Nevertheless, when the need arises and will serve the goals of self-awareness and unblending from extreme parts, some terms are used. For example, if the patient says he feels angry and scared about the diagnosis, the coach may respond, "I am hearing that one part of you is feeling angry and another part is feeling scared about the diagnosis. Does that sound accurate?" The interviewer stays close to the patient's language and feelings, affirming that it is normal to feel ambivalence and have conflicting agendas when making medical decisions and changing behavior (Table 9.1).

Table 9.1 SINHC™ Components

Internal strategies in coach (a through e) (Before starting and throughout)	Interpersonal strategies (1 through 11) (Leading priorities)
a. Connect with a sense of openness/relaxation in mind/body and hold intention to maintain this.	1. Make affective, open energetic contact with the patient.
b. Be aware of the agendas (goals/internal purposes) that might belong to your health care manager parts as different from the agendas of the patient's parts, without letting your activated parts be in the lead.	2. Build attuned connection with patient's presenting parts and find words for emotions.
c. Notice your internal reactions to the patient's specific illness and his attitudes and choices.	3. Begin tracking emotions, content and agendas of the different parts.
d. Focus on maintaining a double awareness with curiosity and compassion toward your internal system and that of the patient.	4. Establish clarity with the patient about the agenda of the meeting and integrate 1, 2, 3 of the above priorities until there is a sense of agreement between you and the patient about the focus of the contact.
e. Notice any internal reactions that signify which part of you has been activated by what the patient is saying about their relatives and care providers.	5. Create an opening for and acceptance of the patient's vulnerability; name it without expanding it or pulling for more.
	(Used in flexible order as indicated by the patient's process)
	6. Interweave credible information guided by the receptivity of the patient.
	7. Invite identification and exploration of beliefs, emotions, responsibilities of parts of the patient, particularly when they conflict or get activated during the interview.
	8. Invite identification and some exploration of conflicting priorities generated by relationships with care providers and family.
	9. Identify and explore factors supporting internal motivation for specific behavior changes and decision making.
	10. Identify and explore cultural, economic and environmental influences.
	11. Establish agreement with patient's parts on an action plan, on follow-up contacts, and referral to a therapist when appropriate.

CLINICAL EXAMPLES

The following three examples are an amalgam of frequent health predicaments that require behavior change and decision making. At key points in each health coaching interview below, we point out which components of SINHC are being used by referring to Table 9.1 above.

Example 1: Behavior Change in Diabetes: "I'm Ready to Give Up"

The vulnerability inherent in life threatening chronic illness is striking. We have heard newly diagnosed diabetes patients express feelings of outrage, betrayal, shock, fear, grief or numbness. From the perspective of IFS, different parts hold these feelings. We have observed physicians and coaches reacting to these same patients with disconnected reassurance, inventories of scientific facts and lectures about complications. In our experience, diabetic patients who are referred for noncompliance provoke intense judgments and are labeled "resistant." A health professional who is motivated by a part intent on teaching facts to diabetic patients will miss the opportunity to connect with the patient's parts. But it is exactly these parts in the patient who determine whether new information will be taken in and whether changes in health behaviors will occur. The diagnosis of diabetes 2 is life changing. Because it affects the entire body, with potentially life threatening complications involving the heart, blood vessels, eyes and kidneys, it requires many specific behavioral changes to lower health risks. In the beginning, the need to track physical issues and institute changes may feel overwhelming for the patient. Areas of concern include four physical items that need to be followed: blood pressure, cholesterol, AIC (average three to four month blood glucose) and renal function; and four behavioral changes to be made: lose weight, increase physical activity, modify nutrition and quit smoking. The clinical vignette below illustrates the use of SINHC with a patient who had a recent onset of diabetes 2.

The patient, a 55-year-old widow speaking on the phone with her SINHC-trained coach, expressed frustration (a part) over wide oscillations in her blood sugar scores. Although her primary care doctor had assured her that wide oscillations in sugar level were normal at this point in managing her illness and had urged her to focus on monitoring blood pressure, changing diet and quitting cigarettes, she said to the coach, "My sugar scores are ridiculous compared to my sister's. I'm ready to give up" (a part). Before responding, the coach checked her own internal state. She noticed tightness in her chest, which was making it hard to breathe fully and feel grounded in her body. By checking inside she realized that one of her own parts had tensed in response to the patient saying she was ready to give up (see Table 9.1: Internal strategy c). She was familiar with this part. It protected her from feeling like a failure, an issue from her childhood. The coach also had an older sister and was familiar with another one of her parts who felt competitive. She recognized that her parts had been activated by the part of the patient who was similar. She put her hand on her chest, allowing its pressure to open her breathing and settle her body. She acknowledged each of her parts, saying, "I'm here. I'll check with you later. Right now I'm going to do my job." She felt her chest open and her breathing begin to move again. Now she became fully curious about her patient's experience (see Table 9.1: Internal strategy e). First she helped the patient label her feelings, saying, "It sounds like you feel frustrated and discouraged—is that close?" The patient agreed. So the coach asked, "What is the most important thing about your scores being different from your sister's scores?" (see Table 9.1: Interpersonal 2, 3, 8).

The patient stopped to think before replying, "She's always been ahead of me. We didn't really get to be friends until we grew up. I'm afraid she'll deal with her illness and I won't."

The coach checked inside to see how she was reacting to the patient now (see Table 9.1: Internal b). She noticed curiosity and compassion. "Can you tell me more about this fear?" (see Table 9.1: Interpersonal strategy 5).

"My grandmother had to have her leg amputated because of diabetes. It was awful," the patient said.

"So does it make sense for you to feel scared?" the coach asked (see Table 9.1: Interpersonal 5).

"Yes, my sister was told that if she didn't get her blood sugar under control, her circulation would be affected and she could lose both her legs."

"It's really important for us to be aware of all your fears," the coach said. "And when we talk about something scary, we can slow down to notice what's happening in your body because that's where feelings start."

"It's kind of hard to breathe when I think about having my legs cut off," the patient said.

"Would it be OK just to breathe calmly together for a minute, then?" (see Table 9.1: Interpersonal 5).

"Yes, I'll try it."

"OK. Let's slow down. Notice that you are inhaling and then slowly turn it around and exhale. Now take a deep breath letting it go all the way inside. Then let it out slowly. How're you doing?"

"Better. My heart is slower. I feel calmer."

Sensing that the patient might now be ready for Information Interweave, the coach asked, "Would you be open to hearing about research on circulation and blood sugar? You may have already heard it and if you forgot that's OK"

With the patient's consent, the coach explained, in user-friendly terms, research indicating that other issues such as blood pressure and blood cholesterol are more associated with peripheral vascular disease than daily fluctuations in blood sugar. She added that fluctuations in numbers for sugar level were common in the beginning of regulating blood sugar. Then she said, "To be sure I'm clear, would you let me know if what I just said made sense?" (see

Table 9.1: Interpersonal 6). The patient sighed with relief and repeated the pertinent research findings.

The coach, aware that relational dynamics often trump credible information, then asked, "What is it like to hear that your sister didn't understand all this information?" (see Table 9.1: Interpersonal 8).

"I feel irritated," the patient replied. "And I guess surprised too. She always sounds right."

"Irritated and surprised," the coach repeated. "What is it like to pay attention to these feelings?"

"Oh it helps me slow down. I see I'm just beginning to learn about diabetes and I know my sister wants to help. There's so much for both of us to learn—it can be overwhelming."

"Would written information about complications be helpful?" the coach asked (see Table 9.1: Interpersonal 6).

"I'm open to learning more," the patient replied.

The coach did not tell the patient to stop smoking or change her diet at this point, however. She offered to send her written information and a DVD that they could go over another time. Because the interview was almost over and the coach knew that acknowledging extreme statements lowers the risk of maladaptive behavior, she returned to the patient's opening statement.

"When we began talking, I heard you say you felt like giving up. How are you feeling now?"

"Oh I'll keep checking my blood sugar numbers every day. And I'm going to see my doctor next week. I'll ask her about complications too."

The coach and patient agreed to be in contact as she visited her doctor. They also agreed to focus one by one on the eight items that are key in controlling diabetes over time: four to monitor and four to change. Finally the coach asked, "Would you be interested in joining a group to support your learning?" (see Table 9.1: Interpersonal 11).

"If I could find one near home and maybe one that my sister could come to as well, I think I'd like to try it."

In a 55-minute encounter this nurse health coach helped the patient process strong emotions and integrate important medical information. In the future, if the patient's busy providers or the group she joined were to disappoint her, she would have this experience as a reminder to call up, not give up.

Example 2: Decision Crisis in Coronary Disease: "Just as Soon Be Done With It"

People with coronary arterial disease (CAD) and the chest pain of angina face possible sudden heart attack and death. Treatment decisions are urgent and complex. It is common for patients to feel overwhelmed by the information they need to assimilate while feeling extremely vulnerable. Culture and custom, family and career factors all affect options and behavior change. A health coach can hold the time and space a patient needs to process emotions and beliefs, then hear and sort out evidence-based information to make a "good enough" decision.

This 59-year-old schoolteacher was the father of two school-age children. He lived in a rural community, was in a second marriage and had debilitating angina. He initiated the first encounter with the health coach, a former intensive care unit (ICU) nurse, saying he "only" wanted more information about angina (presenting part). He said he had spoken with his primary care doctor; what he heard scared him and he had already scheduled a consultation with a cardiologist. They scheduled a follow-up call. He started this second telephone coaching encounter, which followed his first session with the cardiologist who had supplied him with abundant information on his condition and treatment options, by saying, "I'm not enjoying my life very much; I'd just as soon be done with it."

The coach responded, "You're not enjoying your life. What is it like to feel that you could be done with it?" (see Table 9.1: Interpersonal 2). At the same time the coach noticed her own body stiffening and identified a managerial part who had the agenda of saving his life. She went inside for about seven seconds and asked this part to soften so she could stay with the patient's unhappiness and hopelessness (see Table 9.1: Internal c, d). Knowing that the patient's opening statement came from one part, she wanted to hear more of his story.

But first she helped him find words that fit his emotions, "It sounds like the words 'discouraged' and 'hopeless' might fit what you're feeling about having so much information and having angina pain—what is your sense?" She did not try to talk him out of this state with facts about successful treatment nor did she ask about past experiences of surmounting discouragement. Instead she held space and time for his feelings without rushing him (see Table 9.1: Interpersonal 5).

The patient then shifted and began to describe how talking to the cardiologist about treatment options had left him feeling confused and hopeless. "When he started listing the survival rates, I felt completely overwhelmed and realized I would never be able to sort it all out," he reported.

"Is that what you meant when you said you feel 'done with it'?" she asked. When he confirmed, she went on, "What words would best describe your experience with the cardiologist?" (see Table 9.1: Interpersonal 5). He thought for a moment before answering, "Confused—disappointed—annoyed—hurried."

"You know I've talked with a lot of folks in your position and that response is not uncommon. All of that information and pressure to decide can be overwhelming."

He let out a sigh and said, "It was daunting."

She repeated, "Daunting." Then to explore and track his parts, she asked, "What was the hardest thing about your conversation with the cardiologist?"

He replied, "It was the pressure to make a decision quickly because I could die. And then he can't guarantee relief from the angina anyway. I wanted to make a decision but I just couldn't."

She asked, "What's the most important thing about your angina?" (see Table 9.1: Interpersonal 5, 7).

"It's about my daily life. My boys love soccer and want me to play with them and my wife likes having sex—so do I. Right now I'm failing them all."

The coach helped him find a feeling word for this thought. It was "sad." She acknowledged the emotion and also the importance for him of being active with his sons and wife. She held the space for him to honor what was important and then asked whether "more information about relief from angina might be useful at this point" (see Table 9.1: Interpersonal 6).

"Yes," he replied.

She knew that the cardiologist would have given him most of the information already, and she heard that he was stuck on the disclaimer about no guarantee of relief from angina. She explained slowly that all possible choices (meds alone, bypass, angioplasty, bypass surgery) offered some angina relief, and bypass offered the most. She had looked this up ahead of time so she would not disrupt their connection by reading it to him from her database. As he heard the information, he felt surprised, which moved to his next concern: that he would die during bypass surgery. "One day that's my biggest fear," he said. "The next day it's about a stroke and failing my family. Then the next day I'm terrified if I don't do something right now I'll die from a massive heart attack on the soccer field or while having sex."

"What is all this like for you?" she asked.

"Crazy making!" he said. "How can I decide? My wife wants to go the angioplasty route because she's afraid of heart surgery. But if I don't get angina relief with angioplasty, I'll have to do the bypass someday anyway. It's too much!"

"It makes sense that you have many different feelings and responses. Your wife has strong feelings too. All of this may not feel good, but you are in a normal process of making the decision that will be good enough for you and all your emotions and priorities; it's a process that needs enough time and consideration. But it usually saves time to take the time" (see Table 9.1: Interpersonal 7). "Let's go over the story so far. Tell me if this seems right. For you, an active life is very important. You also take responsibilities seriously. You don't want to die and leave your children without a father and your wife without a partner."

"No I don't. That's what happened to me. My father died when I was eight."

"So you are recalling that experience? Anything you want to share right now about it?"

"It was like a hole in my heart," he said.

She acknowledged the intensity of his feeling. "Does it make sense this decision would be extra hard for you?" she asked (see Table 9.1: Interpersonal 5).

"Yes," he said.

As important as traumatized parts are, the adult who needs to make a decision in the here and now is at a disadvantage when blended with vulnerable young parts, so the goal of the coach was to stay with the present. At the same time she was aware that he might not be able to unblend from his vulnerability right now. So while they talked, she was evaluating the need to make an immediate referral for therapy. If he were able to unblend enough now, she would remember to offer him information about IFS therapy at a later time (see Table 9.1: Interpersonal 11). To see if he could stay in the present, she asked, "Would it be OK to ask your feelings about your father's death to step back right now, letting them know that you are not forgetting them and setting the intention to come back when you have time?"

When he agreed, she returned to a respectful review of the conflicts between his parts about his treatment choices—a process of "shared decision making" guided by SINHC. As they neared the end of the appointment, she offered, "We can speak again soon to summarize all this. It usually helps to go over each option and assess how you feel one step at a time with just as much medical information as you may need for each step" (see Table 9.1: Interpersonal 6).

"Here's what I want to know," he said. "How can I reduce my chances of dying during bypass surgery? And what is the best choice to decrease angina? Then I need to talk with my wife."

"OK, I'm hearing that you are clear about what you want to know," she replied. "Shall we talk again this week to develop questions for the cardiologist and your primary care doctor so you can get this information at a pace that is reasonable for you?" (see Table 9.1: Interpersonal 9).

They followed this phone call with four more sessions, each about 30 minutes, over a period of three weeks. The patient returned to his doctors with specific questions to slow the process down and to assimilate what research showed: a 98 percent survival rate for bypass teams that were doing over 400 cases per year, with a 95 percent chance of not having a heart attack and a 99 percent chance of not having a stroke from the procedure. Angina relief was 90 percent five years out from bypass but only 80 percent with angioplasty. At the same time, bypass has a 10 percent to 30 percent chance of causing cognitive impairment that could persist for five years. Having learned that all CAD patients need medication in any case, the patient also needed to process his reaction to the potential side effects of over eight medications, for example, statins, angiotensin-converting enzyme inhibitors, calcium channel blockers and so forth. He processed many pieces of this kind of unnerving information with the coach and some with his doctors.

In a joint telephone call, the coach helped both the patient and his wife to start speaking for their fears rather than to act them out (see Table 9.1: Interpersonal 8). His wife shared that her uncle had died on the table during surgery for a heart condition. After the coach interwove some relevant statistical information, the wife stated, "That sounds much better than I expected. My uncle's surgery was a long time ago." She was encouraged to continue honoring her fear verbally, and the patient was encouraged to listen with compassion but without blending with her fearful part or with his part who wanted to rescue her from feeling fear.

Once the patient had listened to his wife's fears as well as his own feelings and beliefs about his options and risks, the decision could unfold as the product of a holistic process. He said, "I guess I've heard from most of the feelings of my parts and I understand the information."

He chose coronary bypass at the city hospital. However it might turn out, he had a strong sense that he had considered all the essential information and had done his best to be prepared emotionally and relationally. This shared, "good enough" decision was a product of the SINHC coaching process.

Example 3: A Decision About Having Cervical Spine-Fusion Surgery: "Upset and Confused"

A patient who is in a state of vulnerability from pain and physical limitations is likely to be very frightened when shown structural malformations in a spinal X-ray and an MRI. Under such circumstances the patient will tend to believe the doctor's interpretation of the malformations along with whatever prognosis is offered, even if the doctor does not understand how the patient's lifestyle and history could affect the prognosis and is therefore not well prepared to orchestrate shared decision making. Lack of communication about the patient's needs may make it hard, in turn, for the patient to give consent for treatment that is truly well informed.

In this example, a 65-year-old woman thought she needed to make an urgent decision about cervical spinal fusion surgery. She had spinal congenital stenosis with ankylosing spondylitis and bulging discs that extended from her lumbar to her neck region, for which a metal rod that stabilized her spine from her lumber to thoracic region had been successfully inserted. Although she had a good relationship with her surgical team, a neurosurgeon and an orthopedic surgeon, she had moved to a different city and, feeling worried about numbness, tingling and weakness in both arms, had made an appointment for evaluation with an orthopedic surgeon in her new city.

After reviewing her MRI of two days prior, this new surgeon had recommended immediate cervical surgery to fuse destabilized discs. If she did not do this, he said she would run the risk of irreversible damage. Moreover, she should not drive without a stiff neck support because if she were rear-ended she could be paralyzed. As she left this appointment, she felt upset and confused. She called the health coach and shared her story. The coach validated her presenting dilemma. "I hear the urgency in your voice. It sounds like one part of you is feeling really anxious and is hearing the immediate need for surgery, and another part is confused about this procedure and needs more information about recovery, especially since you live alone with two pets. Is that right?" (see Table 9.1: Interpersonal 2, 7).

"Yes," the patient replied.

"Would it be OK if we slow down and acknowledge these different feelings to see what more they might need you to know?" (see Table 9.1: Interpersonal 3).

"Yes, I'm so upset about the speed of this decision. I don't even know how to plan for it. The surgeon was like a cowboy—he walked in shooting facts from the hip. I had no time to ask questions. Now I need answers but feel I don't have time to get them because he said I have to do this right now."

The patient was well informed about her medical condition and was as actively invested in a healthy recovery as she had been with her former surgery. When the coach asked her how she felt after this experience, she said, "Terrible."

"Do you understand this doctor's diagnosis and recommendations?"

"Well, he's the big expert in reading MRIs. He has a reputation for seeing things that nobody else sees. And, he says that I need surgery now."

"And what is that like for you?" (see Table 9.1: Interpersonal 5).

"He was extremely self-confident and I didn't feel any connection with him. He didn't ask questions about me, or what I might need for recovery; he just told me what I should do and left. Frankly, he scared me. I don't want this surgery but if I need it, at least I want to know what to expect so I can take care of myself afterward. That's also scary. I did get a stiff neck brace for driving."

"That makes very good sense," the coach said. "Would you feel OK about calling the doctor's office to get your questions about surgery and recovery answered?"

The patient said she would do so the next day. In their follow-up call she reported that she did not get her questions answered by the surgeon's staff, instead she felt pressured to schedule the surgery, which she was not ready to do. She felt more anxious.

"What did you discuss in your previous surgery?" the health coach asked (see Table 9.1: Interpersonal, 9).

"It was completely different. You know, I actually travelled to this hospital three years ago to see this surgeon and left without scheduling surgery for another year because he scared me then, too. I saw a bunch of other surgeons at different places and finally scheduled with the ones who seemed concerned about me and explained everything, and then a nurse even called to ask if I had other questions. She was willing to walk me through the surgery and the recovery in detail. They were warm and also confident—and they listened!"

The coach had to work within herself to relax a part who wanted to help the patient (see Table 9.1: Internal a–e). "May I ask how you decided to return to the surgeon here?" she said (see Table 9.1: Interpersonal 8).

"I moved and so I live closer to him now. It's supposed to be the best teaching hospital and he's supposed to be the best at reading MRIs."

"And how important does reputation feel to you right now?" the coach asked (see Table 9.1: Interpersonal 7).

"I guess it's not enough to make me feel confident when he behaves that way. I'm scared and I can't bring myself to schedule surgery with him."

"What do you need to feel as confident now about your treatment as you felt with your previous surgeon?" (see Table 9.1: Interpersonal 7).

"I need surgeons who are willing to answer questions and collaborate. I wish I could speak to my other team about this surgery."

"Can you send your MRI to your former team and have this discussion with them?" (see Table 9.1: Interpersonal 9).

"Wow!" said the patient. "That's exactly what I need to do. I feel better already." Later she reported to the coach that she had an appointment with her former surgeon who had taken a careful history and discovered the following: she had been lifting and bending due to her recent move in ways that aggravated her spinal condition, but because of her move she had resumed physical therapy and the numbness, tingling and weakness in her arms was actually abating. Although he saw the same condition the other surgeon had seen on the MRI, he observed that things were moving in the right direction. Together they reviewed her symptoms and shared the decision that she should schedule surgery immediately if the symptoms got worse, but if she continued to improve she could take some time. This seemed right to her and she now had time to create a post-op recovery plan should she need surgery. At one-year and two-year follow-ups, the patient had continued to improve and did not require further surgical intervention.

As we have seen in the three examples above, coaches are trained to make and maintain affective contact with the patient with a friendly tone and willingness to listen. The coach acknowledges the patient's presenting emotional and cognitive states (parts), leaves space for emerging vulnerability rather than breaking relational contact by switching to an informational mode, facilitates the patient in being aware of internal reactions to medical providers and family members, and acknowledges all emotions and beliefs, including contradictory ones, that the patient experiences about making behavior changes and decisions. In addition, the coach helps the patient to identify cultural and economic influences and to clarify what he wants and needs from health providers now and in the future.

CONCLUSIONS

The key to SINHC coaching lies in a compassionate listener who is clear about her goals guiding activated parts of the patient to unblend. In our experience, unblending decreases unwarranted treatment choices, unstable decisions, postdecision remorse, discontinuation of medication, behavioral paralysis and relational conflict between patients, their providers and families. Internal disagreement between parts inside the patient or between a part of the patient and a part of the health provider is normal yet is often misinterpreted as noncompliance. Repeated polarizations of this kind between healthcare professionals and patients over normal behavior are a loss to health programs for all involved. By decreasing misunderstandings and miscommunications and enhancing information transfer, SINHC can help to increase economic efficiency in health care.

Our health care system has made nationwide efforts to improve the quality of medical decision making as well as the prevention and management of chronic conditions. Despite improvements in evidence-based decision aids (Informed Medical Decision Making, n.d.), these programs continue to be hampered by lack of a valid, comprehensive model that takes account of the emotional, physical, cognitive, intra- and interpersonal experience set in motion by illness and efforts to change health behavior. Going beyond the recent emphasis on relationships and emotional states in behavior change (Donadio, 2011), SINHC is a comprehensive model of health behavior change and decision making for health coaching, evidence-based medicine and patient-centered care that integrates the direct access approach of IFS with Information Interweave and synchronizes the power of attending to emotions, beliefs and bodily sensations with the power of knowledge.

REFERENCES

Appel, L. J., Clark, J. M., Yeh, H.-C., Wang, N.-Y., Coughlin, J. W. Daumit, G., . . . Brancati, F. L. (2011). Comparative effectiveness of weight-loss interventions in clinical practice. *New England Journal of Medicine, 365,* 1960–1968.

Braddock, C. (2010). The emerging importance and relevance of shared decision making in clinical practice. *Journal of Medical Decision Making, 30*(Suppl. 1), 5–7.

Donadio, G. (2011). *Changing behavior.* Boston, MA: Soul Work Press.

Informed Medical Decision Making. *Decision aids.* Boston, MA: Author. Available at http://informedmedicaldecisions.org/shared-decision-making-in-practice/decision-aids/

Institute of Medicine. (2001). *Crossing the quality chasm: A new health system for the twenty-first century.* Washington, DC: National Academies Press.

LeBlanc, A., Keeny, D., O'Connor, A., & Legare, D. (2009). Decision conflict in patients and their physicians: A dyadic approach to shared decision making. *Journal of Medical Decision Making, 29*, 61–68.

Livingstone, J. B., & Gaffney J. (2011). *Health-related behavior change & decision making: Survey of relevant theories, methods and research since 1950.* Available at jlivingstoneservices@comcast.net

Livingstone, J. B., Portnoi, T., Sherry, S. N., Rosenheim, E., & Onesti, S. J. (1969). Comprehensive child psychiatry through a team approach. *Children, 16*(5), 181–186.

Lowenstein, G., & Lerner, J. (2003). The role of affect in decision making. In R. J. Davison, K. R. Scherer, & H. H. Goldsmith (Eds.), *Handbook of affective science* (pp. 619–642). New York, NY: Oxford University Press.

Ottawa Decision Support Framework. (2006). *Ottawa decision support framework to address decisional conflict.* Available at www.decsionaid.ohri.ca/docs/develop/ODSF.pdf

Sanbonmatsu, D., Uchino, B., & Birmingham, W. (2011). On the importance of knowing your partner's views. *Annals of Behavioral Medicine, 41*, 131–137.

Wennberg, D., Marr, A., Lang, L., O'Malley, S., & Bennett, G. (2010). A randomized trial of a telephone care-management strategy. *New England Journal of Medicine, 363*, 1245–1255.

Wolever, R. Q., Dreusicke, M., Fikkan, J., Hawkins, T. V., Yeung, S., Wakefield, J., . . . Skinner, E. (2010). Integrative health coaching for patients with type 2 diabetes: A randomized clinical trial. *The Diabetes Educator, 36*, 629–639.

Zikmund-Fisher, B. J., Couper, M. P., Singer, E., Levin, C. A., Fowler, F. J., Ziniel, S., . . . Fagerlin, A. (2010). The DECISIONS study: A nationwide survey of U.S. adults regarding 9 common medical decisions. *Journal of Medical Decision Making*, 30(Suppl. 1), 20–34.

TREATING PORNOGRAPHY ADDICTION WITH IFS

Nancy Wonder

Internet pornography, which includes violence and sex with children, is a billion dollar industry that generates more revenue than all of professional sports combined (Maltz & Maltz, 2008). Addictive parts can spend hours looking at and forming relationships with erotic images, which can impede an individual's functioning at work and in love. Pornography addiction is physiological and these images are arousing even if someone is not interested (Maltz & Maltz, 2008). As a result, clients can have great difficulty quitting. There is always a strong polarity between the firefighter parts of clients who use pornography and the critical, shaming managers who try to stop them.

A 68-year-old man named Herb came to me for help with a pornography addiction. He wanted to figure out how this addiction had happened and he wanted to stop. He was a bright, educated man who had been given the diagnosis of panic disorder in addition to bipolar disorder in his early 40s. His mother, who also had a diagnosis of bipolar disorder, had disappeared into her bedroom for days at a time throughout his childhood, and he wanted to manage his illness more responsibly. So he left a stressful job to work on computer programming at home. But working at home soon became a problem because he could turn to online pornography whenever he felt frustrated. In addition to losing hours to the computer he also lost interest in having sex with his wife. Herb tried psychotherapy but it had no effect on his addiction.

When I asked Herb to focus on the urge to look at pornographic images, he had a vivid memory of being in first grade and seeing the underpants of his classmate, Sally, when, as she took off her snowsuit, her slacks came off by mistake. Herb had begun fantasizing at night about those white underpants. He had liked this mental picture so much that he invented a multiplying machine that could create as many Sallys in white panties as he wished. At age ten, he had discovered masturbation and quickly learned to enhance the experience by looking at images of movie stars in Parade magazine from the Sunday paper. In high school he found an "electrifying" cache of photographs of women dressed in shorts and tight sweaters or bikini bathing suits behind a panel of loose wallpaper in his bedroom closet. With these images in hand, Herb became a compulsive masturbator, a secret life that generated great shame and precluded interest in real girls. Over the years he masturbated in library stalls after looking at college girls, in adult theaters where he could view people having sex or watch women onscreen disrobing. With the advent of Internet pornography, he continued at home during his first marriage, and, with increased intensity, after the end of his marriage and on into another marriage until his second wife finally confronted him.

As with many who are addicted to pornography, Herb had a hard time locating parts in his body. Instead, he noticed them in his head and at first they could not give Herb any space to be there as well. Early on we met a part called Rational Man. This part did not believe the pornography addict was a part, much less that it was trying to help Herb. "It's pure chemistry," Rational Man said. "A short skirt or panties simply make me feel sex in my crotch."

"If that were the case, what would it mean?" I asked.

"That the urge just has to be controlled," Rational Man said.

"What makes you so sure the urge to look at pornography is not a part who is doing something important for Herb?" I asked, using direct access to speak to Rational Man.

"It's a bad habit that I got into because of my DNA," Rational Man replied. "It's just the way this body is."

"You may be right," I said, "but if it were another part and Herb could help that part, would that be good for you?"

"I suppose so, assuming by 'help' you mean stop it," Rational Man replied.

"Let me explain how I view this," I said. "I believe Herb looks at pornography for a reason, so we could say the porn addiction started as a solution to a problem—and then unfortunately it became a problem, too. My experience says if we can solve the original problem there won't be a need to look at pornography anymore."

"Well," Rational Man said with a shrug, "nothing else helps."

"So it's OK with you if Herb and I ask the part why it urges him to use pornography?" I asked and Herb nodded.

But despite this permission, Herb now noticed a growing fear located, as usual, in his head. When I asked the fear if it would unblend, Herb said, "I feel like this fear is me."

"OK. Can we try inviting the fear to give you the space to be there, too?" I asked.

After some deep breaths, Herb relaxed visibly and reported that he could feel the fear separate a little bit.

"How do you feel toward it?" I asked.

"Interested," he said. After some moments, he reported, "It's afraid of getting caught." Herb validated this concern and assured the part that our therapy was confidential. The fearful part then gave us permission to continue and I asked if he could notice the part who liked white panties.

"I cannot locate it. I just imagine the panties and feel aroused," he said.

"Do you notice anything else?" I asked.

"I notice that I feel really embarrassed talking to you about this," he said.

At this point I decided to map Herb's parts to help the embarrassed part. Mapping is a powerful unblending tool that helps parts to differentiate, which is particularly important with embarrassment and shame. "OK," I said, getting out a clipboard with blank paper and markers, "so right now we know that one part is afraid of getting caught, another loves white panties, and another is embarrassed that you're telling me about it. Can you draw these three parts? What size are they and where are they in relation to each other?" Herb drew a large pink cloud in the center; above the cloud in black he wrote the word *fear* and below he wrote *shame*. "When you look at that what do you notice?" I asked.

"I drew the white panties in pink because pink feels feminine and soft," he said. "The panties are a fluffy, soft cloud I could float on. The cloud is warm and comfortable, like being in the arms of a woman you know and love."

"OK," I said. "What do you notice about the part who feels shame?"

"That part is less clear. I feel it like a fog at the back of my head but I have no image. And this fear has been around since high school; it's a buzzing in the front of my head. If anyone knew that I was jerking off to pornography I would have been the laughing stock of the whole school, but especially the girls," he said. "The fear part would show me the girls looking repulsed and disgusted after finding out what I was doing in secret. It's the worst punishment I could imagine."

At our next session Herb described developing a twitch in his right eye and mild tightness in his chest. He said he had been feeling irritable and anxious after looking at pornographic images on the Internet. "Would it be OK to pay attention to that?" I asked. He nodded. "OK then take a couple of deep breaths and notice the chest pain," I said.

"I am angry that I lost control," Herb said.

"How do you feel toward that anger?" I asked.

"I understand it. This part feels it's important to be in control all the time. It demands that I be perfect. Before I went freelance, my job at the firm was very competitive. I began to have panic attacks when I was preparing a project or had to present my ideas to the group and this part got furious with me."

"What happens when it gets furious?"

"It tells me I'm a failure and a phony and I'll never be able to compete."

"It shames you?"

"Yes," Herb said.

"How old does it think you are?"

Herb, whose eyes were closed, was quiet for a moment. "About 10 years old."

"Can you let the angry part know that you are not the 10-year-old but that you can help the 10-year-old?"

"OK it's relaxing. I don't feel so angry. But now I am noticing anxiety in my chest."

"Would it be OK to focus there?" I asked, anticipating that this anxiety would lead either to the other side of the polarity or to an exiled part who had been chronically shamed.

After a minute Herb reported that the anxious part was afraid of having a panic attack. He had compassion for the part and reported that it always felt inadequate, spent most of its time in hiding and did not want him working in an office with coworkers.

"This part has been ashamed my whole life," he said. "He's telling me he got it from my mother. She was an anxious person but especially about bodies and sex. He just soaked up her shame and embarrassment."

"How old is he?"

"Maybe 6 years old? He's showing me how he feels bad about his genitals."

"How do you feel toward him," I asked.

"I want to tell him that he's fine," Herb said.

"Go ahead."

After Herb explained that there was nothing wrong with his body, the boy perked up. He was not ready to unburden these feelings and questions about himself but he did want to go on showing Herb about his experience. At the end of the session, Herb observed that all sex and intimacy with women evoked feelings of shame. He could only soar into orgasm when he was completely alone.

The next week we went over the parts we had met so far. There was the exile who carried his mother's shame and anxiety about bodies and sexuality; the firefighter who encouraged Herb's addiction to pornography; and then, polarized with this firefighter, there was an intensely critical, shaming manager who attacked Herb for his lack of self-control with pornography (Rosenberg, this volume; Sweezy, this volume). Herb said he could now understand them all. "I really get how much I wanted to help my mother as a child. I could feel her embarrassment and pain," he said. "And I believed her embarrassment meant something about me, that I must be causing it somehow."

"Is there anything else he needs to show you about his experience?"

"Not about this."

"What needs to happen for him now?"

"He just wants to feel love for his mother," Herb reported.

After this session Herb noticed a black hole around his heart that was about the size and shape of a football. "It is something that wants to be a feeling but is hollow instead," he said. Herb noticed this black hole between sessions and, although he was almost too ashamed to speak of having slipped, he finally admitted that he had been using pornography to masturbate again since finding it. I explained to Herb that I expected upticks in addictive behavior to occur as we began to locate and unburden his exiled parts. The challenge for the therapist in a case like this is to not manage the firefighter but instead to calm shaming managers and attend to the exile. We spent a whole session getting to Herb's Self-energy and his ability to feel curious toward this emptiness around his heart, which he discovered held many memories of being shamed in grade and high school. As he started to work on historical shame, he found a part who feared criticism.

"OK to notice this part?" I asked.

"Yes," Herb said. "He protects a younger one who looks like me as a little boy. He's with my family but he's got a shell around him. He's the youngest and everyone is talking and laughing and telling stories but when he tries to join in nobody wants to hear his story. His brother is telling him to shut up. And when he gets mad about that his father tells him, 'Shhhhhh!'"

"How do you feel toward him?" I asked.

"I had a part that wanted to hide him at first but I got that part to relax and now I'm asking him to tell me his story. His shell is dissolving."

The next week Herb reported that his compulsion for pornography had relaxed and he felt relieved. "But," I predicted, "it may come back as you get close to this little boy or to other vulnerable parts. Don't worry, once you have taken care of the ones this protector looks after, the urge for porn will go."

As I had predicted, in the next session Herb said that his pornography compulsion was back strongly. "Is it OK to notice the urge?" I asked.

Herb said it was just outside his head on the right. He felt frustrated toward the porn part, which seemed out of control again. "But I feel frustrated toward outside people, too," Herb said. "The frustrated part rehearses things he will say to people who are arrogant or pushy." After getting curious, Herb reported, "He's showing me how I was bullied by another kid every morning in fifth grade walking to school."

"How do you feel toward the fifth-grader?" I asked.

"I feel sad for him. It was so hard walking to school every day with this bully slapping him around and making fun of him." Herb helped the fifth-grader escape the bully and come to the present, where he unburdened his fear and shame.

After unburdening an exile we always returned to check in with the pornography part. While looking at porn, Herb now noticed that he was having a conversation with a faceless female. She stood behind him and watched the images too. This female part understood exactly what Herb liked and shared his pleasure. She was his personal madam who procured women and directed them for him, reading his thoughts, approving his whims and never judging him. Watching porn with her, Herb felt free and relaxed, the opposite of his experience with real women. These parts, the ones who pushed porn and the inner critic, represent a classic addictive polarity between firefighters who relieve shame and managers who stir it up again with criticism. As with all polarities, we would eventually find an exile underneath.

But in the meantime we were in a delicate moment of the therapy. As the client forms a relationship with an exiled part, protectors tend to become more extreme and more polarized. Between sessions Herb found he was either blended with the critic who told him he was doomed to a life of pornography and shame, or the pornography part who plagued him all night with intrusive fantasies. The intensity of this polarity was so hard to bear that another part emerged, a part who analyzed my actions, criticized me, questioned the effectiveness of internal family systems (IFS) and instructed Herb not to go inside or listen to me during sessions. I assured this part that its doubts were welcome and I encouraged Herb to get to know the part, which he called the Closet Snob.

Herb had always been a great student and had gone to elite schools. The Closet Snob had long helped Herb to feel better by looking down on others and questioning their intelligence. Although the Closet Snob had been comforting, Herb now saw how toxic his contempt was for relationships. "He keeps me from connecting," Herb observed. "He doesn't believe I know how to interact with people."

Herb also noticed other protective parts who precluded intimacy. There was Front Man whose job was to hide Herb's dark side by presenting a pleasant, friendly, inoffensive face when interacting with others. He wanted Herb to be seen as a contributor to society so that nobody would dream of viewing him as an outcast or a menace. And then, most important, Herb discovered a part who was protecting him from a bone-chilling fear, which turned out to be the feeling of Peter Pain.

"Peter Pain is showing me something that happened in second grade," Herb said. "When Alice was threatened by the Queen of Hearts in *Alice's Adventures in Wonderland*, I cried. The teacher sent me out into the hall where I couldn't escape these older kids who always teased me." Peter Pain showed Herb his big discovery. If he focused on feeling his genitals and called up feminine images while he was being humiliated he became aroused and distracted from his shame. Unburdening Peter Pain calmed the pornography part and, in turn, the critic. Although all of the exiled parts described above carried shame and were important to unburden, Peter Pain, who carried experiences of being shamed by peers in school, turned out to be the linchpin exile for Herb's pornography habit.

CONCLUSIONS

The key to IFS work with pornography addiction is for the therapist, and eventually the client, to hold Self-energy while exploring the client's central polarity: the part who loves porn and the part who hates the client for looking at porn. Traditional sexual addiction therapy sides with the managers who try to shame the client out of using porn to self-soothe. In contrast, IFS offers both therapist and client a way to care about the parts who love porn as well as the parts who hate the client for being weak and embarrassing. Right from the start with Herb, I was curious and nonjudgmental about the part who looked at pornography. When the porn part explained to us that it longed for the comfort of pornographic pictures, Herb's critical, shaming managers immediately surfaced. The beginning of an addiction therapy always revolves around this polarity between firefighters and shaming managers. It is crucial not to side with the managers.

As with most pornography addicts Herb started treatment with little awareness of his body and, therefore, of his emotions. He initially located all parts in his head. The exercise of mapping parts on paper helped him to differentiate his protective parts by their roles as either managers (trying to prevent emotional pain) or firefighters (trying to suppress emotional pain). Direct access, another IFS technique that is effective with skeptical protectors, was also helpful with Herb. When the therapist addresses skeptical parts directly they will usually relax enough for the client to experience them as separate, or differentiated. Once the client differentiates and forms relationships with his protective system, through mapping and direct access, these vigilant parts will gradually give him more access to his body and, with enough Self-energy, exiles can begin to surface safely.

The last step in therapy is healing the exiles. But to reach the point of healing, the therapist must anticipate and welcome relapses. Firefighters will be triggered as the client makes contact with exiles who carry terror, humiliation and feelings of inadequacy, and it may look as if the therapy is failing. The therapist who stays present with the client as he reassures and loves his firefighters will hear about these relapses. And the therapist who holds Self-energy, tolerating critical managers as well as relapses with interest and compassion, is likely to get the opportunity to guide the client in witnessing and unburdening exiles, whether that happens explicitly or implicitly, freeing the client and his parts of this compulsive illusion of comfort.

REFERENCE

Maltz, W., & Maltz, L. (2008). *The porn trap: The essential guide to overcoming problems caused by pornography*. New York, NY: Harper/Collins.

WELCOMING ALL EROTIC PARTS: OUR REACTIONS TO THE SEXUAL AND USING POLARITIES TO ENHANCE EROTIC EXCITEMENT

Lawrence G. Rosenberg

INTRODUCTION

The erotic—the myriad carnal, romantic and transcendent ways to experience sexual desire, fantasy, connection, excitement and fulfillment—is core to being human yet too often receives short shrift in psychotherapy discourse. Sexuality, arguably more than any other domain of life, stirs strong reactions ranging from supreme ecstasy to curious wonder to anxiety, shame, horror, disgust, rage, denial, pathologizing and punishment. This chapter is an invitation to welcome erotic parts—ours and our clients'—along with the parts who are activated in reaction to the erotic.

A case consultation will illustrate working with a clinician's judgmental parts who were triggered when hearing about the particular sexual pleasures of her clients. The chapter goes on to explore other kinds of parts who are typically reactive to the erotic: those whose beliefs are so blended with cultural messages that they are barely detectable, those who manage emotional reactions through inhibitions and addictions and those who are caught up in erotically charged attraction to clients.

The lens of polarities is a valuable perspective for exploring the highly diverse and idiosyncratic expressions of the erotic. Parts who are seemingly in opposition create tension that can be distressing but can also, paradoxically,

---

I am grateful to Dennis Balcom, Michele Bograd, Shelley Hartz, John Hubbell, Jennifer Potter, Steven Schwartzberg, Sarah Stewart, Martha Sweezy and Ellen Ziskind for their thoughtful feedback during the preparation of this chapter.

be a source of excitement and delight. The standard internal family systems (IFS) approach to polarities involves healing the wounds of exiles whose pain motivates polarized protectors. This chapter posits an alternate view that the dialectical tension of some polarities is inherent and essential to human nature so that one cannot exist without the other, as with differentiation and integration. From this perspective, the erotic can be understood as a balance of opposing yet complementary forces or energies, such as receptive versus penetrative. In contrast to addressing deeper wounds, this outlook focuses on acceptance ("all polarities are welcome") and finding equilibrium between polarized desires and prohibitions. Although counterintuitive to managerial parts, our negative reactions to the erotic (e.g., shame, disconnection, guilt or danger) sometimes intensify sexual excitement when we experiment with polarities that involve regulating distance, violating prohibitions and playing with power. Finally, the common struggle between lusty and romantic desires is illustrated in a case vignette at the end of the chapter.

CASE CONSULTATION: A THERAPIST'S REACTIONS TO HER CLIENTS' EROTIC LIFE

Corrine, a senior, well-respected IFS therapist, sought a consultation with me because she felt uncertain about how to proceed with a new couple in therapy. She had seen Marjorie and Don three times. They were in their mid-thirties, white, married for six years, and had a four-year old daughter whom Marjorie cared for at home. Their comfortable, middle-class stability had recently been shaken when the company where Don had worked for several years was sold and his position and salary were reduced. Don felt frustrated, powerless to seek another job during a recessive economy, and guilty that he was no longer a sufficient provider for his family. Marjorie was very disappointed because their plans for having a second child were now jeopardized. Under this stress, they were arguing almost nightly and their usual pleasure from their relationship was fraying. The tipping point came when Marjorie threw a cup, which just missed Don and smashed against the wall. This very uncharacteristic action frightened them both. They decided to seek therapy.

Corrine was a confident couple therapist who felt within two sessions that she had a grasp of their relational problems and the fundamental strength of their loving marriage, as well as their historical vulnerabilities. But in the third session the couple began to talk about the deleterious effect arguing was having on their sex life, which had always been lively and fulfilling. They wanted to use therapy to help rekindle their erotic spark. Corrine, who acknowledged to me with some embarrassment that she does not usually get much information about her clients' sex lives, tentatively asked them to say more. She described how they smiled nervously at one another before Marjorie disclosed that they regularly incorporated pornography into their sexual activities. In particular, both were turned on by scenes of men dominating women, such as a woman being handcuffed to a bed while a man penetrated her, and they delighted in enacting these scenes.

They had been consensually and safely playing out a variety of similar power-themed scenarios for years; this shared desire had always been central to their mutual attraction. Marjorie said that she had masturbated to these semiviolent fantasies since puberty. Don shamefully added that since his job demotion, he could not maintain an erection or his role as the "top" or dominant partner to "humiliate" Marjorie. And Marjorie was extremely frustrated at Don's losing his willpower to subordinate and "take" her. She admitted to Corrine that this upset her more than their financial stress. In fact, Marjorie had felt her anger building along with the bodily agitation that comes from ungratified sexual yearning and had thrown the cup.

As Corrine described their bedroom preferences during our consultation, she struggled to get the words out. She was flustered and uncertain about whether she could work with this couple. Not only was talking about sexuality in general somewhat uncomfortable for her, but she was shocked to hear about the specific nature of their erotic passion. The idea of women being hurt as a source of sexual arousal was abhorrent to her feminist and ethical principles. She thought that using pornography was the sign of a problem. She speculated whether Marjorie and/or Don were replaying hurts from unresolved trauma, although nothing in their histories indicated abuse. She wondered about the effects of such behavior on raising a child.

Yet, Corrine was also aware that neither Marjorie nor Don had expressed any concerns or misgivings about their sadomasochistic erotic play. No one seemed to be actually getting hurt, both clearly wanted this pleasure back in their lives, and both appeared to be caring and responsible parents to their daughter. She hoped that she had effectively hidden her reactions from the couple and felt both relief and worry when they scheduled another session. Anxious and judging parts within her wanted them to go away while intrepid and intrigued parts wanted to persevere. To her credit, the contradiction between her strongly negative reactions and her perception of their contentment made her puzzled and receptive to learning more—about herself and about the erotic.

When she finished speaking, I invited Corrine to get to know the parts of her who were reacting to this couple's sex life. Corrine had worked with me before and was comfortable using IFS for personal exploration of countertransference. I guided her to go inside, open space for any feelings, parts or sensations and notice what wanted her attention.

She observed, "The loudest part is against people being hurt and women being used by men for their selfish needs. This part was startled and somewhat disgusted and wanted to shout at Don and especially at Marjorie to stop that abusive behavior."

I asked whether this part's attitude made sense to her. She nodded vigorously. "How do you feel toward this part?" I asked.

Corrine said, "I admire and value her. She's been my moral compass for most of my life." She added that this part had become fully formed during her twenties in the women's liberation movement, although her core beliefs had developed earlier.

I said, "I, too, have a part who strongly shares your part's principles. I know that sometimes my part can be so certain that it blends with me so I will take action, sometimes stridently. It's often right. But when it relaxes I can see a broader perspective. I wonder whether your part is blended with you now?"

Corrine paused, "Yes."

I asked, "Would this part be willing to separate a little bit and give you some space?"

Corrine said, "A little."

I suggested, "Thank her for softening. Let her know that she can remain nearby and jump back into our conversation if she gets concerned." Then I asked Corrine, "Please ask your part what she is afraid would happen if she were not so active with regard to your therapy with Marjorie and Don."

Corrine hesitated in a moment of confusion, "At first, the part was going to say that Marjorie will get hurt. But, from what Marjorie said, she wasn't getting hurt. She said that she really enjoyed being tied up and told to serve Don. I don't get it. It still creeps me out. But, they say that's what they want."

Corrine now had space for a part who was polarized with the first, judging protector. This second part was trying to be phenomenologically present with Marjorie and Don, meeting them where they were rather than imposing judgments on them. I asked Corrine whether she recognized this other part, which was holding considerable Self-energy. She did and very much appreciated its contribution to making her a well-attuned therapist. With this second part, Corrine was in touch with some curiosity about Marjorie and Don's sexuality and how aggression and violence can become eroticized. She was surprised that once her anxious, judging part relaxed, she was considering a new perspective on basic drives and behaviors.

However, her curiosity stirred a third part who realized that Corrine was not well-educated about sexuality, that she was unclear how to take a sexual history or even how to talk with clients about sexual matters—to use clinical jargon or colloquial slang words. She felt embarrassed toward this prudish part, identifying it as an important gap in her clinical knowledge and in her ease as a therapist. She reflected that she had unconsciously veered conversations away from sexual material in her therapies with other clients. As I guided her to get to know this part, she was surprised. She had assumed that as a feminist she would be comfortable about sexuality, especially the full range of female sexuality. Corrine realized that her involvement in the women's movement had always been political: she had advocated for women's socioeconomic equality, even for women's rights over their bodies, such as legalized abortion, but saw now that she had been naively blind to sexuality.

This part reminded her that the subject of sex was ignored in her parents' home, that her parents rarely touched in front of others and that sex was almost never mentioned. She saw that a cloud of shameful secrecy had hovered over sexuality in her childhood, and that she had carried this cloud into her adult, conventional sex life. Corrine brought compassion to this young part who had grown up confused and untaught about the diversity and complexity of erotic arousal. With Self-energy, Corrine helped this young part to let go of (unburden) some shame and denial and invite in their place curiosity and openness to learning more about sexuality as well as her own reactions to the erotic.

I asked Corrine whether she would like to try an exercise to notice what parts come forward in reaction to sexual language. Initially hesitant, after some discussion, her reluctant, embarrassed parts softened and she agreed. I explained that I would say a sexual word and her task was to repeat it aloud, sit with it and notice any feelings, associations or reactions. Then we would gently work with those parts and help them relax so she could be present with Self-calm until she was ready to proceed to the next word. (You, the reader, may want to follow along and notice your associations and parts.) I started with *intercourse*. She repeated *intercourse* and described her feelings, thoughts, body sensations or images. As her mildly anxious parts relaxed and more curiosity arrived, we continued on with a few of the following words: *clitoris . . . tits . . . cock . . . jerking off . . . transgender . . . orgy . . . going down . . . vulva . . . pregnant . . . same-sex marriage . . . menstruation . . . swinging . . . fist fucking . . . kissing . . . sadomasochism . . . affairs . . . sucking . . . polyamory . . . love.* I explained the meanings of unfamiliar terms, such as *fist fucking*, in which one person inserts his or her fist and arm into the other's person's well-lubricated and receptive anal cavity, which, for some people, is highly stimulating.

Corrine noticed that slang words, especially those describing nonmainstream behaviors, stirred anxious, confused or disgusted reactions. These diminished as her initial response of startle at hearing unfamiliar sexual words became desensitized. She also noticed that a few of the words, such as *kissing*, stirred some mild excitement and slight genital arousal. Although some parts enjoyed these sensations, others were unnerved to feel them while sitting with me in my office. Corrine was discovering the varied, contradictory feelings stirred by sexual and erotic thoughts. She breathed a sigh of relief at the end of this exercise. She said that it was challenging, eye opening and offered her trailheads for further introspection.

At the end of the consultation, we reviewed goals for the couple therapy with Marjorie and Don. Corrine began with a goal for herself: to work with relaxing her judging and anxious parts before her sessions with them so that she could be in Self as much as possible and be welcoming of their erotic parts. She also planned to read an excellent book, *The Erotic Mind* by Jack Morin (1995). I suggested two other resources for further education: courses offered by the American Association of Sex Educators, Counselors, and Therapists (AASECT) and Dan Savage's frank sex advice column, "Savage Love." Corrine intended to begin the next couple session by asking Don and Marjorie what it had been like for them to tell her about their sex life and problems. And, depending on their reactions, Corrine thought she might speak for some of her parts, explaining that much of what they had described was new to her and that she aimed to learn with them as well as on her own (just as a therapist taking a multicultural perspective might express unfamiliarity with and interest in clients' different cultural beliefs and behaviors). She planned to listen carefully to how they talked about their sexual relationship and not to frame their erotic activity as pathological or requiring change unless Marjorie or Don expressed a concern.

In addition to tracking the sequences of their communications (Herbine-Blank, this volume), we discussed helping Don to work with his shaming, blaming, emasculating parts to foster his power and virility, while acknowledging his very real job and financial stressors. Based on his history, we hypothesized that his disempowerment was protecting hurt, young parts who could be unburdened. Similarly, Marjorie could help her disappointed and angry parts who appeared to be rooted in earlier developmental injuries about broken expectations. Corrine recognized that the overarching goal was to help them both return to and strengthen the former satisfactions of their relationship, particularly their sex life, while bringing compassion, calm and creativity to the parts who were frustrated with their current financial limits. We agreed that she would follow up with me as the therapy with Marjorie and Don unfolded.

REACTIONS TO THE EROTIC ARE BLENDED WITH CULTURAL MESSAGES

The consultation with Corrine illustrates that therapists are as susceptible as anyone to viewing sexual behavior and erotic arousal through the lens of familial and cultural conditioning. Many therapists do not receive comprehensive education about the diversity and complexity of human sexuality. They rely on informal social knowledge, personal exposures to sexuality and prejudiced psychiatric models to form their beliefs about what constitutes "healthy" versus "abnormal" sexual motivations and behavior. In the United States, where the dominant culture is polarized between sex-obsession and sex-phobia, we receive messages that vacillate between the extremes of hedonistic libertinism (*gratify yourself; sex sells; boys will be boys; anything goes; if you're sexual, you're popular*) and restrictive Puritanism (*you'll get . . . hurt, diseased, pregnant, ostracized; it's sick, sinful, deviant, illegal; if you're sexual, you're a slut*). The culture invokes shame and guilt as well as physical restraint and violence to control people's sexual urges and to define what specific sexual desires and actions are judged to be right or wrong, blessed or damned (Rubin, 1984). The Biblical creation story can be seen as conveying the Judeo-Christian bottom line about sexual vitality: when the innocent young parts of Adam and Eve are curious to know the erotic Tree of Life, God banishes them from the Garden of Eden, where Self-energy resides, and they enter exile in self-conscious shame about their bodies. This could be the template for Corrine's story.

There are many topics that can trigger therapists' parts and prevent bringing nonjudgmental curiosity to their clients' erotic lives. In talking with therapists about sexuality over the years, these topics include: erotic fantasies, discrepant sexual desire between partners, sexual dysfunctions, pornography, extrarelational affairs, lesbian/gay/bisexual/transgender/queer concerns, gender transitions, polyamory, norms in sexual subcultures, fetishes for arousal, conflicts between religious values and sexual identity, clients who are sex workers, eroticized power and violence, out-of-control and addictive sexual behavior and the effects of sexual trauma on the development of erotic orientation. When faced with the unfamiliar and the unconventional, parts come forward to help with the anxiety of not knowing by creating a story of what must be happening, by assigning labels of good and bad. Corrine began formulating a story that Marjorie and Don's sadomasochistic sex must be an enactment of past abuse. Along with the narrative, other parts may react with disgust, fear, anger or blaming (pathologizing). These parts may blend so transparently and convincingly that we are sometimes unaware of how our story is interfering with truly getting to know clients' erotic parts and their parts who judge or shame their erotic parts. This is especially probable when our story matches the outlooks put forth by the larger mental health and sociopolitical systems so our parts have no reason to step back and consider a different perspective.

When a therapist is not in Self, other parts take over. These may be avoidant parts who do not raise and follow up on sexual questions for fear that they will make the client—or the therapist—anxious. They might be relieved to ally with parts of the client who are embarrassed or hesitant to talk about private sexual subjects. Or, therapist parts could be excessively curious and intrusive, attending to clients' erotic activities for personal titillation or anthropological fascination. If the therapist is the recipient of the client's erotic attention, a variety of conflicting parts could get activated, ranging from squirmy discomfort and genuine fear to narcissistic pleasure and arousal. As with any IFS intervention, the fundamental step is for the therapist to ask him or herself, "How am I feeling toward my client's erotic parts?" If the answer points to reactions that are not qualities of Self, the therapist should explore these reactive parts through introspection or consultation to bring Self-energy to the therapeutic work.

PARTS DEVELOP EXTREME ROLES TO MANAGE OUR REACTIONS TO EROTIC DESIRES

In addition to our reactions to our clients' erotic expressions, people develop parts to manage their reactions to their own erotic feelings. These protector parts fear losing control over erotic impulses, being attacked or abused by others or feeling vulnerable and ashamed. They take over either by inhibiting our sexual desire and behavior and/or by compulsively addicting us to sex. Inhibiting protectors raise anxiety, impose judgments, numb desire, dissociate the body from the mind, interfere with attention or block the functioning of genital parts in the sexual moment (i.e., males not able to get or sustain erections, ejaculating too quickly or not reaching orgasm; females not lubricating, feeling pain, having involuntary vaginal contractions or not reaching orgasm). Addicting protectors compel a person to follow a ritualized repetitive sequence of thoughts and actions for arousal and gratification without regard for harmful consequences, to rapidly alter sensation (provide a "high" or a "fix"), distract from distressing emotions or use sexual contact as a conduit or substitute for tentative intimacy. A person's inner system may be governed primarily by one type of protector or a combination of both. These protectors can operate in the shadows and are frequently polarized against each other, such as a judging inhibiting part who tries to restrict the acting out behavior of an addicting part, who spends hours cruising the Internet for hot masturbatory images. If unsuccessful, the inhibitor dishes out self-loathing and a hangover following the behavior (Wonder, this volume).

THERAPISTS' ATTRACTIONS TO CLIENTS

Another arena potentially rife with challenge is the therapist with erotic feelings for his or her client. Although this was not the case in Corrine's couple therapy, I would like to address some of the parts who are present when it does occur. Although the incidence of actual therapist–client sexual behavior is low, it is common for a therapist's erotic parts to get stimulated in response to some clients. Yet, frank discussion of this subject remains fairly taboo (Bridges, 1998; Pope, Keith-Spiegel, & Tabachnick, 1986). Judging parts, who know of the ethical and legal prohibitions against therapist–client sexual contact, can stir dread, blame, shame and guilt. These critical parts can be powerful enough to prevent therapists from recognizing and addressing the attraction, which puts them at risk of acting on the feelings

Table 11.1 Clues That a Therapist Has Not Acknowledged His/Her Erotic Attraction to a Client

- The therapist feels physical tension or nervousness while with or thinks about the client.
- The therapist feels annoyance or frustration with the client for no apparent reason.
- The therapist talks in a neutral or dehumanized manner.
- The therapist views the client as a diagnostic label rather than as a person.
- The therapist misses or cancels sessions to avoid the client.
- The therapist thinks obsessively about the client's treatment.
- The therapist thinks about the client during sex with his or her partner.
- The therapist gives the client undue special treatment.

Drawn from Bridges (1998) and Pope, Sonne, and Holroyd (1993).

(Pope, Sonne, & Holroyd, 1993). Parts serving as clues that a therapist has unacknowledged attraction to a client are listed in Table 11.1.

Once aware of having sexual feelings for a client, the therapist can be stymied by various strong reactions including shock and surprise, confusion between genuine caring/liking and attraction, anxiety about unresolved personal issues, fear of losing control, fear of being criticized by peers or supervisors, frustration at not being able to speak openly about the feelings or act on them with the client, confusion about boundaries (e.g., "Are these feelings coming from the client or from me?"), anger at the client for eliciting sexual feelings and anxiety about frustrating the flirtatious client's sexual wishes (Pope et al., 1993). The therapist can ask these reactive parts to unblend to hear from the parts who hold the attraction and then work with possible underlying conflicts, such as longings to be loved or admired, a reenactment of an earlier traumatic boundary violation or protection against parts holding other intolerable urges such as rage, sadism or dependency (Bridges, 1998). This process of awareness, acknowledgement and exploration of erotic feelings toward a client requires considerable Self-compassion and courage and often the assistance of a trusted, nonjudgmental peer, supervisor or personal therapist.

CORRINE EXPLORES EROTIC IMAGERY

After three more couple sessions with Marjorie and Don, Corrine returned for a follow-up consultation. She reported that her judging parts had relaxed enough for her to focus on the couple's communication patterns and each partner's internal work. She added that our consultation had stirred her curiosity, and she asked for help with more self-discovery. I guided Corrine through the following imagery exercise, reminding her parts that they were welcome to participate to whatever degree they wanted and that it was fine for her to keep her experience to herself and not describe the imagery aloud.

"Let yourself be comfortable in the chair. Take some slow breaths in and let them out slowly. As you do, open up space inside, bringing your Self-energy and open curiosity. Welcome into this space one of the ways that you experience the erotic. This may be a memory of a past sexual experience, a fantasy, sensations, an image of people or things or a situation. This may or may not be explicitly sexual. If various ways are showing up, try to focus on one, asking the others to relax back. Notice the particular features that make this erotic or sexually exciting for you. What are the main ingredients and what may be hidden in the wings? Notice what you are feeling and thinking in reaction to being with this erotic experience. Maybe you sense some genital stirrings or other bodily signs of arousal. Do you feel fully absorbed? Or, are parts watching how this experience is going for you?"

At the outset, Corrine was aware of feeling self-conscious, which she noticed in tightness around her chest and midsection. She spoke for a judging part who was wary of her focusing on anything erotic, especially in my presence.

I assured her, "I am not holding any judgment and I'm welcoming whatever you experience. Ask the judging ones to let you know about their concerns and see if they make sense to you. Then, ask them to soften back and let you be as fully present as possible with your erotic experience."

Corrine's body visibly relaxed and she was quiet for a couple of minutes. Then, with a light smile, Corrine opened her eyes, "I've never really done that before—just be with some sexual thoughts and feelings, especially with someone else in the room. I felt nervous but it was also nice. I was thinking about a time during a vacation with my husband. We had gone sailing with another couple. It was a beautiful day and I remember being on the boat and looking at Mark and thinking he was still handsome. I felt a little turned on, with the sun, the gentle movement of the boat in the water. This feeling stayed with me during dinner with our friends. Then Mark and I went back to our hotel room. Maybe he had been feeling it too because we just started kissing and ended up making love slowly but with more passion than usual. Even now, as I remember that day, I feel some excitement."

I asked Corrine, "How do you feel as you tell me this?"

Corrine said, "A little embarrassed but OK." She paused. "But," a worried part who was slightly blended with Corrine wanted to know, "is it OK?"

I said, "It is OK and you can ask the worried part what it's concerned about."

She listened to its concern about revealing this private memory and it softened.

I asked whether she would like to learn more about the erotic, from my didactic part who likes to teach about sexuality. She was interested and her curious, learning parts perked up.

CONSIDERING THE EROTIC FROM THE PERSPECTIVE OF POLARITIES

We usually think of the erotic as that which we think, feel and do to stimulate and heighten sexual and intimacy desires, arousal and orgasm. The cliché that the brain is our most erogenous organ is true; we filter all the sensory moments of the body through the meanings, fantasies and scripts we create, based on genetic predispositions, personal experiences and culturally constructed standards (Leitenberg & Henning, 1995; Mosher, 1980; Stoller, 1979). The erotic encompasses a huge range, including sensation, imagery, emotional intimacy, tantric and spiritual realms that extend beyond rationality and logic (Collins, 1993; Muir & Muir, 1989; Steinberg, 1992). The concept of polarities offers a broader perspective to understand and enhance erotic experience. After first explaining how polarities are used in IFS, I extend this concept and apply it to the erotic.

THE IFS PERSPECTIVE ON POLARITIES

According to IFS theory, parts develop polarized relationships in response to developmental wounds and traumas (Schwartz, 1995). For example, a client, Rose, held intense shame about her body due to her parents' having punished her as a child for touching (and enjoying touching) her genitals. To cope with her mortification, one of her protector parts took on an obedient role in which she ignored her body and suppressed her erotic experimentation to try to win her parents' attention and love, while another protector became angrily defiant and developed a secretly promiscuous sex life with men and women but always faked orgasms. Although Rose appeared to win approval for being a "nice girl," her flirty, provocative part always waited in the wings to take over. As a result of this polarized conflict, she had veered into dangerous, life-threatening encounters.

"My flirty part hates that nice girl. Really hates her," Rose reported early on.

By following the standard IFS treatment toward polarities I helped Rose bring curiosity, calm and compassion to facilitate communication between these parts so that over time their relationship changed to be less embattled.

"They can see that they were both trying to protect me. The flirty one wanted to say 'Fuck you!' to my parents. 'How dare you!' While the nice girl wanted to capture their love."

Through a lengthy process of establishing a trusting relationship between her Self and these wounded protectors, Rose got access to the underlying hurt, the shamed little girl, and helped her to unburden shameful beliefs about her body and her own desire to explore it. This helped the furious flirty part and took the steam out of its polarity with the nice girl. Both of these protectors eventually became cooperative advisors, allowing Rose to practice sensual self-touching exercises so she could experience orgasm and realize greater stability in her life.

POLARITIES AS ESSENTIAL DIALECTICAL TENSIONS

However, there is a kind of polarity that emerges from life's essential dialectical tensions rather than from wounds. One universal polarity, both for individuals and societies, is security versus freedom: as we seek greater security, we feel safer but live with stronger controls and reduced liberties. In contrast, as we seek greater freedom, we may do more of what we want but risk conflict, danger and insecurity. Another basic polarity is autonomy versus dependency or being separate versus being connected. Every person in a relationship grapples with achieving the best balance between these opposing needs. IFS itself is founded on the polarity that differentiation (of parts from Self and from each other) is necessary for assimilation (into a whole harmonious system of balanced multiple parts). Each of these polarities is a paradox: although some of our parts gravitate toward one side, we cannot live without the other. We all face the inherent push–pull of these seemingly contradictory forces. Although there may be early hurts associated with these essential tensions, the goal here is less toward unburdening and more toward accepting the natural and inevitable nature of these opposite pulls. Rather than suffering from the clash of polarized parts, we can use Self-energy to appreciate and play with them to find our own Self-led equilibrium. All polarities are welcome!

THE EROTIC AS ESSENTIAL POLARITIES

As with other polarities, the erotic is a composite of complementary polar forces or energies essential in sexuality and in life. In western thought, this is the interplay of eros (loving, unifying, and life creating and sustaining energies) and Thanatos (aggressive, differentiating and life destroying and ending energies; Freud, 1920/1961). In Chinese philosophy, this polarity is the balance between the forces of yin (earth, soft, female, dark, passive and absorbing) and yang (heaven, hard, male, light, active and penetrating; *New Encyclopedia Britannica*, 1997). These competing principles exist within all of us to varying degrees. The particular give-and-take tensions between these forces result in the idiosyncratic ways in which each of us experience not only sexual desire and excitement but everyday events as diverse as watching a sunset or handling a business transaction. Virtually every polarized dimension of life has been a source for stimulation and passion, such as the animate to the inanimate, the whole person to objectified body parts, private to public, harmonious to torture, magic to realism, safe to dangerous, pleasure to pain, freedom to slavery, the sacred to the profane, and the known to the unknown. As with the other universal polarities, the goal is to be aware of the competing erotic forces from an outlook of curiosity, courage and compassion to experiment and find the best balance.

POLARITIES FUEL EROTIC EXCITEMENT FOR INDIVIDUALS AND COUPLES

A paradox of polarities is that although protective parts aim to reduce the distress arising from strong reactions to sexual desires, the push–pull antagonism among these parts can enhance sexual excitement. Protectors relegate erotic wishes, ranging from silly and ridiculous to dark and dangerous, or spacious and transcendent, to the shadows of the "inappropriate," "undesirable" or "unknown." When our Self is genuinely curious about the parts who hold ashamed, anxious, guilty, angry, inhibiting or addicting reactions, we can ask them what they fear would happen if they were not doing their protective jobs. The answer often directs us to concerns about losing control, being bad, getting punished or hurt or feeling alone and abandoned. Although we can use IFS to heal these basic vulnerabilities, we can also experiment with these seemingly undesirable reactions to provoke erotic tension. A modicum of anxiety, guilt, embarrassment, disappointment, anger, pressure and even pain goes a long way to escalating sexual passion (Morin, 1996). As one client realized, "Doing what is shameful is exciting." But if our parts (or our partner's parts) push us too far, then we are turned-off, overwhelmed by a backlash of fear, shame, disgust or too much pain, and can feel traumatized. The optimal balance between eros and Thanatos or yin–yang energies varies widely across situations and among people. A scenario or erotic style that exhilarates one person completely shuts down another. Experimenting with the polarized concerns of our protector parts from a Self-led perspective allows us to discover our most exciting paths to erotic delight.

Although playing with polarities promotes growth as individual sexual beings, when two (or more) persons bring Self-energy for imaginative investigation together, they have the power to create enthralling sexual pleasure. In long-standing domestic relationships, passionate parts are often exiled due to some parts' fear that sexual desire will destroy attachment (McCarthy & McCarthy, 2009; Morin, 1996; Perel, 2006; Schnarch, 1997). In IFS, we ask our parts to "step back" to make space for their relationship with our Self; we need to be separate to be together. Differentiation is essential for healthy attachment (Herbine-Blank, this volume; Schnarch, 1997; Schwartz, 2008). Working with the polarities within us and between our parts and our partner's parts facilitates differentiation. If two partners are very similar in their sexual tastes and styles, they may enjoy a pleasant and comfortable sexual connection but the repetitive familiarity may jeopardize their early zest, attraction and sexual desire. An erotic charge can be maintained when each partner brings a somewhat different and independent set of desires, fantasies and tastes and is open to changing an established pattern. When our anxious parts relax enough to trust ourselves and our partner(s) and we can approach sexuality with Self-leadership, we establish the safety necessary to be aware of what we want—and don't want—and to communicate these to our partner(s). For example, a person with shy and reserved parts, who plays with being seen by showing off his or her exhibitionistic parts in front of a partner, brings a new equilibrium to his or her inner system, fresh erotic treats to their relationship, and prompts the partner to explore new styles (Queen, 1995). The shared investigation of hidden wishes enriches a couple's sex life, while the trust required in taking risks without fear of being judged deepens their emotional intimacy.

Let's look at three common polarities, each of which relies on approach–avoidance tension for a couple's sexual delectation: creating longing through distance between partners, violating prohibitions and playing with power through dominance and submission (Morin, 1996). The first involves physical or emotional separation between partners that stirs yearning and excited anticipation of being together. Although being close seems like the natural position between partners, too much closeness can feel claustrophobic and prevent knowing one's own erotic wants and limits. This feeling of enmeshment kindles protective impulses to withdraw or to push a partner away through a fight. In a good relationship, actual distance such as when a partner is away on travel, and emotional distance, perhaps caused by a temporary argument, exacerbate the urge to reconnect and be in one another's arms. Corrine's memory of the building erotic tension between her and her husband on their sailing vacation is an example. Romantic parts who appreciate the aphrodisiac power of distance might say, "Absence makes the heart grow fonder," while lusty parts might crow, "Absence makes the cock grow harder." Partners can build mounting sexual anticipation into their relationship by, for example, undressing each other very slowly during foreplay (Morin, 1996), or by living apart and seeing each other only occasionally. Slowing down the sexual encounter also encourages partners to notice any parts that are interfering with staying present in the moment. When partners limit the stimulation of touch to, say, each other's pinkie fingers, they can more clearly sense—with some humor—the parts urging closeness and those seeking distance.

For some people, violating prohibitions is an excellent strategy to heat erotic frisson by working polarities involving guilt, shame, and fear. One polarity exploits the tension between innocence (*I am good and I should be good*) and guilt (*I like being naughty or dirty*). Another variation toys with staying safe (*We should follow the rules so no one gets hurt*) versus risking the forbidden (*Let's break taboos, push boundaries and chance consequences*). Rose had struggled with an extreme version of this polarity. To hazard the dangerous (e.g., unprotected intercourse between strangers), the possibility of being caught (e.g., having sex in public) or an internal backlash (e.g., a shame attack after a provocative sexual encounter) is very compelling for some whereas these anxiety-inducing ingredients restrain others. Fantasy invites us to "release moral, social, and pragmatic constraints" to "push the boundaries further than we would in real life" (Morin, 1996, pp. 90–91). The mysterious power of fantasy resides in simultaneously forgetting the taboos and remembering that we're violating them (Morin, 1996).

Every sexual encounter involves the negotiation of power. This is implicit and unspoken in many relationships yet is clearly defined by the roles that partners automatically take during sex, such as the traditional missionary position with the man on top and the woman on bottom. When the power dynamics are explicit and considered openly between partners, there is a rich opportunity to use this dimension for fantasy role-play to stir much erotic excitement. This polarity is between dominance (*I want to be in charge and have control*) and submission (*I want to surrender control*). Marjorie and Don embraced this polarity to spark their sex life. Each partner chooses his or her role as a top or a bottom to enact a scene. The partners consent to rules, which are often established by the bottom, about safety, limits on subjugation and pain, desired actions, and use of accouterments such as leather, bondage, or other objects of domination (Morin, 1996). "A forceful partner demonstrates with his or her passion the value and desirability of the one who submits. A submissive partner demonstrates through his or her surrender the irresistible erotic powers of the aggressor" (Morin, 1996, p. 97).

The distinction between playing with power responsibly (e.g., in sadomasochistic role-play) and nonconsensual violation, such as rape or child molestation, is crucial. For many people, including therapists such as Corrine, their protector parts go on high alert when hearing about S and M erotic play. Corrine was able to bring Self-calm and curiosity to this subject and relaxed her part who had assumed that Don and Marjorie's sex life was necessarily a traumatic re-enactment or proof of past sexual abuse. A careful history will reveal themes of nonconsensual activity and past experiences of being forced or of forcing another. Although being humiliated is a major turn-off for many people (and might be a sign of past abuse), some people, such as Marjorie and Don, find consensual humiliation a turn-on. Playing with power involves the paradox of partners respecting and caring for each other regardless of the overt text of their script.

TENSIONS EMERGING FROM POLARITIES BETWEEN ROMANTIC AND LUSTY PARTS

A challenging polarity is between lusty parts seeking hot sex and relational parts wanting a successful romantic partnership. Everyone faces the question, is there room for erotic passion, fantasy and aggression in an enduring, respectful, caring, intimate and loving relationship? Are all erotic and reactive parts truly welcome? Yours and mine?

Lusty parts seek sex for recreation and the highly reinforcing psychophysiological sensations that come from touching, stimulating erogenous areas and having orgasm. These parts may be testosterone driven and also socially conditioned. Lusty parts objectify the other person (sometimes as a "type') and focus on particular physical features (e.g., large breasts, a big cock) or a particular manner (e.g., preppy, tough, soft) to stir arousal. *Relational parts* seek sex for emotional attachment, intimacy and romantic love. In contrast to lusty parts, which want Mr. or Ms. Right Now, our relational parts seek Mr. or Ms. Right to form an enduring and loving (monogamous or polyamorous) relationship over time. Relational parts yearn to see and be seen, to feel safe enough to reveal our vulnerabilities and desires and trust that our partner will accept them (Schnarch, 1997). If our lusty parts are strong but sense that other parts internally or in the partner are not welcoming, then the lust may either recede or seek outlets away from one's partner.

CASE ILLUSTRATION: JUSTIN'S CONFLICT BETWEEN LUSTY PARTS AND RELATIONAL PARTS

By mid-adulthood, Justin was living with housemates and eking out a living. His occasional brief dating relationships with men began with initial pleasure but faded as he grew disenchanted over waning sexual attraction or incompatible interests. Returning to being single, Justin liked having time for himself and the freedom for on-the-spot sexual hookups yet he felt lonely, sometimes depressed and longed for a steady companion. Justin sought therapy with the hope that he would stop repeating this long-standing ambivalent pattern and sustain a good relationship.

At the outset of treatment, I had to attend to some of my parts. On seeing Justin's hunky body when we met in the waiting room, my lusty part purred "hmmm" inside. I quickly brought Self-calm to this reaction, which remained inactive and in the wings throughout the therapy. Then, reflecting on the repetition themes in Justin's story, I relaxed my part who was convinced that entrenched ambivalence cannot be altered. I invited Justin to consider that "All parts are welcome here." Drawing on the dialectical principle that trying to change a distressing pattern (or "repetition compulsion") intensifies the polarity between parts who insist on change ("I'll never feel happy and be truly alive if I continue to vacillate.") and parts who maintain the pattern ("Since either partnering or singlehood means psychic death, I choose neither."), I suggested that Justin accept ambivalence as his home base rather than viewing it as a problem to change. Accepting the pattern undercuts arguing about how to resolve it and, paradoxically, opens the door for change.

Justin was surprised by this idea but receptive. I guided him to gradually invite all of his wishing parts (wishing for solitude, partnered intimacy, erotic fulfillment) and the parts carrying judging or anxious reactions toward the wishing parts to gather around a table with Justin at its head for a "greet and meet." With my guidance, he told them he wanted to get to know them all and asked them to soften and take turns so he could hear one at a time. He also said that regardless of his decision about being single or partnered, there would always be space for each of them and he would continue to take their wants and fears into consideration. We repeated this round table exercise over a number of sessions. I was persistent in patiently encouraging his system to make room for his Self, and Justin's parts tentatively began to trust that he wasn't going to ignore the needs of some while pursuing the desires of others.

During this early phase of therapy, Justin met Mike through a mutual acquaintance. Justin smiled as he described Mike as friendly, warm, thoughtful, with a strong body and a good-sized penis. While they felt an initial mutual chemistry, Justin's disappointed parts anticipated that his dating involvement with Mike would run its course similar to his previous truncated relationships. Nevertheless, by continuing to relate to these parts and validate their concerns, Justin was remaining in the relationship and began to have tentative hope.

Not surprisingly, in reaction to this deepening connection, Justin's polarized parts began to feel trapped and they activated his lusty part's urges to seek sex with other hot men. Fit men with big cocks turned on this lusty part, who also had pushed Justin to work out over the years to develop his own well-built physique. Although this part appreciated Mike's penis, it worried that Mike's pleasure in desserts and inconsistent exercise habits would eventually turn Mike's body to flab and Justin's attraction would fizzle. Beginning to panic, the lusty part insisted that Justin extricate himself from the relationship pronto, deal with any hurts that his sudden goodbye might cause to Mike and run for freedom. Other parts of Justin despised and derided this lusty part and stirred strong guilt for merely noticing other guys' bodies. Meanwhile, Justin's relational parts saw his growing intimacy with Mike as the answer to their yearnings for an enduring love and they sought to exile the lusty part permanently. Justin felt paralyzed as these competing agendas pulled him in opposite directions. His lusty part complained of increasing irritation and boredom with Mike.

Justin also was concerned that I was judging his lusty urges. I said honestly that I wasn't and asked him to let me know if he perceived anything judgmental in my expression or tone. My goal was to be steady, compassionate to his distress, interested in the push–pull tension of his parts, and welcoming all. I checked inside and found that some of my parts were in the same polarities as Justin's: some were rooting for his relationship with Mike to succeed whereas others identified with his lusty part and concluded that he should exit the relationship. While asking my parts to relax and trust Justin's system, I also disclosed my parallel process so that he might feel less alone and could see such parts are able to soften. Justin found my self-revelation reassuring.

"Would you like to get to know your lusty part better?" I asked during the next session.

Although other parts were nervous about the lusty part gaining influence if it were heard, they were also beginning to trust Justin's Self-energy and so they did agree to relax.

"My job," the lusty part said, "is to keep Justin sexually turned on so he will stay lively, young and powerful." It had been working hard to fulfill this mission at least since early puberty. It liked the job but was angry about the scornful treatment it got from other parts.

I guided Justin to ask his lusty part, "What are you afraid would happen if you were not doing this job?"

The part showed Justin a picture of himself as a shriveled, tired old man. This unexpected image made sad sense to Justin as he recalled, with light tears, how often he had felt weak and unmanly as a boy. "I was slightly chubby and I didn't have many friends," Justin said. "When I'm around fit, well-built men where there's some sexual chemistry, I feel strong and more masculine. I can feel a kind of healthy aggressive energy." This was in powerful contrast to the feeling of being inadequate that he had experienced throughout most of his childhood and early adulthood. In his twenties, Justin had begun working out and, as an enviable, desirable body blossomed, he had also developed confidence for the first time.

"I'm so grateful to this part," Justin said near the end of the session. "It saved me." As he said this he could feel the oppositional parts, who had been paying close attention, softening their judgment as well.

At our next session I asked Justin, "Will the lusty part allow you to make direct contact with young Justin, who carries those beliefs about being weak and undesirable?"

After getting permission from Justin's protectors, the young part reminded him of the pain of growing up with erotic attractions to other boys and men and the guilty excitement of his secret, compartmentalized sexual life. As a boy and then a teenager, he had tried to hide his gay orientation from his family, and especially from his domineering, rejecting father, whose love and recognition Justin had desperately sought, although other parts had initially denied this paternal longing. During this and subsequent sessions, Justin witnessed, sometimes calmly and sometimes tearfully, memories of hurtful, invalidating, homophobic experiences that had led parts of him to internalize blaming messages from his family and peers. I guided Justin to accompany this young part in surrendering shameful self-beliefs and then inviting in qualities of manliness, playfulness and self-acceptance.

Appreciating this newly deep relationship between Justin and young Justin, the lusty part felt less driven to insist that Justin be with a man whose body was perfect but was still concerned about being trapped in a committed relationship that could lose its sexual fire. This shift by the lusty part to a less extreme position made room for Justin to explore his relational parts. As he worked with the parts who feared intimacy and underlying aloneness, Justin felt increasingly confident about living together with Mike. After testing the partnering waters for a few months and discovering that he could satisfactorily hold his still ambivalent, polarized parts, Justin decided to end therapy, with the understanding that he was welcome to return in case the lusty part reared its head and pushed Justin to seek sex with other men.

CONCLUSIONS

Can we welcome our erotic, opposing energies along with the parts who have polarized reactions to our desires? Because our protective parts judge, inhibit and compel us with strong emotions, this process is challenging. Yet the distressing states of guilt, fear, anger, shame, powerlessness or pain that we try to avoid can be approached to fuel passion under the right circumstances. Being aware of our attractions and reactions to sexual differences also invites the erotic into therapy with genuine acceptance. When we bring Self-curiosity, compassion, and courage to our protectors as well as our exiles, we discover not only that we can tolerate the desires that pull us in different directions, but also we can accept and play with them to heighten erotic excitement and deepen intimacy. Further, when our protectors feel truly calm and able to trust Self, we can open ourselves to transcendent connection, union and bliss with the erotic.

REFERENCES

Bridges, N. A. (1998). Teaching psychiatric trainees to respond to sexual and loving feelings: The supervisory challenge. *Journal of Psychotherapy Practice and Research, 7*, 217–226.

Collins, R. P. (1993). *Blossom of bone: Reclaiming the connections between homoeroticism and the sacred.* New York, NY: Harper Collins.

Freud, S. (1961). *Beyond the pleasure principle* (J. Strachey, Trans.). New York, NY: Norton. (Original work published 1920)

Leitenberg, H., & Henning, K. (1995). Sexual fantasy. *Psychological Bulletin, 117*, 469–496.

McCarthy, B., & McCarthy, E. (2009). *Discovering your couple sexual style.* London, England: Routledge.

Morin, J. (1996). *The erotic mind.* New York, NY: Harper.

Mosher, D. (1980). Three dimensions of depth of involvement in human sexual response. *Journal of Sex Research, 16*, 1–42.

Muir, C., & Muir, C. (1989). *Tantra: The art of conscious loving.* San Francisco, CA: Mercury House.

The new encyclopedia Britannica (15th ed.) (1997). Vol. 12, p. 245. Chicago, IL: Author.

Perel, E. (2006). *Mating in captivity: Unlocking erotic intelligence.* New York, NY: Harper.

Pope, K. S., Keith-Spiegel, P., & Tabachnick, B. G. (1986). Sexual attraction to clients: The human therapist and the (sometimes) inhuman training system. *American Psychologist, 41*, 147–158.

Pope, K. S., Sonne, J. L., & Holroyd, J. (1993). *Sexual feelings in psychotherapy: Explorations for therapists and therapists-in-training.* Washington, DC: American Psychological Association.

Queen, C. (1995). *Exhibitionism for the shy: Show off, dress up, and talk hot.* San Francisco, CA: Down There Press.

Rubin, G. S. (1984). Thinking sex: Notes for a radical theory of the politics of sexuality. In C. S. Vance (Ed.), *Pleasure and danger: Exploring female sexuality.* Boston, MA: Routledge & Kegan Paul.

Schnarch, D. (1997). *Passionate marriage: Keeping love and intimacy alive in committed relationships.* New York, NY: Henry Holt.

Schwartz, R. C. (1995). *Internal family systems therapy.* New York, NY: Guilford.

Schwartz, R. C. (2008). *You are the one you've been waiting for: Bringing courageous love to intimate relationships.* Oak Park, IL: Trailhead.

Steinberg, D. (Ed.). (1992). *The erotic impulse: Honoring the sensual self.* New York, NY: Tarcher/ Perigree.

Stoller, R. (1979). *Sexual excitement: Dynamics of erotic life.* New York, NY: Pantheon.

GLOSSARY

PREFACE

Although parts are considered autonomous and their behaviors motivated, there is no empirical view in internal family systems (IFS) on the nature or origins of psychic multiplicity, nor is there any consensus among practitioners about what a part is. Therefore, the IFS portrait of independently motivated parts at this point remains an invitation from Richard Schwartz to risk acting as if the matter is settled because doing so is clinically effective.

GLOSSARY

SELF: The innate presence in each of us that brings balance and harmony along with nonjudgmental, transformative qualities (see Table 1) to our internal family. Although parts can blend with (overwhelm and obscure) the Self, the Self nevertheless continues to exist and is accessible as soon as parts unblend.

SELF-LED: When an individual has the capacity to hear, understand and be present with parts, acknowledging and appreciating the importance of their roles in the internal family system and with other people.

SELF-ENERGY: The perspectives and feelings (see Table 1) that our Self brings into the relationship with our parts.

PARTS: Internal entities, or subpersonalities, who function independently and have a full range of feelings, thoughts, beliefs and sensations. These

Table 1 Qualities of Self

The 8 Cs

1.	Curiosity
2.	Confidence
3.	Compassion
4.	Courage
5.	Clarity
6.	Creativity
7.	Calm
8.	Connectedness

The 5 Ps

1.	Presence
2.	Patience
3.	Persistence
4.	Perspective
5.	Playfulness

entities, who have their own Self-energy when they feel understood and appreciated, vary in appearance, age, gender, talent and interest. They exist and take on various roles within the internal system. When not exiled or in conflict with each other over how to manage exiled parts, they contribute in a variety of ways to our efficient functioning and general well-being.

THREE TYPES OF PARTS: IFS classifies parts in three broad categories according to how they function in relation to each other. An injured part, or exile, is primary in its influence on the behavior of other parts. Orbiting around exiles are two categories of protective parts. The proactive protector, called a manager, has the role of maintaining the individual's functioning despite what the exiles feel. The reactive protector, called a firefighter, has the role of suppressing the emotional pain of exiled parts, which breaks through despite the best efforts of the manager.

1. EXILES: Revealed in feelings, beliefs, sensations and actions, these parts have been shamed, dismissed, abused or neglected in childhood and are subsequently banished by protectors for their own safety and to keep them from overwhelming the internal system with emotional pain. A great deal of internal energy is expended to keep exiles out of awareness.

Protectors

2. MANAGERS: Proactive helpers who focus on learning, functioning, being prepared and stable, and are therefore vigilant in trying to prevent exiles from flooding the internal system with emotion. As a consequence, they often use a variety of harsh tactics—not least, relentless criticizing and shaming—to keep us task-oriented and impervious to feelings.

3. FIREFIGHTERS: Reactive protectors who share the goal of exiling vulnerable parts and extinguishing emotional pain. Firefighters are activated when the memories and emotions of exiles break through despite the repressive efforts of managers. They tend to be fierce and use extreme measures that managers abhor, such as alcohol and drug abuse, binge eating, excessive shopping, promiscuity, cutting, suicide and homicide.

BLENDED: When a part is undifferentiated from another part or from the Self.

UNBLENDED: The state of being in which no part (e.g., feeling, thought, sensation, belief) is overwhelming the Self. When unblended parts remain present and accessible but are not vying to dominate, we have access to Self-qualities. This state of being unblended is often experienced as internal spaciousness.

POLARIZATION: An adversarial relationship between two protectors who are in conflict over how to manage an exile. Over time, their opposing views tend to become increasingly extreme and costly. However, when the intentions and contributions of each part are acknowledged by the client's Self, polarized protectors generally become willing to allow the Self to take over the job of caring for, protecting and repatriating the exile. Protectors are then freed from an onerous job and can find their preferred role in the internal family.

INSIGHT: The primary approach used with adults to understand parts, insight requires that the client be aware of parts (often aided by visual, kinesthetic or aural experience) and have enough Self-energy to communicate with them directly. When insight is blocked by protectors, direct access can be used.

DIRECT ACCESS: The alternative approach to insight. When a protector will not unblend, the therapist speaks directly to the clients' parts. In direct access the therapist can speak *explicitly* to a part (e.g., "Can I talk to that part directly? OK. Why do you want John to drink?"). Or, when the client rejects the idea of parts, or says, "That's not a part, that's me," the therapist can speak to it *implicitly*, without direct acknowledgment that it is a part. Direct access is the usual method with children (Krause, this volume), although some children are able to use insight.

BURDENED: When parts have taken on painful beliefs and feelings about themselves from external sources and have no relief until they are unburdened.

WITNESSING: The process in which a part shows and/or tells the client's Self about its experiences until it feels understood, accepted and self-accepting.

RETRIEVAL: After being witnessed in whatever way it needs, an exiled part leaves the past where it has been living and comes into the present.

UNBURDENING: The painful emotions and harsh self-judgments of an exiled part are ceremonially released often using imagery that involves one of the elements. After unburdening, the part can invite qualities of its own choosing to fill the space formerly occupied by the burden. The qualities of Self that are listed in Table 1 are common choices.

INDEX

AASECT. *see* American Association of Sex Educators, Counselors, and Therapists
action tendencies, 145–6
addictions, 111, 173; illness interconnected with, 104–5; Somatic IFS with, 93–6; therapy for sexual, 165; *see also* pornography addiction
adolescents, 54; direct access and, 49–53; identity search, 50; polarizations and, 50
adult health, 128–9; *see also* chronic illness
affect regulation, 58–60
affirmations, 6
American Association of Sex Educators, Counselors, and Therapists (AASECT), 171
Ames, L. B., 50
amygdala, 110, 124
angry part, 52–3, 58–60; pornography addiction and, 161
antidepressants, 111
anxious part, 162
approach-avoidance tension, 179–80
arousal regulation, 60
asangkarikachitta (spontaneous action), xxvi

Assagioli, Roberto, xviii
assertive part, 47–8
attachment, 128; healthy, 179; injuries, 33; to outcome, 19; secure, 10; theory, 1; work, 58, 70
attuned communication, 63
attuned touch, 91, 93, 105–6
awareness: of body, 91, 105–6, 165; somatic, 91, 105–6; of tension, 104; of therapist's parts, 146; as tool, 100–2

Bateman, A., 10
befriending, xxiii, xxv, 6, 141
behavior: action tendencies, 145–6; adolescent reactive, 50; harmful, xxv, 25–6; health and, 128; risky, 130, 135; symptomatic, xix; unskillful, xxv; *see also specific behaviors*
behavior change, 143, 145–6, 157; CAD and, 150–4; in diabetes, 148–50
belief, 145–6, 157; health and, 128
biological conditions, 113
biology, 113; parts affected by, 114–15; parts affecting, 115–16; *see also* emotional-biological differentiation; neurobiology
blame, 64–7

blended parts (blending), 18, 187, 189; children and, 45–7; cultural messages and, 166, 171–3; direct access and, 45–7; exiles, xviii; protector, 18, 63

body: awareness of, 91, 105–6, 165; healing relationships and, 141; movement, 18; sensations, 97, 157; *see also* mindful movement

brainstem, 108, 124

breath, 136; conscious, 91–2, 105–6; as tool, 100–2

Buddhism, xx

Buddhist psychology, xxi, xxv, xxvi

burdened parts, xviii, xxii, 11, 37, 190; therapist and, 14–16

burdens, 190; relational, 66, 70; transmitted to children, 35, 36

CAD *see* coronary arterial disease

calmness, xx, 4, 188

Cape Cod Summer Institute, xxi–xxii

caretaker parts, 14, 51; in children, 36

cervical spine-fusion surgery, 154–6

change: within family, 37; parts and, xxv; risk of, 67; after unburdening, 87; *see also* behavior change

cheating part, 47

children, 41–2, 44–5, 47–9, 53–4; burdens transmitted to, 35, 36; caretaker parts in, 36; direct access and, 38–9, 47–9; exiles in, 38, 40; insight and, 38–9; polarizations and, 37–8, 54; protector part in, 38, 40; Self-energy within, 43; Self-led therapist and, 46; *see also* parts (child)

chronic illness, 127–41; framework for application of IFS to, 131; parts related to, 129, 131; SINHC™ and, 148–56; unblending and, 135; *see also* specific illnesses

chronic obstructive pulmonary disease (COPD), 129

clarity, xx, 4, 19, 188

client: clues of therapist's unacknowledged attraction to, 174; prejudice against, 14–15; relations with parts, 4–5; resentment towards, 15–16; Self-energy of, 4–5; sexual life of, 167–71; therapists' parts triggered by, 14–15, 172; therapist's sexual attraction to, 166, 173–4; *see also* dissociative disorders clients; parts (client); Self (client); therapist-client relationship

coach *see* health coach

collaboration, 107, 114

communication, 129, 171; attuned, 63; couple therapy and, 60–4; medication, 120–1; meta-, 12; open, 120–1; between parts, 176–7; *speaking for parts and listening from Self,* 62–3; with therapist's parts, 130

compassion, xx, 4, 33, 188

confidence, xx, 4, 19, 188

conformity, 26

connectedness, xx, 4, 188

connection: breaks in, 12; to client's Self, 8–9; healing, 10; with parts, 132–3; Self-to-Self, 8, 16, 21–2

conscious breathing, 91–2, 105–6

container imagery, 76, 78–9

control, 140

conversation content, 18

COPD *see* chronic obstructive pulmonary disease

coping skills, 73, 76, 80–1, 82, 128; *see also* container imagery; safe space imagery

coronary arterial disease (CAD), 129, 150–4

corrective experience, 5–6

cortex, 108

countertransference, 2, 11–12, 15, 61–2, 81; personal exploration of, 167–8

couple therapy, IFS 48; communication and, 60–4; goals of, 57–8; groundwork for, 55–7; needs addressed in, 67–70; protector parts and, 56–7, 70–1; risk of change and, 67; Self and affect regulation in, 58–60; shame and blame addressed in, 64–7; *see also* sexuality

courage, xx, 4, 19, 188

Courtois, C. A. 81–2

creativity, xx, 4, 188

critics, 29
cultural messages, 166; sexuality and, 171–3
curiosity, xx, 4, 70, 188; imagery exercise for, 175; for unblending, xxv

daily life, xxiii–xxiv
DD. *see* dissociative disorders
death, 131
decision making *see* medical decision making
deep healing, 5–6
delusion, xxv
dependency: on parents, 52; on therapist, 2
depression, 110–11
destabilization, 83
diabetes, 148–50
differentiation, 57–8, 167, 179; emotional-biological, 107, 113, 123–4; internal, 57, 60; pornography addiction and, 161; from protectors, 63
direct access, 48, 189; adolescents and, 49–53; blended parts and, 45–7; children and, 38–9, 47–9; with DD clients, 76; pornography addiction and, 165; SINHC™ and, 144–5; *see also* Self-to-part relationship
disappointed parts, 182
disconnection, 111
dissociative disorders (DD) clients, 72; containers for, 78–9; diagnosis and indications, 74; direct access with, 76; emergence of dissociated exiles and, 86–7; introduction to IFS language, 75; medication and, 81; pace of treatment for, 79; parenting and, 82–3; parts and, 72–3; Self-energy access among, 73; SSI for, 76–8; *see also* phase oriented treatment-IFS integrated approach
Dissociative Experience Scale, 74
diversity, 178
dominance, 180
dopamine, 111

eating, 104; disorders, 50–2; overeating, 130, 135

edgy part, 51
education, about medication, 107, 114, 124
ego state treatment, 76
8Cs, of Self-leadership, xx, 4, 188; *see also specific components*
embarrassment, 161
embodied Self, 90–1; therapist, 93
emotional-biological differentiation, 107, 113, 123–4
emotional response, 66
emotions, 157, 165; be with, 53; health and, 128; *see also* feeling; *specific emotions*
environment, 128; internal experience and, 134
eros, 177–8
the erotic, 166; as essential polarities, 177–8; Self-energy and, 184; *see also* sexuality
erotic desire, responses to, 173
erotic imagery, 174–6
The Erotic Mind (Morin), 171
erotic parts, 166
erotic tension, 178
excitatory neurotransmitters, 110–11
exiles (parts), xviii, 12, 18–19, 32, 66, 188; in adolescents, 52; blended, xviii; in children, 38, 40; dissociated, 86–7; encounter with, 5; implicit memory and, 108–9; negative feelings experienced by, 98; parent-child polarizations and, 38; polarizations and, 38, 164; PTSD and DD 72–3; relapses, 165; relationship with, 164; unburdened, 7, 163
explicit memory, 109, 110
external relational systems, 24–5, 58, 70–1, 130; healing relationships and, 141
external work, 10
extreme parts, 14, 51; emergence of, 11–12

facial expression, 6, 18
family, 35, 53–4; change within, 37; *see also* adolescents; children; parents
fantasy role-play, 180

fear, 32, 131; pornography addiction and, 161

feeling, 145–6; erotic, 173; exiles to experience negative, 98; symptom *versus*, 107, 113, 124

Fenner, P., 21–2

Fine, C. G., 83

firefighters (parts), xviii, 12, 189; in adolescents, 50; explicit memory and, 109; implicit memory and, 108–9; medication and, 119–20, 125; parent-child polarizations and, 38; polarization of managers and, 164; PTSD and DD 72–3; shame and, 27, 30; smoking and, 136

First Parish Church of Cambridge, xvii

5-Hydroxytryptophan (5-HTP), 120

5Ps, 4–5, 188; *see also specific components*

Fonagy, P., 10

Freud, Sigmund, xix

frustrated parts, 64

gamma-aminobutyric acid (GABA), 110–11, 124–5

genetics, 128

Great Traditions, xx

greed, xxv

group therapy, 9

guilt, 26

hatred, xxv

healing process: connection in, 10; deep, 5–6; relapses in, 165; Self-to-Self connection as, 8

healing relationship, 1, 141; connections in, 10; essence of, 22; Self-part as primary, 2–3

health: adult, 128–9; avoidance of facts about, 129; improvements, 131; life experience and, 128; *see also* chronic illness; illness

health care professionals, 143, 144, 156; polarizations of patient and, 157; SINHC™ and, 145

health coach, 144, 145, 157; contact with patient, 156; internal strategies, 147, 148–9, 151, 156; interpersonal

strategies, 147, 149, 150, 151, 152, 153, 154, 155, 156

hippocampal atrophy, 110, 124

historical shame, 26–7; pornography addiction and, 163

humiliation, 65

hypervigilant parts, 114

identity, 33; adolescent's search for, 50; *see also* sexual identity

IFS *see* internal family system

illness: interconnections, 104–5; parts and, 103; Somatic IFS with, 99–105; *see also* chronic illness

imagery exercises, 76; container, 76, 78–9; erotic, 174–6; SSI 76–8

images, xix

implicit memory, 108–9, 110

individual therapy, xxii–xxiii

informational mode, 156, 157

Information Interweave™ 144–5, 146, 157; *see also* self-aware informational nonjudgmental health coaching

inhibitory neurotransmitters, 110–11

insight, 189; adolescents and, 49–53; children and, 38–9; externalizing parts and, 39; *see also* Self-to-part relationship

instrumental shame, 26–7

integration process, 44–5, 87, 167

intentional shaming, 25

interaction, 70; Self-led, 63

internal attachment work, 58, 70

internal correction, 66

internal differentiation, 57, 60

internal family system (IFS): basic assumptions of, 35; chronic illness framework, 131; coaching model and, 144–6; in daily life, xxiii–xxiv; discovery of, xvii–xix; language of, 75, 146; polarities approached by, 167, 176–7; steps, xxv, 73, 88; *see also* phase oriented treatment-IFS integrated approach; psychopharmacology-IFS therapy; self-aware informational nonjudgmental health coaching; Somatic IFS; *specific types and components of IFS therapy*

internal relational systems, 24–5, 58, 130; healing relationships and, 141

internal strategies, 147, 148–9, 151, 156

internal voices, xix

internal work, 10

Internet pornography, 159; *see also* pornography addiction

interpersonal perpetrator, 27

interpersonal strategies, 147, 149, 150, 151, 152, 153, 154, 155, 156

interpersonal trauma, 24

interviewer *see* health coach

intrapsychic perpetrator, 27

judgmental parts, 12, 166, 169, 173–5, 184

Jung, Carl, xviii

Kluft, R. P., 81

Krystal, S., 21–2

left hemisphere, 108

life experience, 128

limbic system, 108, 124

logs, 134

Love's Executioner and Other Tales of Psychotherapy (Yalom), 14

loving companion, therapist as, 9–11

lusty parts, 181–4

managers (parts), xviii, 189; medication and, 119–20, 125; parent-child polarizations and, 38; polarizations of firefighters and, 164; PTSD and DD 72–3; in reaction to erotic desire, 173; shame and, 27, 30; superfunctioning, 98

mapping, 161, 165

masturbation, 160; *see also* pornography addiction

medical decision making, 143, 145–6; CAD and, 150–4; about cervical spine-fusion surgery, 154–6; in diabetes, 148–50; evidence-based aids, 157; shared, 153

medication: DD and, 81; education, 107, 114, 124; manager *versus*

firefighter response to, 119–20, 125; microdoses of, 120, 125; natural, 120; neurobiology and, 110–12; neurotransmitters matched with, 111, 112, 124–5; open communication about, 120–1; parts and, 107, 113–14, 120–1; polarizations and, 118–19; prescription process, 107, 123; symptom *versus* feeling and, 107, 113, 124; for trauma, 111–12; as unblending agent, 113; validation of concerns, 107, 113–14, 116–18, 124

meditation, xxv

memory: dynamics of, 81–2; explicit, 109, 110; health and, 128; implicit, 108–9, 110; trauma and, 108–9

mentalizing, 10

meta-cognition, 10

meta-communication, 12

mind, multiplicity of, xvii–xix, 25

mindful movement, 91, 92–3, 105–6

mindfulness, 10, 104, 108, 124

mirror neurons, 108

mood stabilizers, 111, 124–5

Morin, Jack, 171

motivated fiction, 34

Nathanson, D. L., 65

natural medication, 120

natural state, xx

nerves, 110

neural integration, 108, 109, 111, 112, 124

neurobiology, 110–12

neurogenesis, 108, 111, 124

neuroplasticity, 108, 124

neuroscience, 108, 124, 125

neurotransmitters: balance, 112, 113; excitatory, 110–11; inhibitory, 110–11; medication to match, 111, 112, 124–5

N-methyl-D-aspartate (NMDA) receptor, 111, 124–5

nonrelational therapy, xxvi

norepinephrine, 110–11

numbness, 50, 111, 135

nurturance, 1

obesity, 103–5
orientation *see* retrieval and orientation
overeating, 130, 135
oxytocin, 103

pain: ignoring, 128; inflicted by parts, 30; suppression, 50
paramis, xx
parents: adolescents and, 49–53; burdens transmitted to children, 35; children and, 35–49; DD clients as, 82–3; dependence on, 52; polarizations and, 37–8, 50, 54; Self-led *versus* parts-led, 36, 37; unburdening and, 37
parts, 25, 35, 90–1, 187–8; acceptance of, 140–1; access to, 39; acknowledgement of inherent value of, 128; attack, 17; avoidance of work with, 11; biology affected by, 115–16; biology affecting, 114–15; change and, xxv; chronic illness related to, 129, 131; communication between, 176–7; conflict between, 61; connection with, 132–3; cooperation of, 63; detector, 16–17, 63; experience of, xix, 88; genetic and environmental interplay with, 128; illness and, 103; independently motivated, 187; insight and, 39; medication and, 107, 113–14, 120–1; medication and polarizations, 118–19; multiplicity of mind and, xvii–xix, 25; open communication with, 120–1; in Phase, 1 76; physical pain inflicted by, 30; polarizations between, 114, 128, 131–2, 140; PTSD and DD 72–3; push-pull tension, 183; relationship between, 58; retrieval and orientation of, 80–1; Self interaction with, xx–xxi; sexuality and activated, 166; SINHC™ and, 144–5; speaking to, 12; *see also* blended parts (blending); exiles (parts); firefighters (parts); managers (parts); Self-to-part relationship; unblending (of parts); unburdening (of parts); *specific parts*
parts (child), 37–8; blended, 45–7; burdens acquired, 36; direct access and, 47–9; invitation to externalize,

41–5; naturally externalized, 39–40; unblending during play, 39–40; *see also specific parts*
parts (client): challenging, 19–21; client relations with, 4–5; sensitive detector of, 18–19; *see also specific parts*
parts (therapist), 12–13; addressing, 121–2; awareness of, 146; burdened, 14–16; communication with, 130; judgment and, 166, 169, 173–5; in prescription process, 107; psychopharmacology-IFS therapy and, 121–2; as pushed, 122–3; sexual life of client and, 167–71; speaking for, 46; triggered by client, 14–15, 172; working with, 17–18; *see also specific parts*
past experience, 66
patience, 4, 7, 188
Pendergast, J., 21–2
Perls, Fritz, xviii
persistence, 4, 188; patient, 7
personality traits, 128
perspective, 4, 5, 188; regaining, 13; shift in, 33
phase oriented treatment-IFS integrated approach, 72–3, 74, 87–8; IFS steps in Phase, 1 of, 75–82, 83; IFS steps in Phase, 2 of, 79, 82–7; IFS steps in Phase, 3 of, 87
phosphatidylserine, 120
playfulness, 4, 7–8, 188
play therapy, 39–40, 41–5
pleasing parts, 51
polarities: approach-avoidance tension and, 179–80; cultural, 171–2; the erotic as essential, 177–8; as essential dialectical tensions, 177; IFS approach to, 167, 176–7; internal, 14, 48; pornography addiction and, 164, 165; sexual excitement fueled by, 178–80; sexuality and, 166–7, 170–1, 176, 184; universal, 178
polarizations, 189; exiles and, 38, 164; firefighter-manager, 164; firefighters and, 38, 164; health care professional-patient, 157; lusty-romantic, 181–4; managers and, 38, 164;

medication-part, 118–19; in parent-adolescent system, 50; in parent-child system, 37–8, 54; between parts, 114, 128, 131–2, 140; psychopharmacology-IFS therapy and, 118–19

pornography addiction, 159–65

posttraumatic stress disorder (PTSD), 72–3, 124–5; neurobiology and, 110

posture, 97–9

power, 180; Self and transformative, 21–2

prefrontal cortex, 108, 110

prejudice, against clients, 14–15

prescription process, 107; Self-energy in, 123

presence, 4, 14, 22, 188; regaining, 13

prohibitions violated, 180

protector part, 3, 173; active, 131–2; amusement with, 7–8; attempt to undo what has been done, 33; blended, 18, 63; in children, 38, 40; couples therapy and, 56–7, 70–1; differentiation from, 63; erotic tension and, 178; intolerant, 37; judgmental, 12, 184; reactive, 15; relationship with, 139; respect for, 7; triggers, 12; working back from, 32; see also firefighters (parts); managers (parts)

pseudo-Self, 17

psychic multiplicity, 187; see also parts

psychodynamic psychotherapy, xvii

psychopharmacology-IFS therapy, 107, 123–4, 125; biology affecting parts, 114–15; manager versus firefighter responses and, 119–20; medications and neurobiology in, 110–12; memory and, 108–9; open communication with parts and, 120–1; parts affecting biology and, 115–16; polarizations and, 118–19; therapist's parts and, 121–2; for trauma, 107, 123–4; validating and addressing concerns, 107, 113–14, 116–18, 124; working with medications and parts in, 113–14

psychosis, as reactive part, 32

PTSD see posttraumatic stress disorder

push-pull tension, 183

questions: Self-detecting, 6; specific medical, 153, 155

quitter part, 47

reactive part, 15, 32

reactivity, external from internal, 61–2

reflective listening, 6

regulation: affect, 58–60; arousal, 60; Self-, 60; shame, 25

rehabilitation, 87

relational burdens, 66, 70

relational dynamics, 144

relational parts, 181–4

relational systems, 34; see also external relational systems; internal relational systems

relational trauma, 58

relational treatment, 1

relationship: with exiles, 164; between parts, 58; with protector part, 139; with Self-energy, 22; Self-leadership in, 63, 68, 70–1; therapeutic, 4; see also healing relationship; Self-to-part relationship; therapist-client relationship

repetition compulsion, 181–2

retrieval and orientation, 80–1, 190

right hemisphere, 108

Rogers, Carl, 1

round table exercise, 182

Rule of Thirds, 83

sadomasochistic erotic play, 167–8

sad part, 5, 133–4

safe containment, 3–4

safe space imagery (SSI), 76–8

safety, 4, 18

Savage, Dan, 171

"Savage Love," 171

Schore, A. N., 25

Schwartz, Richard, xvii–xxiii, 28, 57, 64–5, 113, 187

secure attachment, 10

Self, xix–xxi, 35, 58, 75–6, 187; affect regulation, 58–60; embodied,

90–1, 93; experience of, 6; healing relationships and, 141; parts interacting with, xx–xxi; pseudo-, 17; qualities of, 188; reactions and, 172–3; Self-to-, connection, 8, 16, 21–2; transformative power of, 21–2; *see also* Self-to-part relationship

Self (client): connection to, 8–9; trust in, 6–7, 8–9

self-aware informational nonjudgmental health coaching (SINHC™), 144, 157; CAD and, 150–4; cervical spine-fusion surgery and, 154–6; components, 147; diabetes and, 148–50; internal strategies and, 147; interpersonal strategies and, 147; interviewing protocol of, 145–6; summary of, 146–7; training, 146

self-care, 103, 140, 141; habits of, 143; *see also* behavior change

self-compassion, 65

self-criticism, 26

self-directed shaming, 25

self-discovery, 174–5

Self-embodiment levels, 17

Self-energy, xx, xxv, 18, 19, 35, 91, 112, 187; access to, 9, 61–2; within child, 43; of client, 4–5; DD clients and access to, 73; the erotic and, 184; imagery exercise for, 175; neural integration and, 109; neuroscience and, 108; parts access and, 39; in prescription process, 123; relationship with, 22; of therapist, 4–5, 81; trust, 183; *see also specific qualities*

self-hating part, 20–1

Self-leadership, xxi, 2, 4, 22, 187; absence of, 48; break in, 12, 16; caring *versus* care taking, 68; first session, 3; forceful, 19; interactions and, 63; parenting and, 36, 37; relationships and, 63, 68, 70–1; sexuality with, 179; trust restoration, 6; *see also*, 8Cs, of Self-leadership

Self-led therapist, 7–8; children and, 46; in presence of extreme parts, 14

Self-like parts, 17, 76

self-loath, 26

self-monitoring, 16–17, 134

Self-regulation, 60

self-reinforcement, 63

Self-to-part relationship, 28, 30, 38–9, 58; balance in, 43; as primary healing relationship, 2–3

Self-to-Self connection, 8, 16, 21–2

self-worth, 36

sensations, xix; body, 97, 157

serotonin, 110–11

serotonin re-uptake inhibitor (SSRI), 117, 120, 124

sexual addiction therapy, 165

sexual identity, 183–4; illness interconnected with, 104–5

sexuality, 166; as avoided topic, 172–3; cultural messages and, 171–3; lusty-romantic polarization and, 181–4; parts activated by, 166; polarities and, 166–7, 170–1, 176, 184; polarities to fuel excitement for individuals and couples, 178–80; with Self-leadership, 179; slang words and, 170; therapist reactions to client's, 167–71

shame, 24; case study of, 27–33; couple therapy and, 64–7; function of, 26; historical *versus* instrumental, 26–7; instrumental, 26–7; intentional, 25; pornography addiction and, 161, 163; in psychotherapy, 25–6; regulation, 25; relational burden of, 66; self-directed, 25; unintentional, 25

shared decision making, 153

shy part, 47–8

Siegel, D. J., 10

silence, 8–9; direct access and, 46

SINHC™ *see* self-aware informational nonjudgmental health coaching

skeptic part, 5

smoking, 130, 132–3, 135, 136, 140

socializing agent, 25

somatic awareness, 91, 105–6

Somatic IFS 90, 105–6; with addictions, 93–6; with illness, 99–105; tools of, 91; with trauma, 96–9

somatic resonance, 91, 92, 105–6

speaking for parts and listening from Self communication, 62–3
spinning pinwheels, 64–5
spontaneous action *see asangkarikachitta*
SSI *see* safe space imagery
SSRI *see* serotonin re-uptake inhibitor
stabilization, 85, 88
statistical information, 154
stimulants, 111–12
stress, 110, 124, 127, 128, 130
submission, 180
suicide part, 9, 13, 20; approach to, 6–7
symptom, 113; development, 128; feeling *versus*, 107, 113, 124; identification, 107, 113, 123–4; maintained, 131; triggered, 131; unburdening and, 140
synapse, 110

tenacious caring, 7
tension: approach-avoidance, 179–80; awareness of, 104; erotic, 178; polarities as essential dialectical, 177; push-pull tension, 183
Thanatos, 177–8
therapist: amusement with protectors, 7–8; clues of unacknowledged attraction to client, 174; dependency on, 2; embodied Self, 93; as loving companion, 9–11; reactions to client's sexual life, 167–71; relational dynamics and, 144; self-discovery, 174–5; Self-energy of, 4–5, 81; self-monitoring, 16–17; Self-regulation and, 60; sexual attraction to client, 166, 173–4; trust in client's Self, 6–7, 8–9; unnecessary activity, 8; *see also* health coach; parts (therapist); Self-led therapist
therapist-client relationship, xxvi, 1, 2–3, 4–5, 21–2; active side of, 10; collaborative, 10; sexual, 173–4
Three Poisons, xxv
tone of voice, 6, 18
tor-mentors, 17
touch: attuned, 91, 93, 105–6; as tool, 100–2

transference, 1, 11–12
trauma: illness interconnected with, 104–5; interpersonal, 24; medication for, 111–12; memory and, 108–9; neuroscience and, 108; physiological effects of, 124; processing, 83; psychopharmacology for, 107, 123–4; relational, 58; Somatic IFS with, 96–9; *see also* dissociative disorders clients; posttraumatic stress disorder
trust, 3; in client's Self, 6–7, 8–9; Self-energy, 183; Self-leadership to restore, 6

unblending (of parts), xx, 62–3, 64, 112, 189; chronic illness and, 135; curiosity for, xxv; invitation for, 41–5; key to, xxv; mapping as tool for, 161, 165; medication as agent, 113; during play, 39–40; SINHC™ and, 145, 157
unburdening (of parts), xxi–xxii, 33, 69, 82, 88, 190; assisted, 105; coping skills to pace, 73; exile, 7, 163; guided, 138–9; parental, 37; by percentages, 84–5; possible changes after, 87; setup for protected, 83, 84; symptoms and, 140; titrating, 83
unintentional shaming, 25
Upanishads, xix
U-turn, 57, 68, 70

validation: of medication concerns, 107, 113–14, 116–18, 124; request, 81–2
Vedanta, xix
vulnerable parts, 146, 178

WAIT ("Why am I talking?"), 8
Wilde, Oscar, 7
witnessing, 40, 65–6, 69, 79, 88, 190; by percentages, 84–5; setup for protected, 83, 84
word content, 6

Yalom, I.D. 14
yang, 177–8
yin, 177–8
young part, 136–7

MENSANA PUBLICATIONS

CONTINUING EDUCATION FOR MENTAL HEALTH PROFESSIONALS

Routledge
Taylor & Francis Group
NEW YORK AND LONDON

An accredited continuing education component has been developed for this book by the author, in partnership with Routledge and Mensana Publications. The CE offer is worth 6 hours of continuing education credit, and may be purchased from the website below:

www.mensanapublications.com